To our granddaughter

Eva Lee

WHO WONDERS ABOUT
MANY THINGS !!

Love Always
Abuelo &
Grandma

ALICE LOXTON

EIGHTEEN

A History of Britain in 18 Young Lives

MACMILLIAN

First published 2024 by Macmillan
an imprint of Pan Macmillan
The Smithson, 6 Briset Street, London EC1M 5NR
EU representative: Macmillan Publishers Ireland Ltd, 1st Floor,
The Liffey Trust Centre, 117–126 Sheriff Street Upper,
Dublin 1, D01 YC43
Associated companies throughout the world
www.panmacmillan.com

ISBN 978-1-0350-3128-3

1 3 5 7 9 8 6 4 2

A CIP catalogue record for this book is available from the British Library.

Chapter illustrations by Belinda Roberts

Typeset in Minion Pro by Palimpsest Book Production Ltd, Falkirk, Stirlingshire

Visit **www.panmacmillan.com** to read more about all our books
and to buy them. You will also find features, author interviews and
news of any author events, and you can sign up for e-newsletters
so that you're always first to hear about our new releases.

THIS BOOK IS DEDICATED TO EVERY
EIGHTEEN-YEAR-OLD OUT THERE.

May your days be joyful and your future bright.

CONTENTS

INTRODUCTION

The Fountain of Youth

In the UK, eighteen is the age we are officially an adult. The chrysalis of teenage years – with its irresponsible behaviour, terrible haircuts and blotchy skin – suddenly breaks open. Out flies the Beautiful Butterfly of Majority. Childhood is over, and adulthood begins.

Of course, it's not quite as simple as that. The law may flick the switch, but youth is a much more fluctuating, personal thing. The dictionary tells us that 'youth' is the age between childhood and maturity. Maturity. I wonder: what is that? Is it not answering back in a fight? Is it passing the crisps around before helping yourself? At twenty-eight years old, am I there yet? Will I ever get there?

Today, the life expectancy in the UK is seventy-nine for men and eighty-three for women. So perhaps 'youth' is 0–30, young middle age is 30–50, upper middle age is 50–70, and old age is 70+? But what about in the past?

This is a tricky question to answer. Throughout history, all the figures on mortality have been warped by the vast numbers of childhood deaths. It's depressing to realize that many of our ancestors were already shuffling off this mortal coil at a very young

1

age. Everyone in history who lives beyond eighteen is lucky to be there. In Shakespeare's time, Stratford-upon-Avon had an average of sixty-three children baptized and forty-three buried each year. It gets worse in the industrial towns of Georgian Britain. At the dawn of the nineteenth century, 57 per cent of children born in Preston and 53 per cent born in Liverpool died before their fifth birthday. As such, the life expectancy of a newborn Prestonian in a working-class family was eighteen years old. In Liverpool, it was sixteen.

If you discount all those very young deaths, you get a different picture. Between 1200 and 1745, if a man got to the age of twenty-one – and didn't die by accident, go to war, or have a messy night out with his mates – he'd probably live to 62–70 years. Imagine it like a round of job interviews, with each round representing a decade of your life. The first couple of rounds would be brutal, getting rid of over half the applicants. But after that, there are only a few candidates knocked off at each round, with a handful making it to the final stages.

In general, populations in the past were much younger. Today, you walk along the high street of a rural town at 11 a.m. on a weekday, and there are old people everywhere. The supermarket aisles are full of grey-haired Zimmer-framers, the tea shops overflowing with bespectacled knitters, the pubs brimming with conversations propelled by chattering false teeth. But in the past, most people in the street were children or young adults. A silver-haired octogenarian was a much rarer – much more exciting – sight. Of course, there were plenty of old people in the past, dotted around. It's just that today more of us have a much greater chance of getting there.

Imagine you gathered every single person from fourteenth-century England and asked them to stand in a line, in order of their age. The A1 would be a good place to do it, then known as the Great North Road. 'Youngest in Edinburgh, oldest in London please,' you'd shout on the megaphone. It would be a nightmare task, with all sorts of argy-bargy and confusion. ('Where do I stand? All I know is I was born on St Stephen's Day, 203 moons past.')

When everyone was roughly in order, if you picked the person standing in the middle – somewhere near Harrogate – they would be twenty-one years old. So, in the fourteenth century, if you were twenty-two, you'd be older than half the population. If you repeated the process in the late sixteenth century, the chosen Harrogate specimen would be twenty-two years old. In the nineteenth century, they would be twenty-five.

So it's a young crowd. And that doesn't massively change for hundreds of years. At the start of the medieval period, the life expectancy was around thirty. In 1765, that number was thirty-nine. In 1900 – when my great-grandmother was born – it was forty-seven. It's only in the twentieth century that things really picked up. And, in 2024, the average life expectancy in the UK was eighty-one.

With less chance of living longer, it's no surprise people were eager to get on with things while they were still around. In the medieval period, betrothals were often arranged when the children were toddlers. Girls would be married at twelve years old, and boys at fourteen. Many women in their mid-twenties – if they were still alive – might have been married for about ten years and could have given birth five or six times. Some might be widowed – their husbands having perhaps died in battle – and married for the second time.

Medieval boys were expected to work at seven and considered old enough to determine between right and wrong, as they could be hanged for theft. Some were given immense responsibility: at the Battle of Crecy in 1346, sixteen-year-old Prince Edward commanded some 800 men-at-arms, 2,000 archers and 1,000 footmen. Later in the eighteenth century, boys routinely joined ships of the Royal Navy around the age of twelve.

The concepts of 'youth' and 'old age' were seen differently than they are today. In the fourteenth century, a man was considered at his prime in his twenties, mature in his thirties and growing old in his forties. Women had even less time: Chaucer considered a thirty-year-old woman to be 'winter forage' (I look forward to it!). In the time of Elizabeth I, the composer Thomas Whithorne felt turning forty marked 'the first part of the old man's age'. In 1813, Lord Byron despaired at turning twenty-five: 'At five-and-twenty, when the better part of life is over, one should be *something* – and what am I?' He had a point: Byron died at thirty-six, and his fellow romantic poet John Keats died at twenty-five.

The big change came when we stopped relying on children to bring in an income. To eliminate child labour, the 1880 Education Act made school attendance compulsory in England and Wales between the ages of five and ten. It was hard to enforce at first: attendance fell short by 82 per cent. In 1901, there were still 300,000 children working outside school hours, their families not able to forgo the extra income. But as society became more accommodating, attendance improved. Over the years, the minimum leaving age has gone steadily up: eleven years old in 1893, twelve in 1899, fourteen in 1918, fifteen in 1947 and sixteen in 1972, where it remains to this day across the UK.

A new group was emerging in British society: the teenager. These young people who – instead of being smaller versions of their parents – had a new identity between a child and an adult. In 1954, the teenage experience was summed up in *Tatler* magazine as being 'neither fish, fowl nor good red herring – that feeling of being betwixt and between.' They were as capable and energetic as those in their twenties, yet still lived under the supervision of parents or teachers, and had no obligation to work.

The rise of the teenager in Britain largely stemmed from American culture. In 1945, *The New York Times* marked this growing group with an article entitled 'A teen-age bill of rights'. This was a 'ten-point charter framed to meet the problems of growing youth', which included 'the right to a "say" about his own life', 'the right to question ideas' and 'the right to make mistakes, to find out for himself'.

After the Second World War, rapid economic growth meant many people were better off and able to buy houses, giving teens more space and privacy. These young people inhabited a world apart from their parents, at school, or in part-time work – not to contribute to the family income, but for their own pocket money.

Parents soon felt the brunt of this new demographic. 'He's cheeky and he's sulky . . . why should a boy change like this?' one mother wrote to the *Daily Mirror*'s Agony Aunt in 1955. 'He resents any questions. The best I get is a polite yes or no, the worst an angry look which clearly tells me to mind my own business.'

Perhaps it's no surprise that the age of eighteen has become a celebratory moment – for child and parent alike. It is the Age of Majority, meaning parents are no longer responsible for their child, and the child is no longer under their parents' rules and regulations. Freedom for everyone!

Of course, it's not as black and white, even in official terms. Today, governments recognize that this journey to maturity starts much, much earlier. The age of criminal responsibility is ten years old in England and Wales, and twelve years old in Scotland. At eleven, you can open a current account. At thirteen, you can have a part-time job. At fifteen, you can be sent to a Young Offenders Institution. At sixteen, you can leave school, work, serve in the military, change your name, have sex, buy a house and buy aerosol paint (but not get a tattoo or buy alcohol). At seventeen, you can drive a car. At eighteen you can vote, be called for jury service, buy alcohol, stand as an MP, drive a lorry and fly a helicopter. At twenty-one, you can adopt a child.

It's strange how rigidly these turning points are enforced, when so much of it rests on weighty moral judgements. In the eyes of the law, in the space of a second, an act goes from being a criminal offence to totally legal. A child goes from not responsible enough, to totally responsible. Sometimes the moral standard changes as you cross a border. In the UK, the age of sexual consent is sixteen; in France, it's fifteen. In the UK, you can drink at eighteen. In the US, it's twenty-one. Of course, we must have clear rules, but it does all seem a little arbitrary.

What's more, if we look at the reality of British adults, most of us seem to be doing the 'grown-up' bits later and later, whether through circumstance or choice. More people don't get married until their thirties, can't afford a house or don't have children at all. Perhaps it's not necessarily a bad thing. Some neuroscientists reckon we don't become fully 'adult' until our thirties, that moving from childhood to adulthood is a 'nuanced transition that takes place over three decades'. There is hope for some of us yet!

If we look at the long course of history, and modern legalities, choosing eighteen as a big turning point seems pretty random. It should be sixteen, if anything. Almost nothing changes on your eighteenth birthday unless you're desperate to become a local councillor. Considering underage drinking is rife and the chance to vote in a general election usually only comes around every four or five years, the new perks are negligible for most eighteen-year-olds.

Perhaps you are thinking it is a strange argument to make at the start of a book titled *Eighteen*. But that's the point. That's the riddle we're trying to solve. To understand our modern perceptions of what it means to be eighteen, we must break away and examine what being eighteen has meant for over a thousand years.

If you are an eighteen-year-old reading this book the year it is published (2024), you were born in 2006. That was a great vintage for music: 'Crazy' by Gnarls Barkley was the most popular song. At ten years old, in 2016, it was 'One Dance' by Drake (also a banger). You've lived through seven UK prime ministers (Blair, Brown, Cameron, May, Johnson, Truss, Sunak) and possibly another by the time this is published. You were ten when the 2016 Brexit vote passed and fourteen when the 2020 Covid-19 pandemic spread.

Every year, the Oxford English Dictionary announces a word of the year. These are the words (or phrases) that have marked the years of your life: bovvered, carbon footprint, credit crunch, simples, big society, squeezed middle, omnishambles, selfie, vape, [laughing-crying emoji], post-truth, youthquake, toxic, climate emergency, vax, goblin mode and rizz.

You are part of Generation Z, or the Zoomers. You are digital natives who have never known life without the internet. You have lower rates of teenage pregnancy and drink less alcohol. Only 17 per cent of you believe 'political parties care about young people'. Instead, you do politics through digital activism. You live in a world where a TikTok following can be more lucrative than a PhD. You are – to some – the 'snowflakes', viewed as being less resilient and more prone to taking offence than previous generations.

Yet this seems unfair when it's so clear that the human condition doesn't change much, and so much of people's behaviour is shaped by the society they are born in. Those heroes of the Western Front would have been scrolling through TikTok had it existed in 1916. Likewise, had today's young people been born in 1898 and forced to fight in the First World War, there's every reason to think they might have had the same resolve.

On the other side of the coin, when young people do stand up for themselves, they aren't always taken seriously. In 2023, when Keir Mather became an MP at the age of twenty-five, he faced a barrage of mockery. Despite the fact he'd been eligible to vote for seven years, worked several jobs, been to university and lived off a student loan, he still wasn't taken seriously as someone to represent the people. As if – out of 650 MPs – it wasn't worth having just one young person to bring a fresh perspective.

Perhaps Mather's critics might take a moment to consider one of our best prime ministers, William Pitt, was appointed at twenty-four years old. Pitt, too, was mocked for his youth when he arrived in office. 'A sight to make surrounding nations stare,' his opponents scorned, 'A kingdom trusted to a school-boy's care.'

It seems there is a great confusion about the age of eighteen, this apparent turning point between young and old. I set out to write this book hoping to shed some light on the conundrum, hoping to get to know the British eighteen-year-old, discovering what their ambitions, dreams, fears and regrets have been for the past thousand years. I've selected eighteen individuals, each of them remarkable and each bringing a different story to the table.

Of course, the list isn't totally representative, as no list of eighteen people could be. I apologize to all the Neolithic and Roman eighteen-year-olds, who haven't left many sources behind for us to go on. Take, for example, the memorial to a teenage girl, which can be found near the Gherkin in London. She died sometime between AD 350 and 400. It reads: 'To the spirits of the dead/the unknown young girl/from Roman London/lies buried here'. She is one of the millions of teenagers whose stories we will never know.

It was remarkably tricky, too, to find accounts of an eighteen-year-old woman from before the Tudor period, who wasn't in a noble circle. So many – the likes of Margery Kempe or Margaret Paston – have fascinating lives, but their biographies tend to start with a caveat along the lines of 'there is no record of her life before thirty-two'.

But I am confident this is an excellent bunch. On one hand, these are people who have made a real difference, a lasting impact on the world. But they are also my personal favourites: people I'd choose to go on holiday with or have on a pub quiz team.

A few points to note, before we dive in. First, this is a history of Britain – albeit an unconventional one. Today, Britain consists of England, Scotland and Wales. But Britain – and being British – hasn't always been like that. At different points in history, it's meant different things.

In ancient times, 'Britons' were the native peoples, as opposed to the Romans or the Saxons who came from mainland Europe. For the Romans, 'Britannia' tended to mean the area they had control over, which was anywhere south of Hadrian's Wall (basically England and Wales). North of this was Caledonia (basically Scotland).

During the medieval and Tudor periods, the concept of Britain as we know it didn't exist. The Kingdom of England (which, from 1284, included Wales) was separate from the Kingdom of Scotland, between whom wars and disputes often broke out. William Wallace was Scottish, and William Shakespeare was English. Neither considered themselves British, as we might today.

In 1603, all this changed. The English queen, Elizabeth I, died childless. Her heir was the Scottish king, James VI. On inheriting the throne, the separate kingdoms of England and Scotland came under one ruler. Then, in 1707, the Acts of Union, passed by the English and Scottish Parliaments, led to the creation of 'Great Britain'. In 1801, more Acts of Union united the Kingdom of Great Britain and the Kingdom of Ireland. For over a century, the British Isles – England, Ireland, Scotland and Wales – were under one chain of command stemming from Westminster, though each element retained distinct national identities. That's until the Anglo-Irish Treaty of May 1921, which marked the end of British rule, forming the Irish Free State (now the Republic of Ireland) and establishing the state of Northern Ireland.

Today, we have the UK – the United Kingdom of Great Britain and Northern Ireland. With two millennia of varying usage, it's no surprise that the term 'British' is imprecise. Being British is defined in the dictionary as 'people from Britain', or the act of 'belonging to or relating to the United Kingdom of Great Britain and Northern Ireland or its people'.

Like Britain today – a myriad of peoples from across the globe – this selection of eighteen is a mix. Some spent their life in Britain though they had roots elsewhere, such as Ireland, West Africa or France. Some spent most of their young lives abroad, in Germany or India. Some wouldn't have considered themselves a 'Briton' at all. Yet all played a vital role in Britain's story.

It's an interesting lens, looking at Britain's past through our youth. Still passing through the motions of growing up, these young lives are greatly dictated by external forces, rather than on their own terms (which tends to become more important, later). Instead of examining their crowning achievements of later life – their highlights reel – this book goes behind the scenes. We are looking at early moments of anxiety, of vulnerability, of naivety. The rougher, grittier, messier moments of people's lives.

Second, though I hope this is a book that inspires and interests young people, it's a book for all ages that celebrates every stage of life. Eighteen is just the snapshot we happen to be examining, and is not necessarily superior or inferior to any other. The world is full of those who bloom and thrive in later life, when cherished friendships, learnt wisdom and old memories can be enjoyed. Equally, there are the tragic cases of children who never reach the age of eighteen but have still made their mark on the world.

In this selection of eighteen, you'll notice that each figure – though the same age – is at a different stage in their life's journey. Some have achieved incredible things. Some have been thrust into extraordinary situations. Some are totally ordinary, with no idea of the thrills or horrors to come. For some, their fame or success doesn't arrive until many decades later. But this is an interesting point. Did they – at eighteen – have any idea that later in life, they would end up in the history books? At eighteen, could others already tell? Were the signs there?

Third, a question to consider: how do you make a fair judgement of an eighteen-year-old, either today or centuries ago? Perhaps we can look at the year they turn eighteen, and pry apart each day, flicking through their diary, and examining what they wore, ate or talked about. This is useful, but limited in isolation. It's like watching a film from the middle – starting *Titanic* from the point when the ship is already sinking. The backstory – their birth, parents, childhood, historical context, siblings – is everything. Those past eighteen years form the memory and character of an eighteen-year-old (whether they realize it or not).

On the flipside, we can also trace character details from

anecdotes later in life, which shine a light on earlier years. Together, these snippets of information paint a rich portrait. Each snippet offers a valuable insight into the life of our eighteen-year-olds and situates them in the wider course of their life's journey.

It's also worth noting that our view is always skewed when looking at the past. Only a small number of sources survive, and these generally refer to extraordinary people (the rich, famous or downright terrible) or extraordinary and unusual events (battles, plagues or coronations). Most of our ancestors lived ordinary lives that were never written about – as is the case for most people today. That doesn't mean their lives aren't as worthy. They may not have been married in Westminster Abbey or written great plays that have been passed through the ages, but many have achieved something just as – perhaps more – important: a lifetime of loyalty to another person, or years of spreading joy and kindness.

Finally, throughout the book, between each chapter, you are invited to dive into something quite unusual: an eighteenth birthday party. Our eighteen-year-olds will each attend the party, and you will meet them one by one. These are, on one level, extra sprinkles of fun. But there is a serious, important point to this. By bringing these figures from the past into the room with us, they become flesh and blood, not just names in a book.

If you are reading this as an eighteen-year-old, or a soon-to-be eighteen-year-old, I hope this book gives you a sense that these people who went on to become part of the history books were once in your shoes. They shared many of your doubts, joys, anxieties and irritations, albeit packaged in different ways. If you are reading this past your eighteenth year, perhaps you can re-evaluate or reconnect with your eighteen-year-old self and take a moment to reflect on your journey since then.

It has been a great joy to write this book and I hope that comes across. Although history can be moving, tragic and horrific, it can also be uplifting, inspiring and lots of FUN!

Without further ado, this is a story of young people who made their mark and played a part in the story of Britain. Hold onto your party hats. It is much more surprising, exciting and impressive than you might expect. This is a snapshot of Britain through the eighteen-year-olds who have sculpted it. This is what it means to be British. This is what it means to be eighteen.

The First Guest

Everything was ready. The invitations had been sent out, the guests had RSVPed and the table plan arranged.

A long table – draped with an elegant tablecloth – was the centrepiece of the dining room, ringed by eighteen wooden chairs. Eight of them were arranged on either side, with one on each end.

On a side table was a silver weight from which floated two silver balloons – one in the shape of a '1', the other, an '8'. The room was silent and still. And then a handle turned, the door creaked open, and in walked a figure, swathed in a long dark robe.

The party had begun.

1

Bede

IN THE LONG AND tumultuous course of British history, few teenagers have had it as bad as Bede. It wasn't having to wear an itchy robe, or the monotony of monastery life, or even shivering, night after night, on a freezing stone bed. It was something *much* worse. At thirteen years old, Bede came face to face with the living dead. He wrote of this nightmare with startling brevity: 'the pestilence came'.

Bede's tale is worthy of a Spielberg epic. Imagine the opening scene. First shot: an icy Northumbrian landscape with vast grey skies and sleeting rain. Second shot: a hilltop marked by hundreds of wooden crosses, some fallen to the ground. Then, from the swirling valley mist, our protagonist emerges, a scrawny, shivering teenage boy. He drags heavy bundles from a cart, heaving them into shallow ditches. The wind howls and whistles around him, and the wrappings of one bundle blow open to reveal their morbid contents: the pale, gaunt face of a fresh corpse with staring, soulless eyes; bloated limbs twisted unnaturally; blackened, bloodied flesh.

17

The screen turns black. A title emerges from the darkness 'BECOMING BEDE', and the popcorn begins to rustle once more. It would certainly be a gripping start, followed by plenty more heartbreak ('I couldn't believe it when he had to bury his best friend'), and a good dose of gore ('How revolting when the buboes exploded in the soup').

But for Bede, this Gothic horror was the reality of his teenage years. A plague struck the monastery where he lived in AD 686. One by one, the monks discovered their gruesome symptoms: enormous buboes on the groin and the glands. Then, for the next seventy-two hours, they would writhe and squirm in agonizing pain. Black spots would appear on their skin, their buboes would leak rancid pus, and flea bites would become gangrenous. When the disease spread to the lungs, the victim started coughing up blood. Some suffered convulsions – hideous contortions of the arms and legs, so inhuman it seemed the devil had taken refuge. It was a small mercy for the end to finally come, for the soul to escape its tormented body.

Such terrors, caused by sweeping plagues, were endured by millions throughout Europe in the sixth and seventh centuries. Entire swathes of the population were wiped out, as recorded by Paul the Deacon, a Benedictine monk, in his work *History of the Lombards*:

> *You might see the world brought back to its ancient silence: no voice in the field; no whistling of shepherds; no lying in wait of wild beasts among the cattle; no harm to domestic fowls. The crops, outliving the time of the harvest, awaited the reaper untouched . . . pastoral places had been turned into sepulchers for men, and human habitations had become places of refuge for wild beasts.*

For those who lived in close confinement, such as in monasteries, disease spread like wildfire. Here, monks and abbots or nuns and abbesses spent every moment in close quarters, washing, sleeping and eating side by side. In Bede's monastery, everyone 'who could read, preach or say the antiphons and responsories were snatched away'. Only two survived, 'the abbot himself and a lad who had been brought up and educated by him'.

This lad, it's believed, was Bede. In those final months of plague, as the last of their brethren succumbed, Bede and the abbot (a man in his forties named Ceolfrith) continued their duties. They stood in the quire of the church to sing psalms, the deep boom of the man's grown voice alternating with the quivering high notes of the boy. Yet there was no congregation to hear it. No clergy to nod along. 'Why am I still here? Why me?' Bede must have wondered. Had he been chosen by God? And who would be next? If Ceolfrith perished, Bede would be alone. Then, if Bede died, as the very last, would his body be left unburied, his flesh ripped from his bones by scavenging beasts, his eyes pecked to their sockets by wild birds?

Bede was born around AD 673. There is pretty much no record of his early years, so we're left to scramble in the dark. Clue number one: he was born 'on the lands of this monastery', somewhere in the vicinity of present-day Newcastle-upon-Tyne. He was, therefore, an Anglo-Saxon Geordie. Clue number two: his name. 'Bede' was an unusual name, only recorded in high society circles – so more of a 'Fitzwilliam' or 'Augustus' than a 'Gavin' or 'Kyle'. Many historians believe this would suggest he was from a noble family who paid a dowry for his entry to the monastery, perhaps to build the family influence or ensure their son a promising future of learning and prayer in the heart of a powerful institution.

He lived in the Anglo-Saxon era, which is a loose label for the years between the withdrawal of the Romans in AD 409–10 and the arrival of the Normans in 1066. In the early part of this period, groups of people from all over Europe settled in England and Wales, including the Angles, Saxons and Jutes. The Angles gave us the name 'Angle Land', or 'Engla Land', which would turn into 'England'. These tribes were a feisty bunch, first pushing the native Romano-British tribes to the fringes of Cornwall and Wales, then bickering endlessly among themselves. The land was divided into warring kingdoms, such as Kent, East Anglia and Mercia in the south, and Bernicia and Deira in the north.

Bede's family were Anglo-Saxons living in Northumbria, which was a kingdom formed from the unification of Bernicia and Deira. Most people lived in wooden huts with a straw roof, with one room and a central fire. Perhaps this was how Bede spent his childhood. Or, had he been the son of a chief, he would have lived in the biggest house in the village: a long hall with a fire in the middle, shields and antlers on the walls, and rushes on the floor.

It was all hands on deck from an early age: no Norland nannies or Montessori nurseries here. In Bede's time, adulthood began around ten years old, which – when most people were dead by thirty – was a third of the way through your life. As the men headed to the forests with their axes and chopped down trees, Bede might have scurried behind, clearing the wood. There were crops to be sowed, with oxen pulling ploughs up and down long fields. Other days there was fishing and hunting. Was little Bede sent out to sit by the flowing waters of the river, keeping an eye on the wicker eel traps? Or did he help the metalworkers, who forged and hammered and sweated to make iron tools, knives and swords?

As a child, it's likely that Bede never left the village he grew up in, never straying more than a few miles away. He was so embedded in this land, these trees, this way of life. He knew how the worms moved, how the fish darted, how the ice crackled underfoot. His days were shaped by the stars in the firmament, the waning moon, the movement of the sun.

It must have been a shock, at the age of seven, to be sent away for ever. He was to join a world more dynamic and glamorous than anything he had ever known. This was a pioneering experiment, backed by the wealthy and powerful. Seven-year-old Bede, with his muddy fingernails and bony frame, was to be sent to a monastery.

What a moment for a child to bid goodbye to everything they had known. Did a tear trickle down Bede's cheek as he clung to his parents in a final embrace? Did he bring out a handkerchief as he trudged across the Northumbrian country-side: wading through streams and clambering over crumbling Roman walls?

Perhaps a little context is needed here. What was the deal with these new monasteries? They were Christian institutions, and Christianity had, in one way or another, been around for centuries. It was introduced by the Romans, but when the Romans scarpered in the fifth century, Christianity lost momentum and became muddled with the paganism of the native Celts and spiritual practices brought over by the Anglo-Saxon tribes. These faiths co-existed: some going out of fashion, some gaining followers, some only practised through ancient habit. We still live with the remnants of the mix today. The word 'Tuesday', for instance, derives from *Tiw*, the Anglo-Saxon warrior god, and 'Wednesday' from *Woden*, the chief of the gods. The word 'Easter' is derived from *Eostre*, an Anglo-Saxon goddess of spring.

But in AD 563 (a century before Bede was born), a two-pronged Christian Comeback had begun. First, St Columba and his twelve followers sailed across the Irish Sea and landed on the isle of Iona, on the west coast of Scotland. They set out to create 'a perfect monastery as an image of the heavenly city of Jerusalem', building a wooden church, surrounded by a ditch and earthen bank. It was the start of Iona Abbey.

Thirty-four years later, in AD 597, a monk called Augustine travelled from Rome with a team of forty and landed on the south coast of England. Acting on the orders of Pope Gregory the Great, Augustine's mission was to spread the holy word. Soon, ordinary people were turning away from the pagan habits of animal sacrifices, ritual burials and Anglo-Saxon gods. Instead, they turned to Christian priests and bishops. New churches and stone crosses popped up in the landscape and kings gave land away to monks to establish monasteries and schools.

By the seventh century, the Christian bug had spread to Northumbria (by now, the most powerful of the Anglo-Saxon kingdoms). The monks from Iona founded a monastery on the island of Lindisfarne, and by the 670s, there were plans for another. Rumours spread around the villages near the River Wear: 'News! King Ecgfrith has given planning permission for a new monastery!' they gossiped. 'Where the River Wear meets the sea!'

The new Benedictine monastery at Wearmouth was built to be a bustling hub for trade and travel. It was perfectly located for goods to arrive from the continent and bishops to depart to Rome. Stone and rubble were hauled into position, much of it gathered from local Roman ruins. Within a year, the heart of the monastery – St Peter's Church – was up and running. It was two storeys high and topped with a gabled roof, tiled with stone slate. Most excitingly, the windows were filled with a brand-new building material, glass, installed by specialist French masons. This was a mega upgrade: now the monks could keep out the rain *and* have natural light to be able to read. Luxury indeed!

Then came the other monastery essentials: a dormitory (for sleeping) and a refectory (for eating). The complex was run by Bishop Benedict – a kind of headmaster figure – who packed the place with books, relics and paintings from the Pope's private collection.

It was here that seven-year-old Bede arrived to start his new life. The monastery was his new home, the brethren his family (the word 'abbot' comes from the Aramaic word *abba*, meaning 'father'). On balance, for the Anglo-Saxon world, a monastic life was a pretty good deal. Yes, you left your family and spent half your time chanting, but you were guaranteed a lifetime of decent accommodation, above-average meals and a never-ending supply of home brew.

Bede joined the monastery as an oblate, a kind of monk in training. Becoming a monk would come later – if he cut the mustard. And it was tricky mustard to cut. The rules of St Benedict were strict. All personal possessions were to be given up at the door. No trinkets or knick-knacks allowed here. No home clothes either – just the uniform.

'This robe is called a habit,' the abbot might have chimed, as Bede put it on for the first time. 'The sash goes around your waist. That represents chastity. The colour black reminds us of our life of poverty.' It was a daunting and lonely prospect, no doubt. But it was also one of the most exciting days of Bede's life.

Imagine the moment he was first shown around the huge stone buildings, his oversized robe dragging along the floor. What must he have thought, approaching the church of St Peter? First, he heard it: the low, haunting chants of monks. Then, the mysterious smell of sweet incense. Pushing open the huge doors, he walked into what appeared to be a room full of saints.

Was this Heaven itself? Not quite! These were the paintings that Bishop Benedict had brought from Rome, adorning the walls of St Peter's. The Apocalypse of St John on the left, the Gospels on the right and the twelve apostles with the Virgin Mary at the altar. To Bede's amazement, light danced in technicolour through dust and smoke: such was the magic of coloured glass.

Next, Bede was taken to the refectory, lined with long tables and benches. This is where he and his monastic friends would eat in solemn silence, twice a day. The aroma of home cooking wafted towards him – fish, bread, cheese, butter, beans. His nostrils twitched and tingled as he smelt unfamiliar spices, imported from afar.

But there was one space, more than any other, which excited a new oblate's curiosity. In the scriptorium, Bede was shown the true treasures of the monastery. What was this? A large, flat, rectangular shape, which could be opened to reveal sheets of delicate shapes and colourful pictures. 'Don't touch it, boy,' the abbot might have warned him, 'do you know how precious these books are?'

That evening, Bede spent his first night in the dormitory. No doubt he lay awake – not because of the snores of hundreds of other monks – but because his mind was racing. So many new experiences – the paintings, the glass, the spices, the music – and, most especially, that magnificent room full of – what was the word again? – ah yes, books!

So began life in the monastery. Around eight times a day, Bede joined the brethren in prayer. They would chant antiphons and psalms, read gospels and scriptures, and take mass. There were lessons with other boys, sitting in small rooms with dirt floors, on backless wooden benches where they learnt by rote and dictation onto wax tablets. Then there was practical work that kept the monastery going: farming, glass blowing, restoring stonework and preparing meals.

About a year into Bede's monastery life, the monks began whispering more than usual between prayers, with the arrival of some thrilling news. Clearly impressed with the work at Wearmouth, in AD 681, King Ecgfrith gave the order for a sister monastery to be established. The new location was just seven miles north, in Jarrow. It was a similar site, near the sea, and on the south bank of the River Tyne. There were brilliant views of Jarrow Slake, the bustling harbour, and the royal palace at Arbeia, where King Ecgfrith lived. Today, the view is rather less charming, blotted by thousands of Nissan cars, waiting to be exported around the world.

Soon enough, the second monastery was up and running, this time dedicated to St Paul and headed by Abbot Ceolfrith. Bede was transferred to the new site. A church still stands there today, with parts of the original Anglo-Saxon structure still in place. The chancel, with its huge blocks of stone and rounded low arch, dates from the seventh century, perhaps installed by Bede himself. Nearby, in the wall of the tower, is a stone slab. This is the original dedication stone, inscribed in Latin. It records the visit of King Ecgfrith – the money and power behind these new monasteries – at the dedication of the church:

The dedication of the basilica of St Paul on the ninth day before the Kalends of May in the fifteenth year of King Ecgfrith and in the fourth year of Abbot Ceolfrith, founder, by God's guidance, of the same church.

Was Bede there on that day? Did he glimpse royal robes of fur, sweeping across the brand-new stone floor? Did he hear the thud of heavy boots, the clink of a sword, and the booming voice of the king, echoing around the church? If so, Bede was one of the last to see Ecgfrith. Within a month, this mighty king had been ambushed by Picts, and slain.

Thus was the brevity of life in the Anglo-Saxon world – and a lesson worth learning. As Bede sat down to feast in the spring of AD 686, he sat among hundreds of learned men and boys. Boys who laughed, who made jokes, who sneezed and snorted and misbehaved. Yet within the year, this family of brethren would disappear, perishing at the hands of the deadly plague. All gone, for ever, with Bede and Ceolfrith the only survivors.

Take a moment to think of that. Think back to your school hall. Can you see it? Packed with hundreds of pupils sitting cross-legged on the floor, and teachers sitting importantly on the stage. Perhaps there is old gym equipment on the walls or a display of the 'Pupil of the Week'. Can you feel your legs going numb? Can you hear the murmuring? The aggressive 'shhh!' from a teacher at the back?

Now imagine you return to the same hall, six months later. There's been a deadly plague. Everyone has perished, and the hall is empty, apart from you. Oh, wait! The door handle turns! Another survivor! Could it be one of your friends? Or someone from the sports team? Or one of the cooler older pupils? Then, your heart sinks when the truth dawns. In walks the one other survivor: the maths teacher. A bleak prospect indeed.

In light of this, perhaps it's no surprise Bede and Ceolfrith were quick to rebuild the monastery and recruit new members. This is how Bede spent his teenage years, and five years after the plague, he turned eighteen years old.

EIGHTEEN

It was probably around this time that Bede's passion for books began. Eighteen-year-old Bede was a beady, budding bookworm. Today, bibliophiles can scroll through a Kindle and peruse millions of titles from the comfort of a sofa. In Bede's day, it was rather less accessible. If Bede wanted to read a book, he had to make one from scratch with his own hands (the meaning of 'manuscript' is a book that is created by hand, rather than typed or printed).

It's likely that Bede spent much of his eighteenth year engrossed in the manuscript production process. Manuscripts were made from animal skins. Luckily for the monastery library (and less so the cows), Northumbria had an abundant supply of cattle. The first task was to collect the skins of beasts, recently slaughtered for their meat. It was grim work: the untreated skins were slippy, hairy, smelly things, with blood and guts still stuck to them. It was Bede's job to carry them to a shallow, fast-flowing stream, and pin them down with boulders. They were left for a couple of days to be pulled and tugged by the water – like a natural washing machine – until they were clean.

Next, they were packed into wooden barrels or vats, which were filled with a mixture of lime (probably chalk dust) and water. The lime loosened the structure of the skin (essentially opening up the pores) so that after a week, a wooden paddle could be used to scrape the hair off the pelt. Then came another rinse, to get rid of the lime.

After this, the clean, hairless skin was pinned to a rectangular wooden frame, and placed outside in the sunshine to dry. It was smeared with a paste of chalk dust, allowing the monks to stretch it tighter. It was probably Bede's job to stretch it on both sides, with a lunellum (a half-moon-shaped knife without a point, to reduce the risk of puncturing the skin). Once the skin was scraped to an even thinness, it was dried, taken off the frame and cut to size.

Finally! A piece of parchment! What a laborious process: dragging the soaking skins from the water, scraping them down, tightening the frames. One doesn't often imagine monastic dwellers as burly, but there is a chance that eighteen-year-old Bede – under that stinking, damp robe – was a strapping young man.

Once delivered to the scriptorium, the parchment was collated to create a book. Most surviving images of scribes show them with a quill pen in their right hand (made from goose feathers) and a knife in their left, for sharpening the pen when it became blunt. The text was usually in brown or black ink, but a colourful palette was needed to create beautiful images. Indigo ink came from the woad plant grown in the monastery garden, and vivid scarlet came from insect shells. The colours were crushed and bonded with egg white. For illuminations, gold was beaten to leaf-like thinness (to create gold leaf) and delicately applied onto the page surface with a brush.

Sometimes the monks received visits from VIP dignitaries – the high and the mighty from Rome – who came to teach the oblates how to make the swirls and whirls of rounded script. How thrilling it must have been, while working away in the scriptorium, to hear of that 'eternal city', which – at that point – had around 100,000 residents. Bede might have heard of the monuments of Rome's imperial heyday – triumphal arches, baths, palaces, theatres, aqueducts, fountains – all lying in ruins. 'You must visit St Peter's,' the visitor may have told the boys, 'the basilica built by the Emperor Constantine is big enough to fit three thousand worshippers.'

So, at eighteen years old, Bede proved to be intelligent, hardworking and comfortable with life in the monastery. He was soon to be ordained a deacon; a position usually reserved for people over twenty-five. It was clear this boy was going places.

Or was he? Bede later wrote:

EIGHTEEN

I have spent the whole of my life within that monastery, devoting all my pains to the study of the Scriptures, and amid the observance of monastic discipline and the daily charge of singing in the Church, it has been ever my delight to learn or teach or write.

It all sounds . . . rather dull. Not the usual makings of a superstar. Yet, it's an inspirational lesson. From one room, in a monastery in Jarrow, Bede made it big. Just as gaming enthusiasts might make millions from their bedrooms today, or as sixteen-year-old Luke Littler reached the final of the 2023/24 World Darts Championship, from regular, sustained practice in his living room.

Over the next four decades, Bede became the greatest writer of his day, perhaps the most famous and enduring name of his time. He wrote or translated around forty books across his life, covering everything from science to grammar, history to biography. He also wrote a guide to the Holy Land, despite never leaving Northumbria.

His biggest hit was *Historia ecclesiastica* (A History of the English Church and People). This book is probably the most important account of the Anglo-Saxon world, and the medieval chroniclers – William of Malmesbury, Henry of Huntingdon and Geoffrey of Monmouth – relied heavily on Bede's work as source material – whose writing, in turn, informed the likes of Geoffrey Chaucer and William Shakespeare. So, for over a thousand years, it is through Bede that the British have understood their origins. Where – or who – would we be without him?

Bede was venerated as a saint shortly after his death (you can still visit his shrine in Durham Cathedral). From the ninth century onwards, he was known as the Venerable Bede (meaning 'Honoured' or 'Esteemed'). In around 1107, the chronicler Symeon of Durham recorded his immense impact: 'Bede lived hidden away in the extreme corner of the world, but after his death he lived on in his books and became known to everyone all over the world.' In the fifteenth century, Bede made a cameo in Dante's *Divine Comedy*, cast as a resident of Paradise.

Today, academics pontificate over whether Bede's legacy is either 'immense' or 'immeasurable'. It was Bede who adopted the Dionysian method of dating, essentially establishing 'Anno Domini' or 'AD' as the go-to system in Europe. He was, above all, a biblical scholar of international repute, and his Latin translations have been used for centuries (including at the Second Vatican Council in the 1960s).

Could that eighteen-year-old boy – soaking the animal skins in the river – have imagined that people would read his name in a book – this book – centuries later? What would he have made of modern books, made not by human hand, but bound and printed by machines?

I recently visited Clays printing factory in Suffolk, the largest single-site printing factory in the UK. Even to modern eyes, it is a marvel, with enormous, endlessly whirring machines and conveyor belts churning out two million books each week. What would Bede have made of it all? He'd be shocked and completely overwhelmed, no doubt – even with earplugs. But he would have been familiar with some stages of the process. Still, books are sprayed with coloured vegetable dyes, and decorated with swirls of golden foiling. An Anglo-Saxon scribe would have certainly appreciated that.

At eighteen years old, there was no way that Bede knew his place in the history books. But perhaps something clicked in those devastating months of plague: a determination to seize the day and never waste a moment more. A determination that would stay with him until the very end. As he lay dying in May 735, at the age of sixty, he weighed up his life, considering 'what good or evil' he had done and 'what judgment his soul [would] receive after its passing'. Bede needn't have worried about such judgments. For still, over a thousand years later (yes, a thousand years later!), his legacy is celebrated and those years of toil in that drafty scriptorium are still paying off.

An Introduction

The clock struck six. Bede heard the commotion before he saw it – outside, below the window, were hundreds of horses and carts, with banners fluttering in the wind. Indistinct voices floated up from below: 'Where can we leave the horses, sir? How far are the stables?'

Moments later, the door of the dining room flung open. In strode a striking young woman, bedecked in heavy robes and furs and with a dazzling crown on her head. This was a party outfit like no other.

'Goodness! That was a hellish journey!' she cried.

As the door closed behind her, the young woman – who had held herself so tall and noble – now transformed. She flung her crown onto the table, pulled out a chair and flopped into it.

But this moment of bliss was short.

'Hullo,' came a voice from a dark corner of the room. Quick as lightning, the girl sat bolt upright and whipped her crown back onto her head. 'Who's that?' she demanded.

Bede cautiously emerged. 'My Lady, I'm Bede, a humble oblate.'

'Oblate? I am Empress Matilda.'

Bede gasped and stumbled into an awkward bow.

'Oh, enough with that!' exclaimed the Empress. 'Just call me Matilda.'

They began to chat: his English marked by long vowels; hers tinged with a German drawl. They compared their journeys: his from the north of England, by foot; hers from Germany, on horse and ship.

Bede hoped they were placed beside one another at the table. She had some incredible stories to tell.

2

Empress Matilda

MATILDA WAS A FORMIDABLE eighteen-year-old. Already, she had been married for six years, called herself an Empress, and was familiar with overcoming all the usual problems of grown-up life. Crossing the Alps by the St Bernard Pass – tick. Her husband's excommunication – tick. Civil war – tick.

As she awoke on her eighteenth birthday in her palatial room, in Goslar in Saxony, there was probably more than just cake to worry about. What sort of pan-European crisis would she have to deal with today, Matilda wondered, as she threw on her linen chemise. Yawning, she held out her arms for a maid to don her tunic, floor-length and trimmed with coloured braid. Perhaps it would be her husband, Heinrich V, arguing with the Pope again. Or – she mused as her hair was parted in the centre, brushed and weaved into long, willowy plaits – was it to be another uprising in their German homelands? Either way, Matilda was ready for the fight.

Where did all this gumption come from? Matilda's husband, Heinrich, was not only King of Germany but also held the title of Holy Roman Emperor. For those of us who have no idea what that is, here's a speedy summary (HRE fans, talk among yourselves).

The Holy Roman Empire was a group of kingdoms and principalities in the centre of Europe, ruled over by the Holy Roman Emperor. It lasted over a thousand years, in one form or another, from 800 until 1806, and included some colourful characters (such as Charles the Bald and Charles the Fat). The land the empire encompassed changed over the centuries, but was essentially a large swathe of Central Europe, with the area of modern Germany in the centre.

You had to be a king before you could be voted in as Holy Roman Emperor, where you became *Primus inter pares* – the first among your fellow kings, the cream of the royal crop.

You also had to have a strong neck. The imperial crown was made of 22-carat gold and laden with 144 enormous precious stones. It was octagonal, with a cross at the front, and a large arch that supported it from the back like a mini flying buttress. Long golden pins held it together and could be removed, meaning you could take it apart for easier travel. Incredibly, though it was made in the tenth century, the crown still exists, kept behind lock and key in the Imperial Treasury in Vienna.

The first Holy Roman Emperor was Charlemagne, King of the Franks, crowned by Pope Leo III on Christmas Day AD 800. His legitimacy rested on the concept of *translatio imperii*, that this supreme power was inherited from the ancient emperors of Rome. So, in theory, this was the new Emperor Hadrian, or – if you were unlucky – the new Emperor Nero. The imperial crown passed from head to head until 1806, when the empire was dissolved by Napoleon. Lesson over.

Matilda's husband, Heinrich V, was Emperor No. 19, ruling from

1111–25. But this wasn't all feasting and festivities. The throne Heinrich inherited turned out to be quite the poisoned chalice. There was some serious baggage: a thirty-year-long argument raging with the Papacy, known to historians as 'The Investiture Controversy'. Of course, it wasn't unusual for the Emperor – with his immense power and ability to rule by divine right – to come up against the Pope in Rome. It was natural that the Pope and Emperor might sometimes contradict, undercut, or rival one another, like the captain and a manager of a football team. But at the start of the twelfth century, neither was playing ball.

Luckily for Heinrich, as he sought to steady the ship, he was joined by one of the most capable brains in Europe. There was no one better suited for high-level crisis management and epic family breakdowns than his wife, the eighteen-year-old Matilda. It was in her DNA. Although, to an untrained eye, she appeared to be born and bred from noble German stock, her roots lay in another country, far across the sea. Matilda was something quite exotic: Matilda was English.

Matilda's parents were one of Europe's great power couples: King Henry I of England and Matilda of Scotland. Together, they represented a union between the new Norman rulers of England (Henry's father was William the Conqueror) and the old Anglo-Saxon dynasty (Matilda's great-great-great-uncle was Edward the Confessor).

King Henry had come to the throne by somewhat suspicious means. In August 1100, he was out hunting in the New Forest with his older brother, King William II. Suddenly, out of nowhere, an arrow hurtled towards the king, and struck him in the lung, killing him. Not bothering to tend to his brother's corpse, Henry galloped off to the treasury and seized the crown. The Henrician era had begun.

He proved to be a bullish king, earning the nickname of 'Lion of Justice'. 'No one dared misdo another in his time', the chroniclers wrote. Stories of his heavy-handed approach spread far and wide. There was the incident when he cornered a man named Conan Pilatus at the top of a tower in Rouen and hurled him from the ramparts (the tower was renamed Conan's Leap). This was a king who – in an act of petty vengeance – would order his own granddaughters to be blinded, and their noses cut off.

His wife and queen was Matilda of Scotland, who chroniclers generously recorded as looking 'not too bad'. Following in the footsteps of her mother, Saint Margaret of Scotland, she was fiercely pious. During Lent, Queen Matilda wore a hair shirt next to her skin, went barefoot to church and kissed the ulcers of beggars. Her brother, David, was far from impressed. 'If the King knew', he warned his sister, 'he would never want to put his lips to yours again.' Perhaps brother David was right. While Henry and Matilda had two legitimate heirs, Henry was father to at least twenty-two illegitimate children on the side.

But Henry and Matilda had much to bond over. They were a formidable, feisty pair, born and bred in the political game. It's no surprise that their eldest child – our very own Matilda – would inherit an uncompromising pride, razor-sharp intelligence and dogged single-mindedness. Commentators remarked that she 'displayed her father's courage and her mother's piety'. Another chronicler put it more bluntly: she was 'of the stock of tyrants'.

So Matilda was fierce by nature. But what of her nurture? She was born around 7 February 1102 in a royal palace. Some say at the old capital city, Winchester, or Sutton Courtenay in Oxfordshire. The following year she was joined by a baby brother, William. While Baby William was the heir apparent of the Kingdom of England and Duchy of Normandy, little Matilda was also a valuable political bargaining chip – a prized asset on the European marriage market. From the moment of their birth, these bundles of joy were in the history books. Every aspect of their health and well-being was noted, every sneeze or cough having the potential – if it became serious – to affect the lives of millions of people.

Despite this enormous weight of responsibility from the word go, it must have been a thrilling childhood, with every indulgence of the royal court: William was 'a prince so pampered'. Their playground was a blur of castles, hunting lodges, manors, cathedrals, abbeys and convents. Sometimes the children joined their parents on royal progresses – tours of the country to visit courtiers, indulge in summer sports, and keep an eye on unruly subjects.

This was no small operation. It was akin to a modern rock band going on tour, with lorries filled with lighting equipment, marketing teams and huge stage sets, all managed by lots of people with clipboards and headsets. These royal progresses had feather beds and linen sheets to be transported. Rugs and furs, tapestries and hangings. Among bear-baiters and cock-fighters were bishops and cooks, stewards and trumpeters. And, just a week after arriving and finally settling in, the sewers began to reek and food supplies started to run low, so the entire entourage would move on, once again.

As with many a nepo baby, young Matilda became well-tuned to the intricacies of power politics. She eavesdropped on conversations with earls and bishops. She counted Anselm, the Archbishop of Canterbury, as a mentor. She learnt to avoid blunders, to flatter foreign dignitaries, to charm awkward subjects. It was all good preparation for the challenge ahead.

When Matilda was six years old, a group of men with strange accents and unfamiliar clothing visited the palace. Why did they keep looking at her, she wondered. Why did they keep pointing?

These were the envoys of King Heinrich V of Germany, who, on behalf of their master, requested Matilda's hand in marriage. It was an offer King Henry couldn't refuse, for Heinrich was on track to become Holy Roman Emperor. How wonderful – how valuable – to have his daughter marry one of the most powerful men in Europe. An empress in the family! The proposal was accepted. Henry promised a vast dowry of 10,000 marks in silver (around £11 million in today's money).

Thus, the countdown to Matilda's departure began, and she started going by a new title: 'Matilda, betrothed wife of the king of the Romans'. This was wedding preparation on an epic scale. A new tax was introduced: three shillings on every hide of land (a hide being about 120 acres). By February 1110, when Matilda was eight years old, the same imperial envoys returned to the English court. This time, she would leave with them. They took her to a foreign land to marry a twenty-four-year-old stranger.

It must have been a daunting moment as that first chapter in Matilda's young life came to an end. As she boarded the ship destined for Boulogne, she gazed back at her homeland. Those grey cliffs, soon fading to a distant line on the horizon, then disappearing altogether. She would never see her mother or brother again.

Any homesickness was outweighed by the apprehension of meeting her new husband. Heinrich may have been handsome and powerful, but had a sinister side, too: this was a man who betrayed his own father, leaving him 'despoiled and desolate'. After arriving at Boulogne, Matilda and her English party travelled inland to Liège (now a Belgian city, an hour's drive from Brussels) where they met her husband-to-be for the first time. It was a fractious start. Heinrich's first move was to send Matilda's retinue – a few friendly faces from home – straight back to

England. Matilda, still a small child, was now well and truly on her own.

But her whimpers were of no importance in the political landscape of twelfth-century Europe. Coronation preparations went full steam ahead. On 25 July 1110 – the feast day of St James the Great – Matilda was taken to the magnificent Mainz Cathedral. Under towering sandstone arches, in front of hundreds of strangers, she was held in the arms of Bruno, Archbishop of Trier, and anointed with holy oil by Friedrich, Archbishop of Cologne. The crown was heavy, and several sizes too big. But she was Matilda, Queen Consort of Germany, and still eight years old.

After this, work began. Matilda underwent an empress's training. She was to be 'nobly brought up and honourably served', and 'learn the language and customs and laws of the country, and all that an empress ought to know'. The point was, Matilda wasn't trained to be a passive wife or doting mother. Matilda was to be a power player in her own right, who would take responsibility in politics and governance, and – in the event of Heinrich's death pre-dating hers – act as regent for a young son. Matilda learnt two new languages: Latin, the dominant written language in Western Europe, and a dialect we now call Middle High German, which was the spoken language at court.

Shortly before her twelfth birthday, and now considered an adult, Matilda was taken to Worms Cathedral to officially tie the knot with Heinrich. This was pomp and ceremony on such an epic scale that – as one biographer has noted – it made the rest of her life seem 'something of an anti-climax'.

Wedding guests included such 'a great concourse of archbishops and bishops, dukes and counts, abbots and provosts and learned clergy that not even the oldest man present could remember ever having seen or heard of such a huge assembly of such great persons'.

What's more, so numerous were the wedding presents that 'not one of [Heinrich's] chamberlains . . . could count them'. Perhaps Matilda was beginning to see the perks of German life.

Indeed, her noble upbringing paid off, for she performed at the wedding with aplomb:

Matilda, the daughter of Henry king of the English, a girl of noble character, distinguished and beautiful, who was held to bring glory and honour to both the Roman empire and the English realm. She was born of ancient lineage, most noble and royal on both sides, and gave promise of abundant future virtue in everything she said and did, so that all hoped she might be the mother of an heir to the Roman empire.

In February 1116, fourteen-year-old Matilda joined her husband on a journey to Italy. Preparations were made for the epic journey through the heart of the Alps. What an adventure for this young girl, used to the relatively flat landscapes of southern England, to be bumping along ancient tracks, as the Romans had done centuries before, and gazing up at the snow-covered peaks from her wagon. As she lay in her tent at night, what did she make of the wolves howling through the valleys? Was she frightened and homesick, or thrilled at the excitement? A mixture of both, I suspect.

The group reached the Brenner Pass – the lowest of the eight major passes in the Alps – at the beginning of March, travelled through the St Bernard's Pass, and arrived in Venice on 11 March. Here, Matilda stayed in luxury appropriate to her station: the Doge's Palace.

By her late teenage years, Matilda had undergone a complete rebrand. Any of that English upbringing was stamped out, and she was rebooted as a German queen consort, equipped with the German language, customs, jokes and habits. Credit to her, she had earnt her husband's trust. While Heinrich returned to Germany to deal with rebellions, he left sixteen-year-old Matilda behind, where she spent two years in charge of Italy. This was a major turning point. Matilda had seen power at play her whole life, first as a child in her father's court, then as a young queen of Germany. She had spent years training in etiquette, language and diplomacy. This was the real test. And in this moment of truth – of exercising authority on behalf of her husband, and sitting alone at the head of meetings and hearings – she didn't disappoint.

Matilda proved to be a dab hand at diplomacy and statecraft, confident in how to sponsor royal grants, lead petitions or maintain the peace – a lot of responsibility for a sixth-former. It was lonely of course, no doubt compounded by the news that her beloved mother, Queen Matilda, had died. The chronicler William of Malmesbury despaired at the loss, writing of how 'she was snatched away from her country, to the great loss of her people'. For young Matilda, alone and in charge of Italy, it was another reminder that she was no longer a child.

You can see now that when Matilda woke up on her eighteenth birthday, she had reason to be weary. She was 'Mathildis dei gratia Romanorum Regina' – 'Matilda by the grace of God, Queen of the Romans'. But though it seems like she had achieved so much, she had ultimately failed in her prime duty: to produce an heir. As she washed and dressed that morning, her eyes must have darted to her stomach. Not a bump in sight. How could Heinrich and Matilda ever rest easy in their restive kingdom, without heirs of their own to secure the future?

Yet it was not in Germany, nor with Heinrich, that Matilda's future lay. In the final days of her eighteenth year, in 1120, Matilda received terrible, life-changing news. On 25 November, a ship had sailed from Barfleur, in Normandy, heaving with a throng of 300 passengers. This ship was newly refitted and there was no reason to suspect it would struggle on the short journey across the channel. But in the dead of night, not far from the French shore, its port side struck a submerged rock. Within minutes, the ship capsized. Hundreds of souls perished in those freezing waters, frantically splashing and thrashing, unable to swim.

This was not only a tragic loss of human life. It was a political catastrophe. According to William of Malmesbury, 'No ship that ever sailed brought England such disaster'. Aboard the White Ship, as it was known, was the cream of English aristocratic youth – earls and countesses and, most significantly, Matilda's younger brother, William.

How Matilda must have shuddered, hearing the news, imagining William struggling and spluttering helplessly in the rough waters, his corpse in the weeds on the ocean floor. And then, in this moment of grief, a sudden shock. She was not only an Empress and Queen, but something more – the heir to the Kingdom of England and Duchy of Normandy.

It was a tragedy, no doubt. But still, Matilda probably expected to continue her life in Germany with her husband Heinrich and a healthy brood of princes and princesses. Yet this future was uprooted, too, five years later, in 1125: Heinrich died from cancer, leaving Matilda 'overwhelmed with grief'. Matilda, still without a child, made plans to return to her homeland, now in hot demand: 'There was not a single nobleman,' the chroniclers noted, 'from Germany to Rome whose most cherished wish was not to become her proud husband'. In England, she was nominated by her father, King Henry I, as his heir. What happened next should have been straightforward: Henry I dies, Matilda becomes queen. Yet – as was becoming a theme in Matilda's life – nothing ever happened the way it was supposed to.

At the death of Henry I in 1135 (caused by eating too many lampreys, against doctor's orders), Matilda's cousin, Stephen, jumped at the chance of seizing the throne, and would stop at nothing to make it his. Before Matilda had even heard the news of her father's death, Stephen had raced from Boulogne to Winchester, where he was crowned. A new power struggle kicked off: Matilda vs Stephen, each with their own claim to legitimacy. For Stephen's supporters, he had undergone the sacred anointing of a man with royal blood in his veins. For Matilda's supporters, they argued she was the only legitimate child of the previous king.

The country was dragged into 'the Anarchy', a period of civil war so terrible it was said that 'Christ and his saints slept'. An anonymous account of the period, *Gesta Stephani* (the 'Deeds of Stephen'), recorded those years of despair:

> *England, formerly the seat of justice, the habitation of peace, the*
> *height of piety, the mirror of religion, became thereafter a home*
> *of perversity, a haunt of strife, a training-ground of disorder,*
> *and a teacher of every kind of rebellion.*

For Matilda, too, they were years of frustration. The truth is, she was ahead of her time. This was a woman breaking boundaries. For she was prepared to become Queen of England – not as a king's wife – but in the unprecedented form of a female king. Despite being qualified and legitimate, her kingly approach – coming from a woman – was too much for many contemporaries to comprehend. 'She at once put on an extremely arrogant demeanour,' the *Gesta Stephani* complained, 'instead of the modest gait and bearing proper to the gentle sex'. Would her father, King Henry I, have put up with such nonsense?

Matilda remarried in 1128 – this time, to Geoffrey Plantagenet, Count of Anjou – and though she never sat on the throne, it was through the reign of her son, King Henry II, that she finally emerged victorious.

Little did eighteen-year-old Matilda know – this bright, brilliant, ambitious teenager – what was to come. That her time in mainland Europe was merely preparation for the mighty challenges ahead: the political machinations of some of England's darkest days.

And yet, throughout her long, difficult life, she proved to be exceptional, never allowing herself to be restricted by the limitations of her sex and always going by 'Empress'. She presided over Normandy, managed political crises (such as her son, Henry II's, rocky relationship with Thomas Beckett), and gave advice to the rulers of Europe. The French poet Benoit de Sainte-Maure struggled to fit his praise on paper: 'More parchment is now needed,' he panicked, 'in order to enable me to continue recounting the noble deeds and great accomplishments'.

Matilda was one of the best politicians this country has ever seen and lived a life true to her name. She was Matilda, in every sense of the word: 'mighty in battle'.

Small Talk

The dining room flooded with the evening sun, reflected around the room by Matilda's crown. It created a speckled effect on the ceiling, reminding Bede of those wide Northumbrian night skies.

He suddenly felt totally out of place, wildly underdressed and wretchedly homesick. But it was too late to back out now, for the sound of footsteps floated up from the staircase. Matilda gave him a quick glance, 'These must be the others! About time!' she winked.

She was right. Moments later, in poured six new party-goers. First came a girl with fiery red hair, dressed in a black and white gown. This was Elizabeth.

Behind Elizabeth came another girl, Fionnghal, with long brown hair and a plaid dress. Then two boys: one with brown curly hair, in a green tunic and extremely tight leggings. This was Geoffrey. The other, a tall black boy, who wore a white shirt over his broad shoulders. This was Jacques. Then came Horace, attired in white trousers and a smart blue coat with gold braiding. He was chatting with Jeffrey, a fellow half his height, wearing a sumptuous red satin outfit.

With the guests bunching in groups around the table, they began to talk.

3

Geoffrey Chaucer

OVER THE CENTURIES, WALES has been the source of all kinds of weird and wonderful innovations. In 1557, a man from Tenby, Robert Recorde, created the equals sign: 'to avoid the tedious repetition of these words "is equal to" I will . . . use a pair of parallel lines of one length, thus: =, because no 2 things can be more equal'. In 1904, Morris and Walter Davies produced the first spare tyre at their shop on Stepney Street in Llanelli, and spare tyres are still known as 'stepneys' in some countries today. Wales is also where the Pot Noodle is produced. Not – as the 2006 advert suggested – from a Pot Noodle Mine, but a factory near Caerphilly, which opened in 1979.

But perhaps the greatest – and most terrible – innovation from those green hills and valleys was the Welsh longbow, made of elm. These bows were 'unpolished, rude and uncouth', but had a devasting effect when their arrows struck the unlucky victim. The writer, known as 'Gerald of Wales', recorded the impact in his 1191 account, *The Itinerary of Archbishop Baldwin Through Wales*:

*William de Breusa also testifies that one of his soldiers, in a
conflict with the Welsh, was wounded by an arrow, which
pierced his armour doubly coated with iron, and passing through
his hip entered the saddle and mortally wounded the horse.
Another soldier, equally well guarded with armour, had his hip
penetrated by an arrow quite to the saddle and, on turning his
horse round, received a similar wound in the opposite hip, which
fixed him on both sides to his seat.*

During the fourteenth century, the English made full use of this
Welsh innovation, putting it front and centre of their military
strategy against France. The result? English victory and French
annihilation. The advantage of the longbow was so great that it
almost seemed unfair. It was akin to entering the Tour de France
on an electric bike or playing a hockey match on a steep hill with
the opponent's goal at the bottom.

While the crossbow could fire two shots a minute, the longbow
could fire ten, penetrating armour from 200 yards away. At the
Battle of Crecy in 1346, the English fired roughly half a million
arrows, which fell 'with such force and quickness that it seemed
as if it snowed'. In 1349, King Edward III banned people from
playing football (imagine the fallout today!), concerned it was a
distraction from archery training. Instead of footballers with toned
calves and blond topknots, England's young men developed enormous, bulging shoulders, able to command the longbow's
draw-strength of 200 pounds.

What was the fighting for? Since 1066, when Normans first sat
on the English throne, England's monarchy and nobility had roots
in Normandy. Despite settling in England, many spoke French,
owned lands in France and were buried in France. Empress Matilda
was buried in Rouen Cathedral, and her son, Henry II, in

Fontevraud Abbey, in Anjou. Anglo-Saxon culture had become low-brow while French habits and customs were now high-brow.

You can still see it in our language today. The words used on a farm – 'cow' and 'sheep' – derive from Anglo-Saxon, but their fine-dining equivalent – 'beef' and 'mutton' – have French origins. The jobs of men responsible for working a ship (boatswain, coxswain, seamen) derive from Anglo-Saxon, while those of officers (captain, lieutenant, admiral) are Norman-French.

But there were bigger problems than a language barrier that resulted from this Norman inheritance. It was politically awkward: English kings still held duchies in France – some from the conquest, others from marriages – making them vassals of the French king. By 1337, tensions reached boiling point. When the French king, Phillip VI, confiscated Gascony, Edward went nuclear: he hammered home his claim as the rightful King of England and France, and in 1346 launched a full-scale invasion. It was something he might later regret, for this was no flash-in-the-pan victory. It set in course the 'Hundred Years' War', a series of battles that dragged on for the next 116 years, until 1453.

Thanks to the longbow, it started off with some stellar English victories: Crecy in 1346 and Poitiers in 1356. So, when the army returned to France in October 1359, morale was pretty high with hopes of more glory. What's more, the French king, John II, was out of the way, locked up in the Tower of London (where he joined David of Scotland, son of Robert the Bruce). The English force was 10,000 strong, trudging 160 miles from Calais to Reims. On arrival they planned an audacious move: they would crown King Edward III as King of France.

But King Edward's hopes for a speedy victory were soon dashed. When the English army arrived at Reims ready to crown their champion, they found the city occupied by Charles, the Dauphin and son of the French King, acting as regent. Charles played a long game. He refused to engage in battle, denying the English another snappy victory and forcing a siege.

So began a miserable winter for the English army, shivering outside the city walls. Somewhere in the midst of it was an eighteen-year-old called Geoffrey, who seemed determined to make himself a nuisance. The news quickly reached the camp: 'My lord, my lord! It's Geoffrey Chaucer! He's been taken hostage by the French!' For days, perhaps weeks, Geoffrey was in the hospitality of his French friends.

There's no record of the conditions he was held in, but his capture could have been either good or bad news. Had the French perceived him as a lousy English soldier, he'd have spent the nights shivering in a dank cell, scratching his name into the walls ('Geoff woz ere'), wondering if it was the last thing he'd ever write. Had the French perceived him as a member of courtly circles (which is more likely), he would have secured a serious upgrade on the miserable conditions of the English tents. No more sleepless nights, with the endless pitter-patter of rain on the canvas! No more soggy food, or damp tunics! But then there was the small matter of getting home . . .

Luckily for Geoffrey, he had friends in high places. He just so happened to be a member of the household of a royal prince, and on 1 March 1360, the king made a payment of £16 towards his ransom. Geoffrey was free to return to the English camp, now a source of great curiosity: 'Tell us, Geoff, what was it like in there? Is French food really as dodgy as they say it is?'

By springtime, the game was up, and the invasion abandoned. As King Edward jumped down from his ship into the shallows of the English waters, he must have felt it a bitter humiliation. After all that effort, no French crown. Geoffrey was relieved to be firmly back on English soil, and buzzing to see his parents: 'Honestly, Mum, you'll never believe what happened in France . . .'

Geoffrey Chaucer was born in the early 1340s. His father, John Chaucer, was a big name in the wine trade, and his family lived slap bang in the middle of London's wine district, Vintry Ward, on the north bank of the River Thames. Chez Chaucer was somewhere between St Paul's Cathedral and the Tower of London, near a little angled street called Elbow Lane. The street was recorded as 'extending in length from the royal street of Thames Street on the south up to the water of Walbrook on the north'. The Walbrook was one of many of London's old rivers that flowed into the Thames, now buried under pavements. In Geoffrey's childhood, it was via the Walbrook that Gascon wine was unloaded into the family cellars.

The Chaucers were a wealthy bunch. Geoffrey's mother, Agnes de Copton, came from a property family. Her uncle, Hamo, was a moneyer at the Tower of London (someone who is officially permitted to mint money). John Chaucer's family were well-off, too, though money was still a point of tension. In 1324, to keep hold of a family property in Ipswich and share out a fortune, young John Chaucer was kidnapped by a Wicked Aunt, who tried to force him to marry her twelve-year-old daughter. The plot was foiled, the aunt imprisoned and fined £250 (now equivalent to about £200,000).

Trading as a London vintner meant being part of an international scene. Had Geoffrey accompanied his father to the portside he would have discovered a wonderland of delights: wine arriving from Gascony, chests containing Spanish leather, German beeswax, Italian glass or silks and spices from the Far East. It was a cacophony of sound: ropes flapping against the wood, sellers shouting their wares, the snorting of pigs, the braying of horses, and the never-ending *Ding! Dong!* of church bells.

Indeed, churches were two a penny in these parts. Within the old walls of the City of London (a square mile), there were a whopping 108 parishes. Giving instructions must have been a nightmare: 'Turn left at the church, then slight right at the next church, then four churches later, turn into the alley, where you'll see a church . . .'

Geoffrey's church was St Martin in the Vintry, which he visited once a week for mass. In the church was an altar, dedicated to St Thomas Beckett, whose shrine in Canterbury attracted thousands of pilgrims each year. Was it in those early years, at church, that Geoffrey cooked up the idea for *The Canterbury Tales*?

Geoffrey's life began in a happy and prosperous fashion, but his family soon faced challenges on several fronts. In 1348, when he was about five years old, Vintry Ward received devastating news. Bordeaux's wine production was decimated. In 1308, 100,000 tons of wine had left the Gascon ports, but in 1348, it was less than 6,000 tons. It wasn't just wine production that was thrown into havoc. The entirety of Europe had succumbed to a disease, spreading with unprecedented virulence. As John Chaucer stood at the quayside, watching ships arriving with no produce to show for the voyage, the horrifying truth must have dawned: it was only a matter of time before England, too, was visited by the Black Death.

Unknown at the time, this 'great mortality' arrived via rat-infested ships. Starting with port towns, it tore through southern England in 1348. By the end of 1349, it had reached central Scotland. Geoffrey le Baker, an Oxfordshire cleric, recorded the spread:

*And at first it carried off almost all the inhabitants of the
seaports in Dorset, and then those living inland and from there
it raged so dreadfully through Devon and Somerset as far as
Bristol and then men of Gloucester refused those of Bristol
entrance to their country, everyone thinking that the breath of
those who lived among people who died of plague was infectious.
But at last, it attacked Gloucester, yea and Oxford and London,
and finally the whole of England so violently that scarcely one in
ten of either sex was left alive.*

Even the royal family were tainted: fourteen-year-old Princess
Joan perished in the fever. Edward III wrote a grief-stricken letter
to Alfonso of Castile, whose son, Pedro, Joan had been betrothed
to marry:

*But see (with what intense bitterness of heart we have to tell
you this) destructive Death (who seizes young and old alike,
sparing no one, and reducing rich and poor to the same level)
has lamentably snatched from both of us our dearest daughter
(whom we loved best of all, as her virtues demanded). No fellow
human being could be surprised if we were inwardly desolated
by the sting of this bitter grief, for we are humans too.*

How terrifying it must have been for the Chaucer family, living
in the heart of this metropolis, where ships continued to come
and go. Fearing the worst, they made arrangements. On 7 April
1349, John Chaucer's half-brother, Thomas Heron, adjusted his
will. He bequeathed all his tenements to his father-in-law, Richard.
But the plague was quick to strike. When Richard updated his
will five days later, Thomas was already dead.

By the end of the year, the family were familiar with tragedy.

John Chaucer lost his mother, stepfather and brother. Agnes lost her uncle and cousin. But, quite incredibly, Geoffrey and his parents came out in the clear. Though they'd endured the terrors of plague, the fortunes of the Chaucers had never been better. They'd just pocketed the collective wealth of all their deceased relatives, an immense fortune. In 1349, for example, Agnes inherited twenty-four London shops from her late uncle.

They weren't the only ones. The world was a different place now. With such a sudden drop in population numbers, the economic and social order shifted. Those who survived demanded high wages and lower rents. Land was plentiful, the countryside dotted with abandoned villages waiting to be filled. With fewer mouths to feed, food costs plummeted. A lack of farmhands sped along the shift from labour-intensive arable farming to sheep-rearing. In the late medieval period, wool emerged as the absolute backbone of the English economy – literally so for some. The Lord Chancellor sat on a wool bale to remind himself of the source of England's prosperity. Now known as 'The Woolsack', it is still the seat of the Lord Speaker in the House of Lords.

In this moment of societal shake-up, Geoffrey, too, took a surprising turn. Instead of joining the family business, he climbed the social ladder. He became a page in the household of the Countess of Ulster, the wife of Lionel of Antwerp, the third son of King Edward III. It was quite a step up. Geoffrey was in the world of the ruling classes, integrated into a system of royal patronage. Here he would be educated as the medieval equivalent of a civil servant, learning diplomacy, manners and politics. He would become a worldly man, learning customs and enjoying fashions from across the globe. His climb up the greasy pole had begun.

Geoffrey's teenage years were marked by some of the most dazzling displays of the medieval world. He caught sight of

tournaments, royal weddings and outrageous fancy-dress specta-
cles. This was akin to following a minor royal to all their glamorous
engagements: Royal Ascot, Wimbledon, Trooping the Colour, with
celebrity appearances, paparazzi and hundreds of leftover scones.

Christmas of 1357 was spent at Hatfield Manor House in
Yorkshire, which still exists, and is still lived in. How thrilling it
must have been, in December 1357, for the big names of Yorkshire
to receive an invitation to dine with the royal family, to share
sweetmeats and Rhenish wine with the sons of Edward III. Yet,
as they chatted about the latest wars in France, or discussed the
best way to fix a leaking moat, they couldn't help but be distracted.
'Have you seen what he's wearing?' a bishop may have gossiped
to his neighbour. 'I can't believe the countess would stand for this!
That young man might as well be naked!'

Their comments were provoked by the sight of sixteen-year-old
Geoffrey. He wore an outfit so immodest, so revealing, that some
blamed its popularity among young dandies for inciting God's
wrath and causing the Black Death. It was a tunic with sleeves
(called a paltok), black and red tights (called a hose) and plain
shoes, and was bought for him by his employer, the Countess of
Ulster. But the sartorial shock came from the *very* snug fit. The
paltoks were 'extremely short garments . . . which failed to conceal
their arses or their private parts'. That is the first record we have
of Geoffrey Chaucer. Not Chaucer the Diplomat, or Chaucer the
Poet, but Chaucer the Risqué!

The following year, in 1358, Geoffrey's diary continued to be
jam-packed. Windsor for St George's Day, then London for a triple
betrothal: Philippa of Clarence to Edmund Mortimer, John of
Gaunt to Blanche of Lancaster, and Princess Margaret to John
Hastings. Then to Liverpool, Reading, and back to London, for
the funeral of Isabella, widow of Edward II.

It was a favourable time to be in a royal household, for good news was always arriving from France. Had tabloids been around, headlines would have read something like 'Black Prince does it again!!' and 'Time to take a (long) bow, froggies!!'. Edward III's reign was becoming the stuff of legend, and he was happy to provide some extra PR. In 1348, he founded the Order of the Garter – his very own set of Knights of the Round Table. Windsor was redecorated as Camelot, and Edward painted himself as the new King Arthur, with noble quests and tales of honour.

In 1359, Countess Elizabeth's household merged with that of her husband, Lionel. It was probably as part of Lionel's company that Geoffrey took part in the expedition to France during that winter, where this paltok-wearing pageboy found himself captured by enemy forces. And that is how Geoffrey Chaucer's teenage years concluded.

In his adult life, Geoffrey worked as a diplomat, darting between France, Genoa and Florence. He married Philippa Roet, a lady-in-waiting in the queen's household, and together they had three or four children. Serving both Edward III and Richard II, Geoffrey went through the top positions: comptroller of London customs, MP for Kent, and project manager of royal building projects.

But while he was busy totting up royal accounts, or correcting architectural plans, his quill soon found itself escaping to scratch out lines of text, far from empirical. Was it embarrassing, the first time this man of state admitted his true hobby? 'Don't laugh, Phil,' he might have muttered to his wife, as they tucked themselves into bed, 'but I'd like to have a go at writing . . . poetry'.

With the support of his patron and friend, John of Gaunt, it was his writing that put his name on the map. First came 'The Book of the Duchess', then 'Parlement of Foules', 'House of Fame', 'Troilus and Criseyde' and 'The Legend of Good Women'. In 1387, he began his most famous work, *The Canterbury Tales*, which tells the story of a group of Canterbury pilgrims.

It was a hobby worth pursuing, because Chaucer turned out to be pretty good. Thomas Hoccleve, a contemporary, hailed him as 'the firste fyndere of our fair langage'. Today, he is known as either the 'father of English literature' or the 'father of English poetry'. Indeed, two thousand words of today's English language are derived from Chaucerian manuscripts. There are plenty of Chaucerian phrases too, useful to have at hand in moments of crisis. For soothing a driver with road rage, use 'patience is a virtue'. For backtracking on any mistaken drunken promises, go with 'many a true word is spoken in jest'. And one for break-up advice: 'What is better than wisdom? Woman. And what is better than a good woman? Nothing.'

So where did it all come from? How did the son of a London vintner become one of the wittiest wordsmiths in all of British history? In some ways, Chaucer's world was very similar to our own. As historian Marion Turner points out, he 'grew up in a pandemic and in a time of social and cultural change, witnessing tension between England and other parts of Europe, chaotic parliaments and cost-of-living crises'. But then again, there were so many differences: it was also 'a time of universal religious belief, little medical knowledge, no real democracy, and a much more extreme patriarchal system'.

Chaucer's success – the brilliance and longevity of his writings – lies in his ability to stay relevant, whatever the century. He captured something timeless in his writing. He could shrewdly observe human nature, understand the follies and foibles of humankind, and weave them into gripping stories and hilarious satire.

It's impossible to say where this talent came from. But it is hard to believe that those early formative years, when Geoffrey was playing in the streets of Vintry Ward, and watching merchants from every corner of the world, didn't give him an understanding of the human condition. As a page, he learnt the intricacies of diplomatic nuance and manners. What about his time campaigning in France, where he spent days trudging through the countryside, overhearing the conversations of princes and ordinary soldiers? Then, when he was taken hostage by the French, Geoffrey's antennae were again registering the peculiar habits of humankind.

Today we may perceive Geoffrey as a classic parochial character from *ye olde medieval Englande*. But his life was so much more than that. His was a 'European life', as a recent biography put it, shaped by a mixture of English and international influences. He was – even as a spritely eighteen-year-old – a man of the world.

Hiccups

Bede was struggling.

'It's just that we – hic! – didn't have so many bubbles – hic! – in the wine – hic! – in the monastery.'

Hic . . . hic . . . hic!

Jacques stepped forward. 'Do you mind?' he asked, gesturing with his hands.

Hic . . . hic . . . hic!

Jacques began massaging Bede's temple and neck: 'Breathe in. Now, I'm going to squeeze and, yes, alter the pressure in your ear canal.'

Bede's eyes bulged and widened at the strange sensation – the movement of air inside his head. But sure enough – a miracle! – the hiccups were gone.

'Bravo!' cried Jeffrey, clapping his hands in the air.

'Fascinating,' murmured Elizabeth, deep in thought. 'Are you a herbalist, or an astrologer?'

'No, no, my lady, nothing of the sort,' Jacques laughed. 'I'm a diver.'

4

Jacques Francis

IT IS AN ODD place to meet, at the bottom of the ocean. Yet
this was where fate would place the first meeting of Jacques and
Mary. The location was the Solent, a shallow stretch of tidal water
between the Isle of Wight and the south coast of England, near
the towns of Portsmouth and Southampton. The year was 1546.

Jacques leant over the side of the boat, which bobbed to and
fro, dancing on the waves. Gazing down into the sparkling waters,
he was filled with anticipation at this first meeting. Would Mary
really be as beautiful as the minstrels had claimed? It was Mary,
after all, who had once been the favourite of Henry VIII, King of
England. Was she still in shape, or would she be weathered and
aged by the ravages of time?

Such wandering thoughts were interrupted by a sudden splash.
The anchor was tossed overboard. As it disappeared into the murky
depths below, Jacques returned to the business of the voyage. The
deck was noisy and full of action: sails flapping in the wind, the
endless creak of old timbers, and hurried orders given in thick
Venetian accents.

To the unknowing eye, the boat appeared to have a motley crew. They were shoddily dressed, with barely a scrap of sailing knowledge between them. But these men weren't aboard to just sail the seas.

Once the ship was steadied and in position, Jacques grabbed a weight, took one large, long inhale to fill his lungs, and threw himself into the waves. Within an instant, he was plunged into a new world. The chaos of the ship's deck disappeared. Those orders and arguments, those cries of 'Hurry! Hurry!', the intolerable squawking of sea birds – all of it was muted by the water.

For pretty much anyone else in Tudor England, this situation would be a reason to panic. These would be their last, spluttering, terrifying seconds before they blacked out. But for Jacques, as he descended, fathom by fathom, he felt an overwhelming sense of calm. His heart rate settled and all he could hear was the low rumble of ocean currents.

As Jacques fell deeper, the surrounding pressure of the water gradually increased, and – here was the great skill – he was able to balance the pressure within his ears as he did so. Today this is known as equalization and might involve pinching your nose and blowing gently, forcing air to move into the middle ear. Get it wrong and you'll face permanent ear damage, so it was crucial that Jacques could control the descent to perfection. The light was dimming and, looking up, the ship was nothing more than a large black oval, silhouetted by the sunshine.

After twelve metres of descent, Jacques finally reached the seabed, feeling the sand in his fingers. It was piercingly cold, between 5 and 10 degrees Celsius. The water was oppressively murky: Jacques could only see three metres ahead of him. But in the gloom, he could just about make out Mary. She wasn't a wife, nor lover. This was the magnificent *Mary Rose*, the flagship of the

English fleet. Launched in 1511, she served in action against France and Scotland. For over three decades, her galley and decks had been bustling with life: carpenters carrying out repairs, cooks preparing vast feasts to feed the ship's company.

And now here she lay at the bottom of the sea, in pieces, silent, attended only by this strange aquatic man. But as he explored the wreck, Jacques soon realized they were not alone – far from it. They were being watched. Among slimy ropes and snapped timbers were hundreds of haggard, ghostly faces, with skin peeled away by the seawater, and flesh nibbled away by crabs. This wasn't just a shipwreck: this was a graveyard. Alongside piles of ordinary objects – surgeons' mallets, cooking pots, quills, chamber pots, rosary beads – were disembodied arms and legs, swaying gently among the reeds.

What happened? The previous year, on Sunday, 19 July 1545, England was under attack. A fleet of 235 ships carrying 30,000 Frenchmen clashed with their English foes not far from Portsmouth. It would go down in history as the Battle of the Solent. Not long into the scrap, the English flagship, the *Mary Rose*, ran into difficulty. A survivor recalled what happened:

> *The disaster was caused by their no having closed the lowest row of gun ports on one side of the ship. Having fired the guns on that side, the ship was turning, in order to fire from the other, when the wind caught her sails so strongly as to heel her over, and plunge her open gunport beneath the water, which flooded and sank her.*

The last recorded words of the ship's commander, Sir George Carew, reveal he took his crew to the cleaners: 'I have the sort of knaves I cannot rule'. But it was too late to play the blame game.

King Henry VIII – who had been dining aboard a few hours before – watched in horror from the shore. Lady Carew, seeing her husband sink to his watery grave, fainted. Of the nearly 500 men on board, no more than thirty-five survived.

Tragic though it might be, the ship wasn't going to be left to ruin. Immediately, plans were put in place to retrieve the vessel, along with the ninety-one guns on board. Charles Brandon, Duke of Suffolk, was put in charge. On 1 August 1545, Brandon drew up a list of required equipment. He requested 'Two of the greatest hulks that may be gotten', 'Five of the greatest cables that may be had', and 'Forty tons of tallow'. He needed a team too: sixty English mariners, thirty Venetian mariners and one Venetian carpenter.

The plan was simple but brazen. They were to pass cables under the wreck and, at low tide, attach the ends to empty hulks bobbing on the surface. On the rising tide, the Mary Rose would be lifted from the seabed and transported underwater close to the shore.

It may sound surprising, to try to raise a ship this way, but this was usual procedure. Ships were often finding themselves stuck at the bottom of the ocean: the French flagship, the *Carraquon*, had sunk two weeks before. There were specialist teams with tried and tested approaches to float these ships back to the surface. The *Mary Rose*, however, proved to be a stubborn mistress – even for Henry VIII.

In August 1545, Charles Brandon's Venetian salvage crew began the arduous task of recovering the vessel. By 4 August, some of the sails and yards had been pulled up and laid out to dry. On 6 August, she was pulled upright. But despite this initial success, by the end of the week, all attempts ultimately failed, and – once the main mast was snapped in half – all hopes abandoned. Perhaps this mishap wasn't totally unexpected: while at work, the team consumed a whopping 35,904 pints of beer in less than a month, equating to fourteen pints each, per day (the standard daily Tudor fare was eight pints).

These hiccups were soon reported up the ranks, and the news submitted to the king: his beloved *Mary Rose* was doomed to a watery grave. But recovery efforts weren't over. There were still 'certain anchors and ordnance' to bring up – all kinds of cannons, guns and artillery, worth the equivalent of £2 million in today's money.

The man running the operation was a Venetian named Peter Paulo Corsi, and it was Corsi who hired eighteen-year-old Jacques, along with eight other expert divers, in 1546. It may have even been Jacques who was given command of the team.

To help in the dives, we know they used what were recorded as 'Certain instruments'. What could these be? One particularly expensive piece of kit – which would have cost the same as the average upper-middle-class home, or a merchant ship – was a diving bell. This was a device that captured a pocket of air deep in the water, allowing divers to breathe without returning to the surface. But considering the expense, and the likelihood of its lines snagging on the *Mary Rose*'s masts, rigging and sails, it's probably unlikely it was used by Jacques here. Some historians have speculated whether he used a diving tub – a barrel filled with air that a diver could take a few breaths from.

The options at the time were limited. Leonardo da Vinci had designed various underwater breathing instruments, but, fearful of the 'evil nature of man', refused to test or reveal them, dreading they would be used 'as a means of murder at the bottom of the sea, by breaking the bottoms of ships and sinking them altogether with the men in them'.

So, devoid of much technological assistance, it's easy to see how valuable Jacques' expertise was, and how incredible his aquatic skills were to the people of Tudor Southampton. This was an age when any large body of water was considered extremely dangerous. Swimming was considered a death sentence, and even sailors and port-dwellers didn't bother to learn – what was the point when ships wouldn't attempt to retrieve a man overboard, anyway? The royal physician Andrew Board viewed immersing oneself in water as foolish, declaring that bathing 'allowed the venomous airs to enter' and 'destroyeth the lively spirits in man'. You can never be too careful, it seems, even in the bath.

But Jacques was not exactly a typical Tudor. In his youth, he'd never heard of that strange, cold country of 'England'. Jacques was born far away, on an island near West Africa. We know little about his childhood, but it's thought that his homeland might be Arguin, a small island off the coast of Mauritania. This was a landscape marked by sand dunes, swamps, mudflats, islands and shallow coastal waters. It was a nature haven with pink flamingos and pelicans, sea turtles and dolphins, where millions of birds migrated from Europe.

It was here that young Jacques, as a small boy, learnt to be such a brilliant swimmer. It is his unique swimming ability that has helped us trace his origins. It was common knowledge that people from the West African islands were 'the most expert swimmers in the world', where people could 'swim below the water like a fish'. Sometimes they used their aquatic skills for more nefarious means – seizing the belongings of visiting sailors, as was reported by one visitor:

One of them, who had a pewter tankard of beer in his hand and a soldier's helmet on his head, jumped into the water with them and swam thus a great distance underwater; then he re-emerged and jumped into his little boat, which his companion had to bring to him. Thus he got away with the helmet and tankard, and no-one could overtake him.

Alongside the sandy landscapes and wild natural beauty, eighteen-year-old Jacques probably remembered the island being marked by the presence of an enormous fort. This was a warehouse and trading station, which seemed at odds with the surrounding huts and buildings. The people here had fairer, bronze skin. They regularly arrived and left in their caravels, sometimes wearing enormous feathers in their gleaming silver helmets.

These were, as Jacques came to learn, the Portuguese. They first arrived on the island in 1443, about a hundred years before Jacques was born. It was through this base on Arguin that the immense wealth of Western Sudan was tapped, attracting Arab and Berber merchants who travelled vast distances across the continent to sell their goods to the Portuguese.

The most profitable trade, the Portuguese found, was an abominable one: the trade of people. One Venetian explorer and slave trader, Alvise Cadamosto, who was hired by the Portuguese prince, Henry the Navigator, became familiar with the west coast of Africa. He recorded that, in his time, about 1,000 enslaved people were transported from Arguin to Portugal every year.

When Jacques was born a century later, this trade was still flourishing. It's likely that slavers tore him from his homeland and brought him to Europe. Perhaps, as an eighteen-year-old, he could still remember being snatched from his family, never to see them again. What could he remember of being packed into the stifling depths of that Portuguese slaving ship, and making the journey across the seas? Did he catch a final glimpse of the flamingos bathing from a crack in the bowels of the ship, the last he would ever see of his home?

It's likely he was brought to Portugal and then on to Venice. It was not uncommon to see African people in Venice, from all kinds of walks of life, some enslaved, some in service, some valued for their particular expertise. It might well have been in Venice that Jacques first came under the employment of Corsi, who eventually brought him north to Southampton in England.

It was no doubt a hectic arrival, as Jacques stepped onto the quayside. The ships here were loaded up to the brim with the most valuable export in the country. Not gold, nor diamonds, but wool. In the Tudor period, wool remained a major English export, and England was overrun with sheep. When Sir Henry Fermor died in 1521, he owned 15,500 sheep. In 1533, flocks were getting so vast there had to be a crackdown. They weren't bothered about you smoking, or drinking underage, but you were absolutely not allowed more than 2,400 sheep (that's still four times the number of MPs in the current Houses of Parliament).

Once Jacques weaved his way through the busyness of the port, skipping over ropes and darting out of the way of enormous storage boxes ('Coming through! Coming through!'), he was put up to stay at the Dolphin Inn. It wasn't a bad place to end up. If you visit the Dolphin today, you'll be impressed. It now has a grand Georgian facade. Historic guests include Nelson and Queen Victoria, and Jane Austen celebrated her eighteenth birthday there in 1793. These days it prides itself as the premier Southampton hotel, 'the perfect choice for business or pleasure'.

Along with a team of seven other divers, Jacques was kept in peak physical condition, and supplied with ample food and drink. It made business sense for Corsi to keep these professionals well fed, to sustain them for the formidable task ahead. Together, for three years, they would head out to the Solent, retrieving treasures from the sunken ship, or, as the records put it, 'certain guns out of the ship drowned'.

Jacques grew to become a respected figure in Southampton. Most of the information we have about his life exists because, in his early twenties, he appeared as a witness in a court case. As such, he is the first known African to give testimony before an English court, the evidence preserved in the records of the High Court of Admiralty. Not everyone in Tudor times was allowed to give evidence in court, showing that Jacques had become a trusted man in society, his word honoured in law.

Jacques gave his testimony on 8 February 1548. It was the result of a spat between his employer, Corsi, and other Italian merchants. Corsi had been accused of going out 'craftily in the night' to steal tin and other materials from the wrecks of two Italian ships, the *Sancta Maria* and the *Sanctus Edmundus*. Jacques defended his master loyally. He also revealed something about his status. He declared he spoke 'of his own free will' and identified himself as a 'famulus' (a servant) rather than a 'servus' (a slave).

Indeed, for an African living in Europe, this was the key advantage to life in England: slavery on English soil was illegal. William Harrison wrote about this in 1577, in his 'Description of Elizabethan England':

As for slaves and bondmen, we have none; nay, such is the privilege of our country by the especial grace of God and bounty of our princes, that if any come hither from other realms, so soon as they set foot on land they become so free of condition as their masters, whereby all note of servile bondage is utterly removed from them.

Indeed, people of African origin had visited, worked, made lives and had families in Britain since Roman times. There were North

African soldiers based at Hadrian's Wall, in Northumbria, years before Bede. Although a tiny minority, historians have traced the lives of over 360 people of African origin who lived in England during the Tudor period, dotted across the country, and fulfilling a variety of jobs. They arrived on these shores via a range of routes: some as traders and ambassadors, some directly from Africa, and some via the Spanish and Portuguese empires.

One of these was John Blanke, a trumpeter, who was a respected member of the royal court, performing at both the funeral of King Henry VII and the coronation of King Henry VIII. Mary Fillis, the daughter of a Moroccan basket weaver and shovel maker, came to England as a young child, growing up to become a dressmaker.

In Southampton alone, it wasn't uncommon to see Africans living in the households of English merchants and townspeople. There was Joane, maid to Lawrence and Mary Groce. Maudlin lived in the household of John Andrews. Michael was a servant to the mayor, Thomas Holmes. Once more, other names in Jacques's diving team include John Iko and George Black. These names, along with the expert job in hand, suggest they also had origins in Africa.

So Jacques wasn't totally alone in Tudor England. Of course, that didn't mean he didn't suffer vitriolic abuse from some. In his court trial, Italian merchants decried him as 'a [Guinean] born where they are not christened and hath been for these two years slave and bondman to the said Peter Paulo [Corsi] wherefore he thinks that no credit should be given to his sayings or depositions'. This was said in an attempt to deliberately discredit Jacques' testimony, and had Jacques really been enslaved he would never have been able to testify in court. Despite the flaws in such accusations, it gives an insight into the slurs that were likely thrown at Jacques as he lived his life in Southampton.

EIGHTEEN

Despite the upheaval of his childhood, by the time Jacques was eighteen, he had achieved something quite incredible, something so impressive that it still amazes us five centuries later. Retrieving those cannons was an Olympic-level feat no king of England or wealthy duke could ever boast of. Yet had it not been for his chance involvement in the court case, the name of Jacques Francis would likely be lost to the mists of time.

He was one of the millions of immensely skilled men and women from our past – stonemasons and metalworkers, bookbinders and farriers, shepherds and glassblowers, of all backgrounds – whose expertise is overlooked and names are forgotten. Big hitters like Henry VIII and the *Mary Rose* may hog the spotlight in the history books, but their stories – and their glories – so often rely on people like Jacques, along with millions of others, to do the heavy lifting.

Pattering Princesses

'Oh! Nibbles!' cried Geoffrey, picking up a cocktail stick and stabbing an olive. Since the hiccupping incident, the boys had been deep in conversation about how exactly to achieve the perfect non-hiccup-inducing fizz. 'My dad would know the answer,' enthused Geoffrey. 'We once had a barrel that exploded in the cellar, when all the pressure built up. Took days to clear out.'

Matilda had cornered Elizabeth, the girl in the black and white dress. 'A princess, you claim? If that's true, we must be related. Which is your favourite palace, then?' Matilda challenged. 'Tower of London?'

Elizabeth flinched at the mention of the Tower. Noticing her distress, Matilda changed tack. 'There's Woodstock, of course. My father introduced the menagerie there. Bit of a mad scheme in my opinion – leopards and camels roaming the gardens. Breadstick?'

To Matilda, Elizabeth seemed serious, intensely intellectual, and guarded with her words – not the liveliest party companion. But equally, it was this reserve, this modesty, this self-control, which Matilda found impressive.

I like that Elizabeth, *Matilda thought to herself.* A woman I could do business with.

5

Lady Elizabeth

IN 1547, A LARGE, flat, rectangular parcel was delivered to Whitehall Palace in London. It contained a portrait of a red-headed thirteen-year-old girl, recorded as having 'a booke in her hande' and a 'gowne like crymsen clothe'.

'A fine portrait of the Protestant princess, of beauty, duty and learning,' some courtiers may have nodded, noting the two books in the painting – one the Old Testament, the other the New. 'She's got Boleyn features, that's for sure, just like her mother,' some of the long-serving household staff might have whispered, noting the pointed chin and dark eyes. 'And the red hair; undeniably she is a Tudor.'

But outward appearances can be misleading. Behind this facade of calm and self-confidence was a child who had endured one of the most chaotic upbringings in royal history.

From the moment Elizabeth was born on 7 September 1533 at Greenwich Palace, she was already a disaster. Her father – King Henry VIII – had put a lot on the line for the birth of this child. He had broken from the Catholic Church in Rome, started the

Church of England and split from his first wife to marry a younger woman who had caught his eye, Anne Boleyn. His actions had uprooted centuries of tradition and thrown the lives of millions into turmoil. All of this had just one purpose: Henry wanted a son.

The birth of a baby girl did not go down well. The mood at court was 'very cold and disagreeable', with 'no thought of having the bonfires and rejoicings usual in such cases'. Not a good start.

The baby was named Elizabeth after her grandmother, Elizabeth of York. At three months, she was sent away to her own household. This was standard procedure at the time (better to keep royal children away from cities, free from noxious smells and bad air). Thus began a relatively normal royal childhood.

Elizabeth settled into Hatfield House, twenty miles north of London (not to be confused with Hatfield Manor House, of Geoffrey Chaucer's childhood). It was a fine red-brick building, built around 1485 (the year her grandfather, Henry Tudor, defeated Richard III at the Battle of Bosworth and founded the new Tudor dynasty). The house had four wings that made up a square around a central courtyard.

Elizabeth was in the care of her lady mistress, Lady Margaret Bryan – her mother in all but name. Lady Bryan was meticulous at updating the king's minister, Thomas Cromwell, with details from the royal nursery. 'My lady has great pain with her teeth, which come very slowly,' Bryan wrote of the three-year-old princess. 'This makes me give her her own way more than I would.'

But Bryan had demands, too. Elizabeth was growing at quite the speed, leaving her with 'neither gown nor kirtle not petticoat, nor linen for smocks, nor kerchiefs, sleeves, rails [night dresses], body stirtchets [corsets], handkerchiefs, muddlers, nor begins [night caps]'. This princess was high maintenance from the start.

As Elizabeth scurried through the corridors of Hatfield, and tumbled through the formal gardens, she must have noticed something was off. Wasn't it strange how – although she lived in a fine house, wore sumptuous clothing and was treated with great respect – she was sometimes sneered at by servants? Sometimes she overheard gossip: 'She's a sweet girl, but what a shame about her mother.' And, whenever Elizabeth brought it up, Lady Bryan tensed and changed the subject.

With these titbits of evidence, Elizabeth began to piece together a horrifying picture. Her father was mighty Henry, the King of England, and her mother was Anne Boleyn, an evil seductress who had committed an array of terrible crimes. As punishment, her mother's head was severed from her body.

In time, Elizabeth would learn that there were two sides to the story. Anne was an intelligent, ambitious and independent woman – qualities Elizabeth could see in herself. False accusations of infidelity had sent Anne to the scaffold. Anne, despite Henry's monstrous behaviour, remained faithful until the last: 'I pray God save the King,' she said, 'for a gentler nor a more merciful prince was there never.' The sword swiped moments later. Henry didn't waste any time mourning. His marriage to Anne was declared null and void and he married Jane Seymour, one of Anne's ladies in waiting, ten days later.

As for Anne, a vicious campaign to eradicate her from hearts and minds was quickly put into action. At the palace of Hampton Court, many of her badges and symbols of heraldry were chiselled away. Boleyn relatives lay low. Young Elizabeth – who was two years and eight months old – was declared a bastard and cut out from the royal succession.

Thus began a childhood of endless change. Henry married six times in the end, and each new wife brought a seismic shift for

Elizabeth. Again and again, her future was redirected, her identity recalibrated, her place repositioned, within her family, in the court, and on the world stage.

How unsettling it was for the young princess! Stepmothers came in quick succession, each playing a different role in young Elizabeth's life. First, Jane Seymour, the Evil Stepmother. Jane was the rival and replacement of Anne Boleyn, so paid Elizabeth little attention. Second came Anne of Cleves, the Fairy Godmother. Anne doted on Elizabeth, confessing their relationship was a 'greater happiness to her than being queen'. Considering Henry was now grossly overweight with oozing leg ulcers, perhaps this was unsurprising.

Third, Katherine Howard, the Troublesome Older Sister. In the summer of 1540, when Elizabeth was six years old, her father married his fifth wife. Henry was forty-nine and Katherine was seventeen. Katherine was Elizabeth's first cousin once removed, and part of the Boleyn family, so Team Boleyn was back on top, and Elizabeth welcomed to the top table.

But this new-found favour was not to last. Queen Katherine was accused of adultery, and at eighteen years old, was executed, along with her lady-in-waiting, Jane Boleyn (Elizabeth's aunt, and the wife of Anne Boleyn's brother, George). The Boleyns were disgraced, again. It was a chilling reminder for eight-year-old Elizabeth, to see two more Boleyn women beheaded on Tower Green, just as her mother had been only six years before. From that day, Elizabeth was said to have vowed: 'I will never marry'.

Fourth, and finally, in 1543 Henry married Katherine Parr. To Elizabeth, she played the part of the Guardian Angel. At least, that's how it seemed to start. Meanwhile, King Henry himself was sometimes a Noble Prince, sometimes a Wicked Villain to Elizabeth, but always her father, and the ultimate reason for her position of power. It wasn't an easy relationship. Apart from the occasional visit to court, they hardly saw each other. Messages from Henry would come via letters, read aloud by a messenger.

All of this made things tricky for her household, who were sticklers for etiquette. 'I know not how to order her or myself, or her women or grooms,' Lady Bryan wrote, in a furious letter to Thomas Cromwell. It had left Elizabeth's Lady Mistress 'succourless', just like 'a redeless creature'.

Blowing around in this reed-less world, two people did provide Elizabeth some rootedness: her stepsiblings, Mary and Edward. These were surprising supporters – though they were Elizabeth's closest loved ones, they were also her greatest rivals. Mary was the daughter of Henry's first wife, Catherine of Aragon, who was cast aside for Elizabeth's mother, Anne Boleyn, who was herself cast aside for Edward's mother, Jane Seymour. To add fuel to the fire, Mary was a hot-blooded Catholic, determined to eradicate followers of the new Church of England, while Elizabeth and Edward were champions of this new Protestant movement. And you thought your family was complicated!

Despite these awkward differences, these three clung together as half-siblings. They had a lot in common. There was the formidable father, King Henry, who they were in distant awe of. They had each lost their mothers in tragic circumstances, and each knew that they were pawns in a dangerous political game.

Even with a seventeen-year age difference, Elizabeth and Mary were close. Mary showered her younger sister with gifts and attention, writing to the king in 1536: 'My sister Elizabeth is in good health, thanks be to our Lord, and such a child toward, as I doubt not but your Highness shall have cause to rejoice of in time coming'.

Elizabeth also adored Edward, who was four years younger

than her. When their households came under the same roof, they prayed, read and studied together, practising languages and discussing politics.

At the start of 1547, when Elizabeth was thirteen years old, her life took a new course, once more. King Henry 'waxed heavy with sickness, age and corpulence'. Lying in bed in Whitehall Palace, he mumbled to an advisor: 'I will first take a little sleep, and then, as I feel myself, I will advise upon the matter.' He was never to advise on the matter, for these were his last recorded words. The next morning, Henry lost the power of speech. He died in the early hours of 28 January 1547, aged fifty-five.

The following day, Elizabeth and Edward were informed of their father's death. Newly orphaned and fearing for their future, it's said they wept and clung to each other. The age of Henry VIII – with his cruel and erratic temperament, and tyrannical kingship – was finally over. But the new chapter would bring dangers of its own. The royal children were easy prey for ambitious counsellors, keen to profit from their vulnerability. As nine-year-old Edward took the throne, they swarmed around him like bees to honey, armed with false flattery and offers of counsel.

Elizabeth lost her father, and a brother too: Edward was now her anointed king. An invisible barrier of formality and etiquette now parted them: 'The ceremonies observed before sitting down at table are truly laughable,' one ambassador noted. 'I have seen, for example, the Princess Elizabeth drop on one knee five times before her brother, before she took her place.' Again, Elizabeth had lost one of her nearest and dearest to the political machine.

It was as the Edwardian era dawned that Elizabeth had the portrait painted that was sent to hang at Whitehall Palace. Her outfit of choice was a gown of crimson silk, shimmering with metal threads, and an elaborate pomegranate pattern. The sleeves were made of a cloth of silver tissued with gold. This was quite the statement, and technically illegal. According to the sumptuary laws (which regulated who could wear what), Elizabeth was dressing far above her station. She was technically illegitimate, yet wore materials reserved for the king and his closest relatives. It was a pointed move: Elizabeth was determined to override the technicality, presenting herself as King Henry's daughter, and reminding the world that she was still a player in the game of thrones.

Along with the portrait, Elizabeth wrote a letter to her brother, sent in May 1547. She missed him, wishing to be 'oftener in your presence'. She describes the painting, but admits she disliked how her face was painted: 'For the face . . . I might well blush to offer'. But she also made an important distinction – that this painting only showed the 'outward shadow of the body', but not her 'inward mind'.

So what was the 'inward mind' of the thirteen-year-old Elizabeth? What was going on beneath that French hood, underneath that layer of fiery red hair, inside that big Tudor brain?

A lot of space was taken up with verb declensions, lists of vocabulary and theories on syntax. Elizabeth had a great mind, and was brilliant at languages. In the spirit of the new humanist movement, Elizabeth (a girl!) received a rigorous education, fit to rival any prince's. This meant long days of intense rote learning and study. She excelled in Greek, Latin, French and Italian, and practised double translations: translating classical and religious texts from Latin to English, then reverting them again.

But this wasn't just a nerdy obsession, or a dogmatic curriculum. This linguistic mastery was to be her most effective weapon. At the age of six, she had impressed a courtier, speaking 'with as great a gravity as she had been forty years old'. Now in her teens, she had in her arsenal some powerful ammo: witty turns of phrase, studied metaphor and sharp ripostes, all of which could be used to flatter, persuade, conceal or bribe.

Elizabeth had been a precocious, intelligent and spirited child, but, as a teen, she was becoming increasingly distrustful and constantly on the edge of a nervous breakdown. She knew full well her life was tied up in irrational and ruthless political machinations. As she lay in bed at Hatfield, she must have been terrified by the creaks of the house. Was that a door in the wind, or the arrival of the king's men, here to take her to the Tower? Was this letter to be one inviting her to court for Christmas, or informing her of some unknown treason? She was right to be wary. Elizabeth would soon face her greatest challenge yet, one that would see her fighting for her life.

In the early months of Edward's reign, fourteen-year-old Elizabeth was sent to live with Katherine Parr, her newly widowed stepmother. They lived in a manor house in Chelsea on the outskirts of London. It was a happy arrangement. Katherine was an intelligent woman, a vigorous supporter of the English Reformation, and a keen patron of the arts, being the first English queen to write and publish her own books. She had been a good wife to Henry (despite not wanting to marry him) and had a healthy relationship with his children.

But Katherine made a terrible mistake. After Henry's death, she married again. Her new husband was Thomas Seymour, the uncle of King Edward VI. Seymour was devilishly handsome, extremely flirtatious and outrageously ambitious. This man was not to be trusted. In the position of Lord Admiral, one of his duties was to suppress the gangs of pirates who preyed on shipping in the English Channel. But, according to several merchants and sea captains, it was Seymour himself who – while pretending to crack down – was encouraging the pirates and taking a cut.

In 1548, his unscrupulous tactics reached a new low. You'd have thought marrying King Henry VIII's widow was a good enough prize . . . but then his eyes fell on another glittering jewel: the Princess Elizabeth. How eligible she was, the half-sister of the new king, now blossoming into a beautiful young woman.

Seymour began wildly flirting with Elizabeth. He abused his position – playing the part of a father figure who cared for this troubled, lonely teenager, while manipulating her with charm and flattery. How confusing for Elizabeth, for this older man to seek her out when she was alone, compliment her clothing, stroke her face, or comment on her blushing cheeks. Was she overthinking things, or was this behaviour . . . weird?

Seymour's intentions became crystal clear when he and Elizabeth were caught in an embrace. Poor Katherine, who was pregnant, walked in and caught them red-handed. Elizabeth was sent away in disgrace. She would never see her stepmother again, as Katherine Parr died in childbirth later that year. Again, Elizabeth lost a mother and became more vulnerable than ever to the ambitions of powerful men.

Single again, Seymour was free to pursue his young prey. He met with Elizabeth's financial advisor, Thomas Parry, to enquire about her estates and income. He visited the princess, offered her his rooms, and again, bombarded her with flattery and kindness. Word soon got out that Seymour was planning on Elizabeth's hand in marriage. 'My Lord,' the Lord Privy Seal warned him, 'if ye go about any such thing, ye seek the means to undo yourself and all those that shall come of you.'

But Seymour was blinded by ambition, and his 'disloyal practices' were discussed by the Privy Council. Evasive action was taken. Seymour was dragged to the Tower of London, shortly followed by Elizabeth's two closest companions – her governess, Kate Ashley, and financial advisor, Thomas Parry. 'I would I had never been born, for I am undone,' cried out Parry, on realizing he was entangled in Seymour's treacherous ambitions. Elizabeth, too, was distraught: she 'was marvellous abashed and did weep very tenderly a long time'.

The charges were devastating. Elizabeth and her household were accused of being compliant in a 'marriage plot', where she had intended to marry Seymour without royal permission. They were accused, in effect, of going behind King Edward's back. There was no evidence for this, but during the testimonies of Elizabeth's household, something else much more sinister came to light. Elizabeth's treatment in Katherine Parr's household was worse than ever believed.

While living together in Katherine Parr's Chelsea household, Seymour had the keys to Elizabeth's bedroom. In a total affront to propriety, he would often visit her in the early hours, while she was still in bed, and 'strike her upon the back or on the buttocks familiarly', forcing her to 'go further in the bed so that he could not come at her'. On other occasions, she 'ran out her bed to her maidens', to hide from his advances. Then, there were times when Katherine Parr, too, seemed to encourage it. On one occasion, Seymour 'wrestled with [Elizabeth] and cut her gown into a hundred pieces, being black cloth', while Katherine held her down.

Armed with these shocking revelations, Sir Robert Tyrwhitt was ready to squeeze a confession of the 'marriage plot' out of the princess. Tyrwhitt was utterly convinced of her guilt: 'I do see it in her face that she is guilty.' For days, Tyrwhitt tormented Elizabeth and insulted her, happy to remind her of the brutal consequences of a guilty verdict: 'I did require her to consider her honour and the peril that might ensue,' he reported to London. Elizabeth needed no reminding: her mother had been sentenced on much flimsier evidence.

At sixteen years old, Elizabeth was at a perilous point. She was not only alone but surrounded by enemies and spies, who were determined to trip her up. She was interrogated, manipulated and grilled for five days. She was confronted with licentious gossip that was impossible to disprove. Tyrwhitt also brought in false friends, hoping Elizabeth would drop her guard in the presence of a seemingly sympathetic ear.

But Tyrwhitt had bit off more than he could chew. He had underestimated this quiet, thoughtful teenage girl. All those years of study had made Elizabeth a master of words and formidable in argument. She would have made a brilliant lawyer today. Even under immense pressure, Tyrwhitt failed to break her: 'I do assure your grace she has a very good wit,' he admitted in a letter to the Lord Protector (who was also Seymour's brother) in London, 'and nothing is gotten off her but by great policy.' After days of this torment, with Elizabeth convulsing into bouts of weeping, Tyrwhitt knew the game was up. The princess was immovable, although his suspicions still held firm: 'I do verily believe that there has been some secret promise between my Lady, Mistress Ashley, and the cofferer, never to confess 'til death.'

Meanwhile, Elizabeth wrote letters that asserted her innocence and dismissed the growing rumours that she was imprisoned in the tower, or pregnant with Thomas Seymour's child. 'My Lord, these are shameful slanders,' she wrote to the Lord Protector. It was a masterclass in PR crisis management, maintaining her image and minimizing the damage.

Thomas Seymour was not so savvy. His reckless ambition would be the end of him. On 20 March 1549, under the orders of his brother, the Lord Protector, he was executed for his part in the 'marriage plot'. Six months after losing a stepmother, Elizabeth's stepfather was gone too, with two strokes of an axe. Elizabeth, it's said, acknowledged the events with these words: 'This day died a man with much wit and very little judgement.'

As the scandal subsided, Elizabeth returned to the calm of her private study. In time, Kate Ashley and Thomas Parry returned to the household, and service seemed to resume as normal. But everything had changed. Elizabeth was no longer the little girl in the bright crimson dress, captured in the Whitehall painting. She had endured the terror of being at the heart of a political scandal, which had ended with even more family members being executed at the Tower of London. It was a brutal push into the adult world.

From that moment on, Elizabeth was taking no chances. She rebranded, playing to perfection the role of the dutiful princess with impeccable virtue. No longer did she don lavish clothing bedecked with jewels or rich colours. It was time for plain and sober garbs, in line with the new Protestant reforms of Edward's government. The young king called her his 'sweet sister Temperance'.

'I am sure that her maidenly apparel,' the Bishop John Aylmer wrote, 'made the noblemen's daughters and wives ashamed, to be dressed and painted like peacocks, being more moved with her most virtuous example'. Others followed Elizabeth's fashion statement. When Princess Mary – who still upheld the Catholic fashion for sumptuous dress – presented their Protestant cousin, Lady Jane Grey, with a rich gown of gold and velvet, Jane refused. Jane thought the dress put her on the path 'to follow my Lady Mary against God's word, and leave my Lady Elizabeth which followeth God's word'.

In the months leading up to Elizabeth's eighteenth birthday, cracks were emerging in the frail family unit. King Edward became increasingly frustrated with Mary's refusal to conform to his religious politics. At Christmas 1550, Mary burst into tears. She explained to the Privy Council: 'I could not contain myself and exhibited my interior grief.' Then Edward – as Mary reported – 'showed the same himself, filling me with sorrow for having caused him to weep'.

As the tide of fortune turned away from Mary, Elizabeth – who favoured the Protestant reforms – sparkled in the limelight. During her eighteenth year, Elizabeth visited her brother in London, riding through the streets with 'a great company of lords and knights and gentlemen, and after her a great number of ladies and gentlewomen'. She was presented as the leading lady of the realm and 'very honourably received'.

At court, Elizabeth – and her marriage prospects – were a hot topic of debate. The brother of the French Duke of Guise was on the cards, as was the King of Denmark's son. Portraits were painted in haste and shipped abroad, where foreign princes may have been impressed by her image: steely, dutiful, beautiful. Eighteen-year-old Elizabeth was one of the most eligible women in Europe.

But what of the real woman behind the royal facade? At various points through her young life, she had been sole inheritrix to the crown, then the king's second bastard child. She had been the bad seed of a notorious concubine, then a shining example of piety. She barely knew her parents, yet their legacies defined every aspect of her life. Her siblings were her closest loved ones but were also a direct threat to her position. There was a constant, changing stream of governesses, stepmothers, step-siblings and tutors. What kind of young woman would this produce? Elizabeth grew to trust no one – her isolation, loss and abuse during those eighteen years taught her valuable lessons that she would never forget.

What's more, she had no idea that – even at this point – everything she knew was to be uprooted, once more. The following year, in 1553, fifteen-year-old King Edward died from tuberculosis. Thus followed five years of unrest and unease, as her sister, Mary, sat on the throne. Elizabeth was forced to outwardly conform to the Catholic faith. She was accused of inciting rebellion and imprisoned in the Tower of London, then spent almost a year under house arrest.

Finally, on 17 November 1558, when a childless Mary died of illness, it was time for Elizabeth to finally step up to the mark and take her throne. At twenty-five years old, she declared her intentions to the Privy Council: 'My lords, the law of nature moves me to sorrow for my sister; the burden that is fallen upon me makes me amazed.' It was the start of forty-five years of Elizabethan rule.

At eighteen years old, could Elizabeth have guessed that she would be sitting on the throne just seven years later? Did she even have a moment to think that far into the future? With such high stakes, could she have dared to hope for anything more than just being alive?

Her reign is often seen as one of the most glorious of them all – the 'Golden Reign of Gloriana' – following in the footsteps of other great queens that came before her: Empress Matilda, Eleanor of Aquitaine and Margaret of Anjou. Yet it was those childhood years of upheaval that equipped her with the powerful tools she would need for queenship.

Unlike the more dogmatic religious approach of her siblings, Elizabeth chose a more moderate 'Middle Way', desiring not to make 'windows into men's hearts'. Did this stem from those years in her youth, when Elizabeth was constantly thrown between political changes, and forced to conform?

She also chose to never marry – to never share her power – and remain the 'Virgin Queen'. Did this emerge from seeing so many of her father's marriages end in disaster? Did she have the manipulation of Thomas Seymour constantly in the back of her mind? Did this turn Elizabeth away from marriage, from childbirth, for good?

Diamonds, as they say, are made under pressure, and the immense pressure of Elizabeth's childhood produced a dazzling diamond in the ruff. These were lessons that made Elizabeth. This was the making of Gloriana.

The Dance Lesson

'Any suggestions?' hollered Geoffrey, scrolling through the phone attached to the speaker. Requests flew in.

'Thomas Tallis,' cried Elizabeth.

'No, no! How about Now! That's What I Call Music 1634,' chirped Jeffrey, while topping up his glass.

'How about "Hearts of Oak"?' begged Horace. 'I know all the words! Every verse!'

'Just put something on, hurry up!' implored Jeffrey.

'Patience!' protested Geoffrey. 'The life so short, the craft so long to learn,' he muttered to himself, trying to reconnect to the Bluetooth.

As Now! 1634 – a series of Baroque instrumental pieces – filled the room, Jeff started reminiscing. 'Now this one,' he laughed, his body swaying, 'this was playing when I was on stage in front of King Charles I, dressed in the most exquisite outfit. King of the Faeries, I think it was.'

Jeff began showing the other party guests his court masque dance routine. 'First, drag your leg across the floor, spin on one foot – yes, that's it – and then a clap. Yes! Jacques, you've got it!'

The party-goers were feeling the effects of the alcohol now and all nerves were gone. Jeff leapt, skipped and hopped, up and down – the life and soul of the party.

6

Jeffrey Hudson

BY THE TIME OF his eighteenth birthday, in 1637, Jeffrey Hudson had already lived a remarkable life. He had been captured by pirates in the English Channel. He was beloved by two queens: Henrietta Maria of England and Marie de' Medici of France. He was the muse of some of the greatest poets, playwrights and artists of the age, including the great Baroque painter, Anthony van Dyck.

So why was Jeffrey such an inspiration, to so many? Jeffrey was an impossibly small young man, just eighteen inches tall. That's about the length of a rolling pin, or a windscreen wiper, or three TV remotes lined up, head to tail. Jeffrey was fifty-two inches smaller than the average man in the UK today.

There were all sorts of theories flung around regarding his height. Some said it was caused by a pickle that became lodged in his mother's throat while she was pregnant: 'Being a great lover of pickled cucumbers, she was once, at Dinner, very near being choak'd only with a bit of a gherkin.' Did this pickled cucumber perhaps cause an internal blockage? Or was it the 'sourness of the pickle itself, vinegar being, as all known, a very great astringent'?

Others accused Jeffrey's parents of stunting their son's growth on purpose, similar to how 'the Chinese women acquire little feet' or 'ladies stunt the growth of their lap-dogs'. The method was to rub the backbones of a child with the grease of moles, bats and dormice. What was their incentive? To 'make a penny of him when he grew old enough, by showing him about in a box'.

Such vicious rumours were, of course, untrue. Jeffrey's condition was a natural occurrence, perhaps caused by side effects of a premature birth (he was born 'beforehand'), and very likely a growth hormone deficiency in the pituitary gland. Quite simply, the hormone that makes us grow wasn't being made. Today, it would be treated by simple injections.

What this meant was that Jeffrey was particularly unusual, even for someone of his height. In most cases of dwarfism, the cause is a rare genetic condition called achondroplasia, which hinders bone growth, resulting in short arms and legs, and a relatively larger head or torso. But Jeffrey's relative proportions weren't affected. He was just extremely small.

High society thought he was a marvel of nature, 'one of the prettiest, neatest, and well-proportioned small men that ever Nature bred, or was ever seen, or heard of beyond the memory of man'. He was admired by dukes and ladies, countesses and earls. But he also caught the attention of the first lady in the land: Queen Henrietta Maria, the wife of King Charles I. Henrietta Maria became obsessed with Jeffrey, and he in turn enjoyed the highest royal favour. He was the best friend of the queen – a position other courtiers could only dream of.

At eighteen years old, Jeffrey's life was a blur of masques and boat trips, riding lessons and clothes fittings. There was adventure, too. In July 1637, he accompanied a military expedition to inspect the siege taking place outside Breda, in Holland. Among the group were 'two noble Lords, the Earl of Warwick and the Earl of Northampton; and with him was the Queenes Majesties Dwarfe, strenuous Jeffrey' – and here was the joke – 'whose Gygantisme body made the bulwarks of Breda tremble'. As the soldiers were scaling walls and digging trenches, they were amazed by this curious visitor: Jeffrey 'made the whole Army to admire his monstrous smallnesse'.

But Jeffrey's day-to-day had not always been this merry-go-round of glitz and glamour. For the first seven years his life, he lived 'one degree above rags'. He was born in Oakham, in, quite appropriately, the country's smallest county, Rutland, in the Midlands.

His father, John Hudson, was 'of a lusty stature' who earned his keep as a butcher. He spent his days herding squealing livestock through pens, draining out carcasses and hanging the meat on hooks – sides of mutton, joints of beef, whole veal calves. It was hot, physical work, tainted with the putrid stench of dried blood filling his nostrils, swarms of flies buzzing about his face, and the cries of housewives, innkeepers and cooks, all wanting the best deal. This butchery brought in a meagre income – just enough to sustain his wife, Lucy, and children in 'a very mean condition'. The family lived in a roughly built hovel, with just one room to eat, sleep and play in.

It was only by the time of Jeffrey's first birthday, that his mother, Lucy, noticed something amiss. Was baby Jeffrey a little on the short side? Or was that just her imagination?

The months went on and it was undeniable. Jeffrey had stopped growing. No amount of broth, or rye bread, or sunshine, or warmth, or prayers, or herbal remedy would change it. What was most perplexing to his parents was that Jeffrey's siblings – a half-sister Joan, and brothers John, Samuel and Theophilus – were all the usual size.

Jeffrey's future must have been of concern to the Hudsons. Would he be the subject of mockery? Would he ever be able to earn a keep, when manual labour was at the heart of their lives? Would he be kidnapped to join a travelling circus, to be put on a pedestal and ridiculed?

The answer lay just one mile away, in Burley-on-the-Hill. There stood an enormous house, belonging to George Villiers, the Duke of Buckingham, who – through charm alone – had risen to power. He was the favourite and trusted advisor of King James I and then his son, King Charles. Buckingham's rise to power was rapid: 'His ascent was so quick that it seemed rather a flight than a growth . . . as if he had been born a favourite, he was supreme the first month he came to court.'

Though his business was conducted in London, Buckingham came to Burley-on-the-Hill for pleasure. He provided his guests with all kinds of entertainment, including bullbaiting, one of England's most raved-about sports. It had drama, pace, and was enjoyed by princesses and paupers alike.

But it was also brutal. A bull was placed in a pit and tethered to a five-metre rope, fixed to a stake. Fierce working dogs were thrown into the pit to attack the bull, clamping their jaws into its flesh, and tearing it from the bone. Thrashing in agony and maddened by the pain, the bull would toss the dogs, sending them high in the air and thudding to the ground. These displays were managed by strong men who scurried around the pit trying to break the fall of the dogs as they plummeted to the ground. They were often butchers by trade, supplying the working dogs and carving up the bull after the fight.

This was the case in Oakham. When Buckingham organized his bullbaiting displays, he called in the local butcher, Jeffrey's father, John Hudson. It was perhaps as John was working in Burley-on-the-Hill that the lightbulb moment arrived.

By virtue of being a 'Rarity of Nature', seven-year-old Jeffrey was taken to Burley-on-the-Hill and presented to the duchess. She was entranced and offered him a place in her household. This was a turnaround of epic proportions. In an instant, Jeffrey went from rags to riches. There were to be no more nights shivering against rugged stones. No more horrible smells of animal carcasses or rotting meat. No more bland, boring broth! The butcher's boy with dismal prospects was given fine clothes of satin and silk, and two servants to tend to his every need.

Meanwhile, there was trouble afoot in London. The new king, Charles I, and his young French wife, Henrietta Maria, were not getting on. Henrietta Maria, a fifteen-year-old French princess, was isolated and alone in a foreign land and trapped in a loveless marriage. When she complained of being lonely, Charles warned her 'to be aware how she behaved, for in England queens had had their heads cut off before now'. Without a husband's sympathy, Henrietta Maria surrounded herself with small pets – monkeys and dogs – for companionship.

To try to smooth the tension and stoke some royal romance, Buckingham made a plan. He organized a series of banquets, with all kinds of plays, pageants, music and marvels. It was pure and opulent razzle-dazzle. And starring in the centre of this luxurious extravaganza was to be Jeffrey Hudson, the butcher's boy from Rutland.

In November 1626, seven-year-old Jeffrey was helped into a carriage on the driveway of Burley-on-the-Hill. As it rolled out of the estate, he bade farewell to the hills and valleys of his childhood. The next chapter began.

They headed south along the Great North Road, which linked London, York and Edinburgh. First, they reached Stamford, marked by the 'lofty large cross', built to commemorate the medieval queen, Eleanor of Castile. The following day, they passed Buckden Palace, where Henry VIII stayed once with his fifth wife, Katherine Howard. It was here that she was supposedly unfaithful – she was executed the next year. Forty miles later, they passed another royal palace, Hatfield House, where Elizabeth I grew up.

Finally, as the carriage rolled into the village of Hampstead, Jeffrey was met with a spellbinding vision. One of the largest cities in the world stretched out before him as far as the eye could see. In the centre was an enormous steeple – the legendary St Paul's Cathedral, still in its original Gothic form.

The carriage pulled up in front of York House, Buckingham's London home (now the location of Charing Cross station). Stepping foot into the heart of London, Jeffrey was amazed by the hustle and bustle of the city. He had never seen so many people in one place, at one time. As he was escorted into the grand rooms of York House, there was more industry: workmen sawing and carpeting, and wigmakers and seamstresses adjusting elaborate costumes. The ducal household was preparing for a feast of epic proportions: a feast for a king.

'Look at the size of you!' the seamstresses likely cackled as they measured Jeffrey up and dressed him in a suit of armour. But still, the day held more surprises. Jeffrey was about to be informed of his role at the heart of the pageantry. 'You want me to do . . . what?' he must have stuttered, eyebrows raised in amazement. 'Are you really sure?'

At four p.m., trumpets sounded, and the pageant began. Candles flickered and earls and ladies craned their necks to see the king and queen process into the hallway, in all their finery, and sit on the raised dais. Next came the French ambassador, Bassompierre, and the showman of the entire evening, Buckingham himself. The banquet had begun.

The guests were treated to some of the most ornate dishes in history. These royal cooks were nothing short of magicians. The pastry chefs, especially, were worthy of acclaim, as Ben Johnson declared in verse:

> *A Master-Cook! Why, he's the Man o' Men,*
> *For a Professor! He Designs, he Draws,*
> *He Paints, he Carves, he Builds, he Fortifies,*
> *Makes Citadels of curious Fowl and Fish,*
> *Some he dri-dishes, some motes round with Broths.*
> *Mounts Marrow-bones, cuts fifty angled Custards,*
> *Rears Bulwark Pies, and for his outer works*
> *He raiseth Ramparts of immortal Crust*

At some point during the meal, the Duke of Buckingham gave the nod. It was time for the pièce de résistance. An enormous, cold pie was placed in front of the queen, causing the tables to groan under the weight. As she was presented with a knife to cut into the crust, Henrietta Maria did a double take. The pastry started moving. Something alive was inside, trying to get out. As the pastry tore, out came a human hand, as small as a child's. Then a shiny helmet, and then – throwing back the crust – out popped Jeffrey Hudson, to rapturous applause.

Jeffrey bowed at the queen, and probably marched up and down the table, waving a flag and darting between Venetian glassware and gold plates. The queen was besotted. A companion at last!

After the dinner, Jeffrey accompanied the queen along the river to her lodgings at Denmark House in London, a classical Italianate building of clean white stone, spread out across the river (now the site of Somerset House on the Strand).

It wasn't surprising to see a person with dwarfism at a royal court. They had played a part at European courts since at least the late medieval period: a page named John Jarvis lived in Mary I's household, while Elizabeth I lived with a woman called Thomasina.

In Jeffrey's time, there was also Sara Holton, Anne Shepherd and Richard Gibson, all of whom had dwarfism. Gibson himself was four years older than Jeffrey, and became an acclaimed minia-turist in the style of Sir Peter Lely. His paintings were so valuable that when the Keeper of the Royal Pictures feared he had misplaced one of Gibson's works, he took his own life rather than admit his mistake to the king.

There were plenty of other people at the Stuart court brought there for their strange or unusual bodies. William Evans, the 'porter of the back stairs', was seven feet six tall, knock-kneed, and splay-footed. On 23 November 1626, he performed with Jeffrey in a court masque. William was cast as a giant, and from his enormous pocket, he drew a loaf of bread. Reaching into his other pocket – as if for a knife, or piece of cheddar – he pulled out Jeffrey, to rapturous applause.

Later, in September 1635, another 'marvel of nature' arrived at court. Thomas Parr, or 'Old Parr', was a man said to be 151 years old. A poem was written about him (ingeniously titled 'The Old, Old, Very Old Man'), where he, William Evans and Jeffrey Hudson were championed as 'the oldest, the greatest and the least' men in the land.

So Jeffrey had plenty of friends at court who endured the same indignities as him. But there were practical problems to look out for, too. On 17 June 1627, 'Little Geffry, the Queen's dwarfe fell last day out of the window at Denmark House'. Jeffrey had clearly made a huge impression in the seven months since his arrival: Henrietta Maria 'tooke it so heavily that she attired not her self that day'.

On another occasion, when 'washing his hands and face', the story goes, he almost drowned in an overflowing sink. Henrietta Maria forbade him from using any vessel larger than a coffee cup. Even outside, the perils were numerous:

> Another time when in a blustering Day, the friendly Arms of a spreading shrub have sav'd him from being blown into the Thames, the Queen, after a full Council, gave strict orders that he should never go abroad in windy Weather without his Leaden-heel'd shoes.

Jeffrey's fame reached new levels in 1630, sparked by tragedy. In 1629, Henrietta Maria had given birth to a baby, who – despite seeming to be healthy – died shortly after. When she fell pregnant once more, action was taken to ensure tragedy wouldn't strike again. In February 1630, a party – including Jeffrey – was sent across the channel to France, to recruit an expert midwife, Madame Peronne.

During the visit, Jeffrey became the darling of the French court, earning the adoration of the queen, Marie de' Medici, who presented him with £2,000 worth of jewels (quite incredible, when his family in Oakham were living off £10 a year). By mid-March, the party were ready to return. Along with a bevy of nurses and midwives, ten Capuchin monks, twelve nuns and chests of jewels, they boarded a ship at Calais and set sail.

Just off the French coast, it emerged all was not well. It wasn't a submerged rock or bad weather. It was another ship, following in hot pursuit. But this was no friendly ally. This was a pirate ship.

'Get beneath deck!' the captain cried as the fearful passengers huddled together, clutching rosaries. Did ten-year-old Jeffrey take comfort from the nuns and monks beside him? Did he hide in the chests, among the jewels gifted from Marie de' Medici? Did he – in those moments that might have been his last – long for the safety of Denmark House? Or the comfort of his mother in Oakham?

The pirates boarded and captured the ship. The news sent London into uproar: it 'caused more upset at court than if they had lost a fleet'. Luckily, once it dawned on these pirates quite how important the prize was, they lost their nerve. The captives were free to go and Jeffrey returned to court, unharmed. A midwife arrived, too, ready to tend the queen. Two months later, after an eight-hour labour, a healthy baby boy was born: the future King Charles II.

With all this adventure, it's no surprise that Jeffrey became a popular subject for portrait painters. He sat for Daniel Mytens, the great Flemish artist, who painted him in a woodland, posing in a bright red suit with shoulder-length blond locks.

At fourteen, Jeffrey became the focus of Anthony van Dyck. This time, he shared a canvas with the queen – a dizzying honour other courtiers could only dream of. Titled 'Queen Henrietta Maria with Sir Jeffrey Hudson', the painting is now displayed in the National Gallery of Art, Washington, DC. As twenty-four-year-old Henrietta Maria sparkles in a brilliant blue satin riding costume and delicate lace collar, Jeffrey stands at her side, again in red. He looks up at the monkey on his shoulder. This was Pug – another of the queen's loyal companions.

For most teenagers of the seventeenth century, being painted by van Dyck would have been a once-in-a-lifetime event. For Jeffrey, it was just another dinner party anecdote.

But what did Jeffrey think of all this? Did he tire of being the endless subject of jest? Did his patience wear thin when he performed in the masques? When, for the thousandth time, he heard such banalities as 'What's it like being so small? or 'Careful, Jeffrey, you might fall through the cracks in the floorboards'?

It was obvious to all – including Jeffrey – that his size was the sole reason he was brought to court. 'Had you been Bigge and Great ten to one,' the popular court playwright Thomas Heywood put it, in a panegyric to Jeffrey, 'you never had proved a Courtier; 'twas onely your littleness preferr'd you'. In van Dyck's eyes, he was a spectacle, a prop, to show off the queen's wealth.

But, since his arrival, Jeffrey had proved to be much more than a visual exhibition. It was his exceptional character that the queen grew to adore: dogged loyalty, sparky wit and an ability to make her laugh. He seemed to have a wider popular appeal, inspiring many authors to champion his name in plays, books and poems. He was championed as 'Lord Minimus', with writers showering him with effusive praise: 'Your loveliness being such as no man can disdain to serve you.'

Little did eighteen-year-old Jeffrey know, as he enjoyed the delights of Denmark House, that he was probably past his best days. Behind court masques and endless entertainment, Charles I was at a crisis point. His Parliamentarian adversaries were at their wits' end, and civil war broke out in 1642. When he was twenty-three years old, Jeffrey became Henrietta Maria's trusted advisor and joined her in exile in France. In these years of peril, Jeffrey's patience wore thin. Frustrated at being the constant butt of jokes, he shot a man in a duel and was banished from court.

But even then, his troubles were only just beginning. Jeffrey had the misfortune to board a ship captured by Barbary pirates. These were Muslim privateers from the North African coast, who terrorized towns and ships across Europe, everywhere from Italy to the Netherlands, Ireland to Iceland. For twenty-five years, Jeffrey was enslaved in North Africa. It was a quarter of a century of 'hardship, much labour and beating, which he endured when a slave to the Turks'.

We don't know how Jeffrey escaped enslavement, or how he returned to England. But by the end, he was, no doubt, a shell of his former self. He returned to his birthplace, Oakham, to end his days in quiet comfort. He was a different man now and the country had changed, too.

After losing the civil war, King Charles I was executed in 1649 (in the shadow of the Banqueting House, where Jeffrey once performed court masques). For eleven years, the country became a Commonwealth, with Oliver Cromwell at the helm. Then, when the experiment proved a failure, King Charles II returned to the throne (the king whose safe birth was facilitated by Jeffrey's mission to recruit the French midwife all those years before).

But still, Jeffrey's troubles were far from over. By the time he returned to England in the 1670s, London was in the grip of anti-French, anti-Catholic sentiment. Jeffrey – as a long-lost favourite of Henrietta Maria (the deceased French, Catholic queen) – was a prime target for the mob. He was thrown behind bars, and though eventually released, died an outcast around 1682, and was buried in an unmarked grave.

So it was a rollercoaster of a life. As he eventually returned to his homeland and saw the Rutland County motto painted on the signpost, he must have smiled to himself, for nobody embodied that motto more than he. *Multum in Parvo*, it read – 'Much in Little'.

The Table Plan

The clock struck seven. The chef popped his head around the door:
'Dinner will be served in half an hour!'

With this warning, some guests took the chance to use the facilities. 'It can take a while when you're wearing ten petticoats,' complained Elizabeth, as she headed out the door with Matilda.

The rest began to find their places. On one side of the table were little folded place names that read, ISAMBARD, MARY, RICHARD, ELIZABETH, HORACE, ROSALIND, GEOFFREY, ELSIE. On the other side were eight more: VITA, JEFFREY, FIONNGHAL, JACQUES, SARAH, JACK, VIVIENNE, BEDE. At the head of the table was MATILDA. At the other end, RAE.

Elsie, a well-mannered young woman, wearing a white blouse and long skirt, was engaged in general polite small talk: 'I've recently moved to Edinburgh. I'm at the Institute for Young Ladies – do you know it? The one on Charlotte Square?'

On overhearing 'Edinburgh', Fionnghal grabbed Elsie's arm and dragged her away.

'Thank goodness for that! Thought I'd be the only Scot!'

7

Fionnghal nic Dhòmhnaill

THERE WAS NO CHANCE of a lie-in for Fionnghal on her eighteenth birthday. Fierce winds whistled in from the Atlantic, racing around her island home. Seagulls swirled above the thatched roof, squawking at full volume. For Fionnghal, brought up on South Uist in Scotland's Outer Hebrides, these sounds were part and parcel of daily life.

'Co-là-breith sona dhut, Fionnghal! Co-là-breith sona dhut!' her three half-siblings, James, Annabella and Florence, must have cried, wishing their sister a happy birthday in their native Gaelic tongue. 'Happy birthday, sis,' added her older brother Angus, grinning and throwing her a present – perhaps the latest historical bestsellers about her heroes Robert the Bruce and William Wallace.

For most teenagers growing up in the eighteenth century, there was nothing remarkable about turning eighteen. The big milestone was still three years away when she turned twenty-one and reached her 'majority'. This is when all the opportunities of adult life would open up for her – entering contracts, owning property and enjoying the delights of legal transactions. And as it would turn out for Fionnghal, when adulthood did arrive, she would quickly find herself in the deep end.

Nevertheless, it was still a special day, not to be wasted. Time to get dressed! Time to get going! On top of her nightgown went a stay – a corset, lined with whalebone to create an elegant hour-glass figure – a petticoat, and a dress. On top of this came her arasaid. This was the pièce de résistance of traditional Highland fashion, a length of plain, striped or tartan fabric that covered the head, wrapped around the body and was fastened at the chest with a silver or brass buckle. This was a vital bit of kit to keep warm, and to mark one out as a true Hebridean woman.

Next up, time for breakfast – porridge cooked on the hearth. Fionnghal's house was small by today's standards. There were

only three rooms, one on each side of the entrance, and the other opening into the kitchen on the south. Though it was thatched and unpretentious, like all other in the islands except the castles of the chiefs, it was furnished and eminently comfort-able.

Indeed, it was a strange mix. Today, it might feature in an interiors magazine, championed as 'rustic chic':

Sumptuous woven rugs and deeply piled animal skins play games with the earthen floor of this rustic island escape. Prepare to rethink everything you know about interiors. Are we back to basics, or stepping into a luxe retreat? Rawness and refinement co-exist in perfect harmony. Turf, heather and thatch are surprising partners for fine landscape paintings, well-stocked

bookshelves, and tables laid with white linen and silver cutlery.
But it's Scotland herself who reigns supreme: deer antlers,
bagpipes and plaid blankets adorn the walls. This is understated
theatricality at its best.

The Outer Hebrides are a landscape formed from the oldest rocks in Britain. After a tectonic jolt millions of years ago, molten material surged to the surface and hardened on the fault lines. The result is an archipelago: islands sprinkled out in a line. The major islands are Lewis and Harris, North Uist, Benbecula, South Uist, and Barra. In Fionnghal's time, they were known collectively as the Long Island. This – apart from the tiny archipelago of St Kilda – is the westernmost point of Scotland and the outer edge of Europe.

South Uist is divided into two distinct landscapes. On the west is machair land: fertile low-lying grassy plains, with mile after mile of Atlantic beaches. The east is more dramatic and jagged, with long hill ridges and a rocky shoreline, offering sheltered coves for incoming sailors. And all of this is in the shadow of the great peak known as Gèideabhal or Beinn Mhòr (meaning 'big mountain').

I often think of Fionnghal trudging across this landscape, a dark speck against the vast expanse of yellow gorse and purple heather, passing grazing livestock, lochs and tiny stone cottages. To city dwellers, this island might seem bleak and barren. But for Fionnghal, who was born and bred here, and knew where to look, this was a show like no other . . .

Look! Look up! High above! Can you see the sea eagle with its white tail? Watch as it dives, straight into the cold waters, and pulls out its prize – a squiggling fish, surprised at being abruptly removed from the salty waters. Now, cast your eyes up again.

There, high up in the gorse, above that long stone wall – do you see? There's a bevy of red deer making their way across the plain, a stag in the centre, proudly displaying its horns. And at the end of this lane, on the gatepost, do you see that sweet little brown bird with chestnut markings on the wings and blue-grey under-parts? Yes? We're in luck. That's the elusive corncrake.

While nature spotting, Fionnghal passed all kinds of strange stones in the landscape. All were postcards from bygone ages, clues to the lives of her ancestors. These Highland markers, with their mysterious origins, made an impression on the Romantic poets. Keats recorded his impressions in verse:

> *There is a pleasure on the heath where Druids old have been,*
> *Where mantles grey have rustled by and swept the nettles green:*
> *There is a joy in every spot made known by times of old,*
> *New to the feet, although each tale a hundred times be told . . .*

As Fionnghal walked north, she caught sight of a single stone, standing tall, a lone marker in the vast expanse of sky. As she drew close, the seventeen-foot standing stone towered above her, as it had towered above neolithic man 4,000 years before. This stone was known as An Carra.

If Fionnghal headed south, she would come upon Cladh Hallan, a set of semi-buried stones, arranged in circles. To the islanders of the eighteenth century, these were shrouded in mystery. In recent years, excavations uncovered the remarkable truth. Here lay prehistoric mummies, the only ones found in Britain. These included a male who had died around 1600 BC and a female who had died around 1300 BC – about the same time as King Tutankhamun of Egypt.

Nearby were strange bumps on the land. Today, we know these

are the remnants of Viking settlers and their thriving community that traded across the continent: archaeologists have found green marble from Greece, ivory from Greenland and bronze pins from Ireland at the site.

What did Fionnghal think of these stones and dips in the land? Were they roundhouses, places of worship, or burial pits? If islanders once lived here, why did they disappear? Was it famine or plague? Or was it something more sinister? Were these the work of the *sithchean*, the fairies who lived in the mounds and knolls across the glen?

Such faerie tales and ghost stories were part and parcel of Fionnghal's life. As she continued her journey around the lochs, she was mindful to keep vigilant. 'Eisdibh a mach air son nan ceilp,' mothers of South Uist warned their children: 'Listen out for the kelpies.'

Kelpies were water spirits, believed to appear sometimes as a horse, sometimes a human. Their whistling tunes would lure their victims to the water to be drowned. There were selkies, too, who shapeshifted between seal and human form. Most ominous of all were the banshees, female spirits with no nostrils and webbed feet, whose wailings or appearance would signal that a family member was soon to perish.

Mixed in with these folkloric beliefs, the islanders of South Uist clung to an ancient religion: Christianity. In AD 563, when St Columba sailed from Ireland to establish an abbey on Iona, his teachings spread seventy miles across the water to South Uist. It was a story Fionnghal might have pondered on as she clambered over the ruins of the Tobha Mòr, a collection of chapels with origins as far back as the ninth century.

Over the centuries, Scottish kings had dispersed their lands among important nobles, giving rise to the clan system. Clans were family groups, each with their territory, each with their chief (often with a nickname such as 'the Knight' or 'the Laird'). In the Hebrides, the clans of the northern islands (Lewis, Harris, North Uist) were predominantly Presbyterian. Those of the southern islands (Benbecula, South Uist, Barra) were generally Roman Catholic. It was unusual, therefore, that Fionnghal, living in South Uist, was of strict Presbyterian upbringing.

Squabbles among clans were commonplace in Hebridean history, but in the seventeenth and eighteenth centuries, there was a greater – and unifying – cause to fight for. In 1688, King James VII of Scotland (who was also James II of England) was removed from the throne and exiled by English Protestants, who feared a Catholic king. Though some Scots enthusiastically supported the eviction, for others, this was an outrage. James was not only the great-grandson of Mary Queen of Scots, he was also descended from Robert the Bruce.

In 1707, in the Acts of Union, Scotland and England united to become the Kingdom of Great Britain. The English and Scottish parliaments were dissolved, and the Parliament of Great Britain met for the first time in London in October of that year. Many Scots were not happy, not least in the Highlands and Islands. Why should they pay their respects to Queen Anne, with her wars in Europe and baroque architecture and vast extensions to some-where called Hampton Court?

In 1715, eight years after the Acts of Union, the clan chiefs staged an uprising in support of their own candidate for the throne. James VII (and II) had died, so the obvious candidate was his son, James Francis Edward Stewart (known as 'Stuart' in England). His supporters across Britain were known as Jacobites (who had existed in some form or another since 1603, named after the Latinized version of James: 'Jacobus'). In the autumn of 1715, they raised the standard and fought in battle against government forces. But the rebellion failed, and Jacobite hopes were dashed.

It was these dramatic events, which occurred seven years before Fionnghal was born, that she would have been reminded of when she came across the ruins of Ormacleit Castle. This was no ancient ruin. It was built around 1701 by Allan MacDonald, the MacDonald clan chief – 'MacDonald' being the anglicized form of 'nic Dhòmhnaill'.

He didn't have much time to enjoy the fruit of his labours. In 1715, Allan MacDonald joined the Jacobite uprising and perished in battle. In a strange twist, on the same day, Ormacleit Castle was gutted by fire, started by cooking venison in the kitchens. What a terrible omen, Fionnghal must have thought, as she sat on the stones, still in ruins. Was it divine punishment? Was it a sign that Jacobitism was doomed?

When Fionnghal was eighteen years old, it had been twenty-five years since the 1715 Rising. The Jacobite cause, with its romantic notions of Stewart revival, must have seemed part of a bygone age. A dream of her parents' generation, not hers. The Hanoverian king, George II, was firmly on the throne and life in South Uist was peaceful and prosperous.

The island was under the feudal control of Ranald MacDonald of Clanranald, better known as Old Clan. Under Old Clan, the land was managed by gentlemen farmers, known as tacksmen (the land they rented was known as the 'tack'). They lived a respectable life in stone houses, dining on roast meat, French wine and brandy.

The mass of ordinary islanders, who the tacksmen sublet to, lived in dwellings that were little more than huts, with a diet of bread, oats, cheese and barley. They raised black cattle, a hardy native breed, to sell in Highland markets. In the summer they grazed the livestock inland, in glens and above the freshwater lochs. In the winter, the cattle came onto the low ground, close to the farms.

Luckily for Fionnghal, her family were tacksmen, of 'gentle' birth – not from poverty as the legends so often put it. Her societal equivalent in England might be the likes of the Bennet family, who feature in Jane Austen's *Pride and Prejudice*.

Fionnghal's mother was a lady of good standing: Marion of Griminish. Her father was Ranald of Balivanich and Milton, who died when Fionnghal was very young. Marion soon remarried. Her second husband was Hugh of Armadale, an army captain who went by the nickname One-Eyed Hugh.

While her parents kept a beady eye (actually, three) on Fionnghal, she grew close to the family of Old Clan. After the fire at Ormacleit Castle, the Clanranalds relocated their HQ to the neighbouring island of Benbecula, at Nunton House. It was here that Fionnghal spent much of her childhood.

Sitting beside the light of a sash window, she learnt to sing, dance, play the harp and spinet. There was reading, writing and embroidery to master. She spoke Gaelic, Scots and English. Most importantly, she learnt the social graces: when to curtsey, how to hold your cutlery, how to address the host. At eighteen years old, there was no reason for Fionnghal to expect much more of life than this. She certainly had no idea of the drama to come.

By 1746, when Fionnghal was twenty-four years old, the Jacobite cause had ignited again. This time, there was a new candidate, the 'Young Pretender' and grandson of James VII, Charles Edward Stewart, later known as Bonnie Prince Charlie. But like his father before him, Charles Stewart's attempt ended in a bloodbath: on

16 April 1746, his forces were defeated at the Battle of Culloden. Bonnie Prince Charlie scarpered.

Along with a handful of loyal accomplices, the prince took cover in the remote Outer Hebrides, with a £30,000 bounty on his head. After two months in hiding, a daring plan was proposed: he was to be smuggled off the islands to Skye, the largest of the Inner Hebrides, by boat. From there, he would flee to France, to freedom.

The escape was probably planned by One-Eyed Hugh, Fionnghal's stepfather, who suggested it to the prince. Being the captain of a pro-British government militia, he was a surprising candidate to orchestrate the escape, but saw in the prince a 'friend in his heart'. What's more, it was best for his family to ensure he wasn't captured on MacDonald territory, in case of reprisals from either the Jacobite or government side.

Where did Fionnghal come into it all? She knew nothing of the scheme until 20 June 1746, when the prince arrived at the shieling – a small hut in the hills – she happened to be staying at, on the nearby island of Benbecula. What a shock, in the still of the night, to open the door and see her stepfather usher the country's most wanted man to the hearth.

Suddenly, this remote hut became a den of secrecy and intrigue. Everyone was compromised. Everyone's life was on the line. Fionnghal was presented with an audacious proposition. She had been chosen – perhaps because she might seem a less conspicuous candidate than her stepfather – to deliver the prince to Skye. It is a great credit to Fionnghal's personality that she was trusted with such a momentous task. It must have been a dramatic moment: all eyes on her, with words of encouragement, or perhaps force. Reluctant at first – for fear of putting those she loved in danger – Fionnghal conceded. She was in.

A daring plan of escape was forged, albeit pantomime in style: the prince was wrapped in shawls and skirts, disguised as a serving maid, and given a character: 'Betty Burke'. With Hugh's position, they could obtain the necessary permits, and be given a heads-up about government search parties.

At 9 p.m. on Saturday, 25 June 1746, with government forces less than a mile away, 'the Young Pretender, Miss Mac Donald, one MacAchran, with five men for the Boat's crew' climbed into a small rowing vessel. As the light of the moon danced on the waves, the little boat was pushed off from the shore, carrying its precious cargo. 'Good luck, Fionnghal,' they might have whispered from the shore, 'Scotland's future is in your hands.'

There was a picnic to sustain the travellers, 'Lady Clan Ronald having provided Provisions for the voyage'. It must have been a low moment for Charles Stewart, who set out with hopes of a crown, a throne and a palace. Instead, he was shivering in a rowing boat dressed in women's clothing, eating soggy sandwiches.

The plan was to deliver the prince to Monkstadt on Skye. This was the house of Lady Margaret MacDonald, a Jacobite sympathizer. Yet to their dismay, after rowing through the night, they found the house surrounded by government militiamen. With the prince hiding on the shoreline below, Fionnghal held her nerve. She breakfasted with the troops, convincing them she was an innocent traveller. When the coast was clear, they diverted the journey, crossing the island to the capital, Portree. The prince was able to escape to safety on the continent. He never saw Fionnghal again.

News of the audacious act spread fast, and Fionnghal was arrested and imprisoned at Dunstaffnage Castle in Oban, then briefly in the Tower of London. The usual punishment – as endured by other Scottish Jacobite supporters – was to be executed before jeering English crowds. Fionnghal's actions were treason of the highest level: she aided the escape of National Enemy No. 1, deliberately deceiving her anointed king. Her involvement – that terrifying night she helped Bonnie Prince Charlie escape across the seas – kept the hopes of a Jacobite revival alive. A rebellion that, if successful, would overthrow the Hanoverian dynasty and potentially dissolve the Anglo-Scottish Union of 1707.

But – miraculously – she was released in 1747. She wasn't derided as a criminal but feted as a celebrity. London high society was fascinated by this good-looking girl with fine manners who played the spinet. They were impressed with her polish: 'one could not discern by her conversation that she spent all her former days in the Highlands'. Samuel Johnson would later record her as 'a woman of soft features, gentle manners, kind soul and elegant presence'. All those dancing lessons paid off! It was an astonishing escape from a grisly fate, surely saved by her sex and class: it's hard to believe the same treatment would have been afforded had she been a rough-mannered Highland boy who only spoke Gaelic.

After some time in the spotlight, Fionnghal nic Dhòmhnaill – now going by an Anglicized version of her name, Flora MacDonald – returned to Scotland. Did she settle into life as a bygone celebrity, making an appearance at Christmas light switch-ons, or appearing in sofa adverts? Far from it.

Fionnghal moved to Skye and married Allan MacDonald of Kingsburgh. This was a bad move: he was terrible with money. In 1774, facing immense debts, Fionnghal and Feckless Allan crossed the Atlantic and bought a plantation in what is now North Carolina. With their son and eight indentured servants, they took on about 500 acres, with grain mills and orchards of peach and apple trees.

When the American Revolution broke out, Fionnghal was active in raising regiments of Highlanders to fight for King George III. As the Loyalists were defeated, Feckless Allan was captured and their plantation ravaged, leaving Fionnghal to lay low in hiding for two miserable years. Having lost everything, she lived in New York, then Nova Scotia, then back on Skye, where she died in 1790.

How strange that the heroine of the Jacobite cause went on to defend the Hanoverian king, and four of her sons and a son-in-law fought for King George III. It all raises the question: why did Fionnghal do it? She was sympathetic to the Jacobites but wasn't an ardent supporter. Why did she help Bonnie Prince Charlie, risking everything, though she didn't care much for the cause? In the end, she claimed it was a straightforward Good Samaritan moment, that she would have done the same for anyone in such a desperate plight.

Perhaps Fionnghal's wishy-washy explanation derived from the fact that, in reality, she was just a cog in a larger plan, doing as she was told. Though she is often championed as a lone hero, saving the prince when everyone else looked aside, there were plenty of others who were instrumental in the action. It was Lady Clanranald who 'communicated the scheme' to Fionnghal, prepared her for the journey and dressed the Pretender in women's clothing. On the night of the escape, Fionnghal and the prince were accompanied by six others in the boat. It's likely that had Fionnghal refused to hop aboard that boat, another would have taken her place.

Fionnghal was no doubt bemused by her sudden rise to fame, considering all she did was follow the orders of her stepfather. Nonetheless, in this moment of crisis, when others would have run a mile, Fionnghal put herself forward and put her life on the line. Her bravery is to be heartily commended.

EIGHTEEN

Did Fionnghal have any idea, as she trudged through the heather on her eighteenth birthday, of the adventure ahead? That in six years, she would be traversing the seas with the last Jacobite hope, a journey that would change her life – and the fate of Scotland – for ever? Could she have imagined that she would become a celebrity, overnight? As she sang songs of Scotland's heroes, did she realize she would join their ranks, with monuments built and schools commemorating her name? For in turn, Fionnghal became the greatest heroine of all, her tale retold a thousand-fold, in the immortal lyrics of song:

> *Speed, bonnie boat, like a bird on the wing,*
> *Onward! the sailors cry;*
> *Carry the lad that's born to be king*
> *Over the sea to Skye.*

> *Though the waves leap, soft shall ye sleep,*
> *Ocean's a royal bed.*
> *Rocked in the deep, Flora will keep*
> *Watch by your weary head.*

Dry Land

The table setting wasn't as immaculate as it was before the guests arrived. A bowl of olives had overturned on Matilda's place, leaving an oily patch on her napkin.

Meanwhile, Vivienne cracked open the bottles of wine in front of her and began generously topping up glasses. 'Red or white?'

Halfway along the table, Horace attempted chit-chat with Elizabeth. 'So, if you had to choose, would you rather sail on the English Channel or the open ocean?' Elizabeth looked bemused. Horace tried again. 'Have you ever spent the night in a crow's nest?' he enquired, tentatively.

'A crow's nest?' she finally murmured, more to herself than to him. 'I'm more used to dry land' was all she said.

It was going to be a long night for Horace. There was only one thing for it: he topped up his wine glass and headed three sheets to the wind.

8

Horace Nelson

THE FIRST THING YOU must know about the young Horatio Nelson? You've got his name all wrong. Sure, when he was baptized, he went down in the books as Horatio. It was a family name, used by his godfather Horatio Walpole. But, until the age of nineteen, he went by the nickname Horace. It was 'an English name for an Englishman'. So, if we're going to become well acquainted, Horace it is.

He was born on 29 September 1758 in Norfolk. It was an idyllic childhood. His father was Rev. Edmund Nelson, a steady, sensible man who came from a dynasty of Norfolk clergymen. His mother, Catherine (née Suckling), was also the daughter of a reverend. She was a strong-willed woman with strong opinions: Horace's enduring memory was that 'she hated the French'.

If Edmund hoped to live out his days in quiet, thoughtful reflection, he was to be bitterly disappointed. All around him – running along corridors and thundering up staircases – was a bevy of young Nelsons. There were three girls, Susannah, Anne and Catherine, and five boys, Maurice, William, Horace, Edmund and Suckling.

They lived in a rectory on a lane outside the village, beside a flowing brook. The house was built in an L-shape, with stone walls and sash windows. 'A picture-perfect dream home,' estate agents would chime today, 'set in the heart of unspoilt Norfolk countryside.'

What fun it must have been for the Nelson children, on long summer's days, splashing in the stream and exploring the surrounding countryside. There was plenty of choice for adventures. One mile away from Chez Nelson were the wild ruins of Creake Abbey. Once a fine Augustinian church, it was perfect for hide and seek.

'Where shall we head today?' cried the more adventurous explorers. 'I vote we head north, let's take a picnic to the beach!' It was a five-mile walk to the coast. On the way, they passed one of the grandest Palladian houses in the country, Holkham Hall. Then came fishermen's cottages, with netting laid outside to dry in the sunshine, the air reeking with the smell of herrings. Finally, they arrived at the beach, with sandy dunes, vast blue skies and – far on the horizon – ships returning from voyages across the world.

The winter months had delights of their own. On Christmas Day 1767, when Horace was nine years old, the celebrations were in full force. After their father's sermon, the children returned to a house decorated with holly and ferns, and a table groaning with dishes of delicious food.

What a spread! After a solemn prayer of thanks, the feasting would begin. A goose was the standard Christmas fare, though some years there might have been beef or venison, or turtle soup, cockles and mussels, caught locally. 'Pass the brawn, Horace!' Maurice might have cried, gesturing to the meat jelly made from the boiled head of a calf and seasoned with spices. 'Hey, Edmund, leave us some of that frumenty,' little Anne may have squawked, her eyes fixed on the porridge-like dish, made with grains, almonds, currants and sugar, which was often served with meat. Then there was plum pottage, a kind of Christmas pudding filled with dried prunes and raisins.

No doubt the Nelson family slept soundly that evening, wholly satisfied and full of Christmas cheer. But the next day, the festive cheer turned to horror: Horace's mother suddenly died. She was just forty-two years old.

A dark cloud hung about the family. Four days later, Edmund and his eight sombre children returned to the village church of Burnham Thorpe. It was a sad sight, the siblings' heads bowed as they trundled through the churchyard to bury their mother. Catherine's ledger stone can be found inside the church, on the north side of the chancel. In Latin, she is remembered: 'She was endowed with conjugal and maternal affection, with Christian charity and with real love.'

More tragedy followed the next week. On 5 January 1768, Horace's maternal grandmother also died. Edmund was not only heartbroken but overwhelmed at the new weight of parental responsibility: 'As it has fallen to my lott to take upon me the care and affectation of double parent, [the children] will hereafter excuse where I have fallen short and the task has been too hard.'

The question of the children's futures – especially that of the boys – was a pressing one. The eldest son, fifteen-year-old Maurice, left home to work as a clerk in the Board of Excise (a kind of trainee in the civil service and as boring as it sounds). At some point in 1768, it was time for Horace to also pack his bags.

With his brother William, he travelled thirty miles along the country lanes, heading to the second largest city in England, Norwich. Here, Horace enrolled at Sir William Paston's Free School in North Walsham, a fine red-brick building that still stands to this day. But this educational stint was short-lived. When Horace reached the ripe old age of twelve, it was time to find a job.

What were the options? Could Horace enter the legal profession? Or become an army officer? The problem was, these jobs required considerable financial backing that his father couldn't provide. What about the Royal Navy? Could he command those ships he saw passing the Norfolk beaches? It wasn't unheard of. From a survey of 1,800 officers who served between 1793 and 1815, 899 were from middle-class families, and many were the sons of clergymen.

Besides, the prospects were good: the Royal Navy was the growth sector of the day, akin to joining an AI development firm or a clean energy company today. With Britain's empire expanding around the world, there were ever-growing shipping routes to manage, coastlines to defend, and wars to be fought. No chance of jobs drying up there!

There were plenty of other perks: a dazzling uniform, prize money, a chance to see the world, glory for king and country, and a place in the history books. You can see why Horace – who had never left Norfolk – might be attracted to life at sea. But the small print here was important: 'Please be aware that death is likely. Chances of disease, loss of eye, loss of limb, loss of sanity, very high.'

But who needs two eyes when immortality is at stake? What use is an arm if you're a nobody? It was a risk Horace was happy to take.

The next challenge was getting the job itself. It wasn't a case of *what* you knew, but *who*. Officer recruitment might have taken place across a dinner table, along the lines of: 'Going to the West Indies, are you? If you need an extra pair of hands, I know just the fellow, my little sister's friend's son. He's never been on a ship, of course, but he's a dab hand at Latin declensions and a quick learner.'

Luckily for Horace, he had an 'in'. His late mother's brother was Maurice Suckling, a naval captain who had found glory during the Seven Years' War, triumphing against the French in the Caribbean. He was very well positioned to guarantee 'interest' for a naval upstart.

This wasn't as horribly corrupt as it sounds. 'Interest' was an accepted method of influence, common in the Georgian period, that could be used to start, promote and enhance someone's position in life. It was through 'interest' (the patronage of Sir Robert Walpole, Britain's first prime minister, and a distant relative) that Uncle Maurice had first joined the Royal Navy all those years before.

All this was essential when you consider the strict social etiquette in place. To meet someone new in the Georgian period – to become 'acquainted' – you had to be properly introduced, in person or by letter. No chance of 'striking up a conversation with' or 'chatting up' strangers (which is a shame – *Sense and Sensibility* would be half as long if they didn't spend so much time looking at each other from the other side of the room).

Horace was itching to join the ranks, and his uncle was the answer. 'Do, William,' he pleaded with his brother, 'write to my father and tell him that I should like to go to sea with Uncle Maurice'. Maurice wasn't so sure: 'What has poor Horatio done,' he wrote, 'who is so weak, that he should be sent to rough it out at sea?' But any concerns for welfare were soon cast aside: 'But let him come, and the first time we go into action a cannon ball may knock off his head and provide for him at once.' Character-building stuff.

To get a sense of life at sea, Uncle Maurice sorted Horace a position on a merchant ship, the *Mary Ann*, which set sail for the West Indies on 25 July 1771. It was a steep learning curve, being sent to sea as a twelve-year-old boy. This was a brutal life of hardship with all kinds of challenges: cramped conditions, disease, bad food and bad weather. The diet was based on a ration of salt beef, pork, cheese, fish, ale and some form of ship's biscuit. This kind of merchant ship probably had a crew of around 130, but the largest Royal Navy ships might have up to 1,000 men aboard, where discipline would be strictly enforced with a clear allocation of duty.

How did Horace fare? Did he flinch when he first saw men tied to the gratings and flogged? Did he squirm eating a ship's biscuit, crawling with weevils? Did he ever manage to get a decent night's sleep, swinging to and fro in a hammock, with hundreds of others snoring beside him?

After around four weeks of travelling at four knots, the crew reached the Caribbean island of Tobago, then Jamaica. Here were crystal-clear waters, stingrays dancing in the shallows, and deliciously sweet mangoes waiting to be plucked. But there was a sinister side to this paradise: Jamaica was a wealthy sugar colony, notorious for the 'barbarous Treatment of Slaves' and 'the cruel Methods they put them to Death'. When Horace visited, there were around 200,000 enslaved Africans on the island.

Tobago was the same story. Here they found an island in turmoil, where a plague of ants was destroying the crops. Some enslaved Africans (known as the 'desperadoes') had openly attacked their enslavers, and maroon gangs (groups of escaped ex-slaves) emerged from the forests to destroy plantation property. It's unlikely Horace would have seen the full horrors of the plantations, but he might have seen clues. On the coastline there might have been rotting corpses hanging in gibbets, the remains of enslaved workers who had been barbarically starved to death. What impression did that make on this twelve-year-old boy, I wonder?

The crew were back in Blighty on 7 July 1772, and Horace stepped off at Plymouth, now sporting a long plait in his hair. After twelve months at sea, his physique was stronger, and he considered himself 'a practical seaman'. Others would beg to differ. The voyage taught Horace a great deal about himself, including his difficulty with seasickness: 'I am ill every time it blows hard and nothing but my enthusiastic love for the profession keeps me one hour at sea'.

Not long after being back on dry land, Horace caught wind of a once-in-a-lifetime expedition. Two ships, HMS *Carcass* and HMS *Racehorse*, were preparing to sail for the North Pole, and explore the possibility of 'A Northern Passage': a direct route to the Pacific Ocean. Horace wasn't going to miss out on that! Despite it (unusually) being adults only, he used 'every interest' to join the trip. His persistence paid off, and he joined HMS *Carcass*, serving under Captain Skeffington Lutwidge.

Georgians prepared for Arctic expeditions by transforming ships into icebreakers: 'these vessels, beside their natural strength, were sheathed with planks of seasoned oak three inches thick, to fortify them against the shocks and pressure of the ice'. They were packed with 'a double set of ice poles, anchors, cables, sails and rigging'. The crew were provided with Arctic equipment:

A stock of warm clothing was laid in, consisting of six fearnought [incredibly thick wool] jackets for each man, two milled caps, two pair of fearnought trousers, four pair of milled stockings, and an excellent pair of boots, with a dozen pair of milled mitts, two cotton shirts, and two handkerchiefs.

The voyage departed Sheerness with 'a fresh breeze' on 4 June 1773, when Horace was still fourteen years old. They sailed north, passing the Norfolk beaches of his childhood, up and up the east coast of England, charging through the North Sea. They picked up provisions where they could: when 'many fishing boats' were sighted near Shetland, 'the men were invited on board, and some fish purchased of them at a cheap rate'.

Instead of the boiling temperatures and sunstroke of the Caribbean, Horace faced new challenges: 'raging seas, tremendous rocks, and bulwarks of solid ice'. The fog could be so dense that the crews had to keep 'firing guns and beating drums' to not lose each other. There were days of exquisite beauty when the sailors seemed to have travelled to another world. On Tuesday 27 July, it was glorious:

> *The very ice in which they were beset looked beautiful, and put*
> *forth a thousand glittering forms, and the tops of the mountains,*
> *which they could see like sparkling gems at a vast distance,*
> *had the appearance of so many silver stars illuminating a new*
> *firmament.*

This was nature-watching like never before, with dolphins, seals and polar bears to spot, and whales 'spouting their fountains towards the skies'. One island was covered with birds: 'geese, ducks, burgomasters, ice-birds . . . almost every other species of birds peculiar to the climate'. Compelled to investigate, Horace's (rather rotund) sailing master went ashore: 'the [master], a full fathom in the belly, endeavoured to waddle after his companions'. But the hilarity took a turn when out of nowhere, he was approached by a polar bear. The captain was paralysed by terror:

EIGHTEEN

His hair already stood on end . . . and he had scarce breath
enough left to call his men to halt. In this critical situation
he unfortunately dropt his gun and in stooping to recover it
stumbled against a goose-nest, fell squash upon his belly
into it . . .

Trapped between a hungry bear and a furious gander, the master
escaped within an inch of his life. But, on 30 July 1773, true
disaster struck. The ships were past the archipelago of Svalbard
(pretty far north – halfway between Norway and the North Pole).
It was the furthest they would go, as the elements were closing
in. The ships became trapped in the ice. They locked in position,
with little chance of escape. Drastic emergency plans were put
into action. Preparations were made to abandon ship and escape
to safety in rowing boats (as Ernest Shackleton would do on the
other side of the planet, in 1916).

At this moment of total crisis (and in the same vein as Geoffrey
Chaucer on the French expedition), Horace made a nuisance of
himself. Hungry for adventure, and joined by an accomplice, he
ventured off the trapped ship to explore. It must have been epic
for the teenage boys: roaming this fairy-tale land with glittering
valleys and sparkling peaks. But soon enough, reality hit home:
a polar bear approached.

Horace pulled the trigger of his musket, but the gunpowder
flashed and the bullet remained wedged in the barrel. With the
bear closing in, Horace – the story goes – cried out: 'Let me
get a blow at this devil with the butt end of my musket and we
shall have him'. Whatever happened next – some say the ice
separated, others that a fellow crew member fired a gun from the
ship – it was a thrilling tale, which became the stuff of Nelsonic
legend. Here – his fans would later chime, with the benefit of

hindsight – you could see all the marks of a future admiral: brazen leadership and stunning bravery in the face of danger. It would be immortalized in paint by the artist Richard Westall in *Nelson and the Bear*. Here, Horace is depicted fearlessly attacking the bear with his broken musket. Horace and the bear are wide-eyed, as bemused by the situation as each other.

'Explain yourself, boy!' Skeffington Lutwidge must have bellowed as the adventurers were brought back on deck. Horace – while 'pouting his lip, as he was wont to do when agitated' – admitted, 'Sir, I wished to kill the bear, that I might carry its skin to my father' (a surprising object for a clergyman to have displayed in his Norfolk home!).

More battles followed. A few days later, Horace was given command of a rowing boat manned by twelve seamen. They were attacked by a walrus, which – unlike the polar bear debacle – Horace was said to have fended off with valour.

Finally, after nine days trapped in the ice, the ships broke free and made a beeline for home. They returned to Deptford, in London, but there was no time for Horace to rest. Within weeks, voyage number three began.

On 27 October 1773, aged fifteen, Horace set out as a midshipman on HMS *Seahorse*. This time, the destination was the furthest Royal Navy base from Britain at the time. It was exactly what Horace wanted: 'Nothing less than such a distant voyage could [. . .] satisfy my desire for maritime knowledge'. Over the following years, Horace saw 'almost every part of the East Indies', stopping off at Madras (now Chennai), Ceylon (Sri Lanka) and Bombay (Mumbai), to name a few ports.

It was in early 1776, when Horace was seventeen years old, that he faced death, again. It wasn't a polar bear or a walrus this time, but something far more deadly. Had you climbed below the deck of HMS *Seahorse*, you'd have found Horace a shell of his former self. Not perusing the charts, nor polishing his buttons, but lying in a pool of sweat, struggling to breathe and shaking uncontrollably. His skin had turned an unpleasant shade of yellow, the spark in his eyes gone. He stared blankly at the ceiling, flies buzzing around his face.

'He'll never make it back to Blighty,' his fellow sailors might have whispered. 'He's at death's door.' It had all come from a single bite of an infected mosquito. Horace had contracted one of the deadliest diseases of the day: malaria.

In light of his perilous condition, Horace was reallocated to the frigate HMS *Dolphin*, to hitch a lift back home to England. This was his best chance of survival. It must have been a harrowing few months, tormented by fever, incapacitated by headaches, and enduring diarrhoea – all while in the sweaty bowels of a ship. What a blessed relief when, in September 1776, HMS *Dolphin* weaved its way up the Thames and docked in London.

Horace recovered physically, but his mental well-being had taken a toll. He began to suffer from depressive episodes, which he would battle with throughout his life. He felt a sense of hopelessness, an overwhelming anxiety that he would never achieve his dreams – a feeling so acute he would only admit to it many years later. It was

a feeling that I should never rise in my profession. My mind was staggered with a view of the difficulties I had to surmount and the little interest I possessed. I could discover no means of reaching the object of my ambition.

Then he would yo-yo to the other extreme, emerging from the gloom with a fiery hunger for glory:

137

After a long and gloomy reverie, in which I almost wished myself overboard, a sudden glow of patriotism was kindled within me and presented my King and Country as my patron. Well then, I will be a hero and, confiding in Providence, I will brave every danger.

Perhaps it was hearing of his family fortunes that lifted Horace out of the gloom. Uncle Maurice had been appointed Comptroller of the Navy – the top position in the Navy Board. Three days before his eighteenth birthday, Horace was appointed fourth lieutenant of HMS *Worcester*, which was gearing up to sail to Gibraltar. And so the next adventure began.

By the age of eighteen, Horace had lived two completely different lives. There was a quiet childhood with his kin in the parsonage in Norfolk. Then there were his teenage years of danger and adventure, where he lived with an almost all-male family, his fellow crewmates. With these brethren, he had travelled the world. He'd crossed the equator and fought off Arctic polar bears. He'd endured frostbite and malaria, scurvy and seasickness – all before reaching his eighteenth birthday.

He was a talented officer, 'with a florid countenance, rather stout and athletic [with] ardent ambition'. But there was a spark in Horace. This wasn't a yes man, happy to follow orders unthinkingly. Horace could be reckless, sometimes brazen in his defiance of authority. It meant he took risks, and in the years to come, his daring approach produced some unconventional – but brilliant – tactics.

How surprised those shipmates would have been – as they watched him shiver and sweat in the grasp of malaria – to know what the future held. That within two decades, this scrawny teenager on the verge of death would have his place in the history books, that young Horace was to lead the Royal Navy to its greatest-ever victory at the Battle of Trafalgar in 1805.

And after that bout of malaria, that brush with death, perhaps Horace thanked God for his miraculous recovery. While waiting for his next voyage, did he head to St Paul's Cathedral to say a prayer, or stroll over to St Martin in the Fields? Had he done so, he would have walked through a patch of land now known as Trafalgar Square – named after his great victory. And had he gazed up to the skies, he'd be looking at a view that would one day be dominated by an enormous column, upon which his own statue would stand.

What would Horace have thought, had he known? Had some soothsayer whispered the future in his ear, that he was to become 'Horatio Nelson, national hero'?

'Of course,' he would have replied, his heart swelling with patriotic pride. 'England confides that every man will do his duty.'

Getting Schooled

After failing to enchant Elizabeth, Horace turned to his left, and tried his charm on Rosalind: 'Have you ever been to the ropery at Chatham? It's a long rope room, full of ropes. Pretty heavenly, don't you think!'

'No, I haven't,' Rosalind replied, 'but I have been to the second-longest continuous indoor corridor in Europe. Can you guess where?'

'The Hall of Mirrors at Versailles?' Horace replied, encouraged that conversation was flowing at last. 'The king's shooting gallery?'

'Wrong and wrong, I'm afraid. It's at my college at Cambridge – Newnham. They built it so us girls wouldn't get our hair wet in the rain. Silly, really!'

Horace was perplexed. 'Women? At Cambridge?'

'On the up and up, Horace,' Jack chipped in. 'I've just gone up to Oxford and we have special colleges – girls only. There's Somerville, Lady Margaret Hall, St Hugh's, St Hilda's . . .'

'Absolutely. The world has changed,' Rosalind said. 'We're not stuck in the eighteenth century any more.'

'Being a girl has never held me back,' piped up Sarah, 'and nothing else has, either!'

Dinner was served.

9

Sarah Biffin

ABOUT A MILE EAST of London's Trafalgar Square is an area called Smithfield. The name comes from 'Smooth Field', referring to the large open space outside the city walls. In the medieval period, it became a bustling livestock market, betrayed today in the quirky street names: 'Cowcross Street', 'Cock Lane' and 'Poultry Avenue'.

Here is one of London's oldest churches: St Bartholomew the Great (or Great St Barts for those in the know). It was founded in 1123 by a man called Rahere, a favourite of King Henry I (father of our Empress Matilda). It's said that, following the White Ship tragedy where young William Adelin perished in the English Channel, Rahere was determined to spend his time in a more worthwhile way. He packed his bags and set off on a pilgrimage.

On his travels, Rahere fell ill. In his delirium, he had a vision of St Bartholomew (a saint often depicted holding his skin, a nod to his martyrdom of being flayed alive). 'I am Bartholomew,' the saint declared, 'who have come to help thee in thy straights. I have chosen a spot in a suburb of London at Smithfield where, in my name, thou shalt found a church.'

True to his vision, Rahere founded a church in the suburb – which in this context meant an area at the edge of a city, still within the city walls. He set up both a priory of Augustinian canons and a hospital. Incredibly, the church still stands today, with many original features. There are rows of muscular Romanesque columns that blend into more elegant Gothic arches. So evocative is the space, it's often used as a filming location (most notably as the location where Charles leaves Duckface at the altar in *Four Weddings and a Funeral*). More importantly, the church still thrives as a centre of worship. It was at Great St Barts that I watched a livestream of the coronation of King Charles III, followed by tea and a good selection of biscuits.

But the great historical legacy of St Barts was something far more frivolous. Ten years after the priory's foundation, in 1133, the friars decided to start a summer fair. It was a small-scale fundraiser – the type that would today have a raffle of unwanted presents, and stalls with homemade cakes where everything cost 50p. Little did they know, this was the start of a centuries-long tradition. St Bartholomew's Fair would continue here, every summer, for the next 722 years. This four-day festival was the Glastonbury of its day and the highlight of a Londoner's year.

By the 1800s – when London's population surpassed a million inhabitants – thousands visited the fair, determined to have a good time. There were attractions of every kind: acrobats and tightrope walkers, boxing competitions and puppet shows. There were snacks, too: gingerbread and nuts, sausages and hot pies.

The poet William Wordsworth was one of the visitors. His romantic sensibilities were alarmed at the chaos: 'What a shock For eyes and ears! what anarchy and din, Barbarian and infernal,—a phantasma, Monstrous in colour, motion, shape, sight, sound!' Alongside the cacophony of shouting and fiddle playing, of drums and rattles, Wordsworth wrote (in his 1805 'Prelude') of clowns, 'grimacing, writhing, screaming' and 'chattering monkeys dangling from their poles'.

But there was a more sinister side to this entertainment. There were 'Albinos, painted Indians, Dwarfs' to be gawped at. There were famous acts, such as 'the learned Pig, The Stone-eater, the man that swallows fire, Giants, Ventriloquists, the Invisible Girl'. For Wordsworth, and for many visitors, it was a 'Parliament of Monsters', a perverted, Promethean jumble of 'freaks of nature'.

Had Wordsworth visited the fair in the early years of the nineteenth century, there is a chance that one of these 'freaks of nature' was a talented young woman, Sarah Biffin. She had a 'comely Appearance' and was skilled in 'the polite Art of Drawing, and Miniature Painting' – a skill that was 'truly astonishing, even to the most eminent Artists'. She could make clothes, too, able to sew 'extremely neat, and in a most wonderful manner'. Stories of her accomplishments spread far and wide, and PR campaigns heralded her as the 'Eighth Wonder!'

For fans, Sarah was a marvel. They were desperate to see her in the flesh, paying extra for a portrait of their own to take home as a token. Watching her at work was quite extraordinary. This young woman was unlike most artists: she was 'born deficient of Arms, Hands, and Legs', making her 'only 37 Inches high'.

Without hands to hold a paintbrush, she had developed her technique. The paintbrush was held in her mouth, then passed through a loop of material attached to her dress, enabling her to control the brush by moving her body. All of this she conducted with a cheery disposition and determination.

Sarah was born far from the fracas of London's masses. Like young Horace Nelson, her family lived in a little village, East Quantoxhead in Somerset, a short walk from the sea. But the beaches here weren't flat and sprawling for miles on end, as in Norfolk. Instead, Sarah grew up beside towering cliffs and little coves, with water-falls and rock pools with crabs scuttling around. On the horizon, when looking out across the Bristol Channel, was a view of a distant stretch of land: the south coast of Wales.

Life in agricultural communities was a difficult one. There were about 10.5 million people living in Britain at the turn of the nineteenth century, 80 per cent of whom were residing in the countryside, and a third were employed in agriculture. However hard these people worked, their welfare and prosperity were deter-mined by random external factors. Some years, they endured bitterly cold winters, with temperatures low enough to freeze over rivers. Other years, after weeks of rain, they might dig up an entire field of rotten vegetables.

This was the world known by Sarah's parents, Henry and Sarah. They were ordinary village folk who lived ordinary lives, so the birth of their new baby girl may have caused them some shock. 'What shall we do, Henry?' Sarah might have whispered to her husband. 'What will people in the village say? They shall suspect us of wrongdoing!'

Sarah was baptized at six days old, on 31 October 1784. The village church still stands, a charming stone building with sand-stone dressing and slate roof, set back from the road, bordered by a low wall and nestled in green fields. Here, the priest dowsed her in water and welcomed her to the holy family. Her record in the register has a notable addition: she was 'born without arms or legs'. Today this is known as phocomelia, a condition brought into prominence in the 1960s as a common side effect of pregnant mothers taking the drug thalidomide.

Sarah may not have had arms or legs, but – unlike many other children – she had a loving family. She was brought up 'with much care and tenderness under the eye of an affectionate mother, and in the society of four brothers and sisters'. Contemporaries recorded her as 'a dear little girl, with fair curls, blue eyes and a sweet disposition'.

But Sarah's ambitions were greater than being just a *dear little girl* – something her parents didn't seem to pick up on. When she asked to be taught how to sew, her parents refused. And so Sarah began in secret:

> *At the age of eight years, I was very desirous of acquiring the use of my needle; but my parents discouraged the idea, thinking it wholly impractical. I was not, however, intimidated, and whenever my father and mother were absent, I was continually practising every invention, 'til at length I could, with my mouth – thread a needle – tie a knot – do fancy work – cut out and make my own dresses.*

Disability was a familiar sight to the people of Georgian Britain, with records of the time peppered with those in the streets being 'deformed', 'stunted', 'crooked' or 'crippled'. In 1804, the physician William Buchan reported that 'every narrow lane' in London 'swarms with rickety children', who would grow up in a world where 'every third man is a pigmy' and 'many of the women are evidently stunted in their growth'.

Many of these disabilities were a result of poor working and living conditions. In 1785 (a year after Sarah's birth), a report was compiled to review the dangers of chimney sweeping on the bodies of young children. It described one twelve-year-old boy, already dependent on crutches, and 'hardly three feet seven inches in stature'. Other causes came from 'pernicious' air, which was 'a poison to young children'. On other occasions, the mother was blamed, for 'indulging herself in Indolence while with child'. 'In all cases of dwarfishness and deformity,' the report declared, 'ninety-nine out of a hundred are owing to the folly, misconduct or neglect of mothers'.

Sarah was determined not to let her disability, family doubts or underprivileged background define her. But East Quantoxhead – that small, sleepy Somerset village – wouldn't hold the answer. At some point in her life – her late teenage years, or perhaps a little later – a stranger called Emmanuel Dukes made himself known to the Biffins. Dukes was fascinated by Sarah. In her twinkling eyes, Dukes saw a spark.

Dukes was a showman who ran a travelling fair. He persuaded Sarah to join his company, where 'a comfortable living might be obtained by Public Exhibition'. And so it was, young Sarah left her parents' country cottage and joined a travelling show. What did the Biffins think, to know their daughter was part of a circus, where she might be mocked, scorned and degraded? What if the Dukes were cruel, and Sarah was ill-treated or turned out to become a beggar on the streets?

The Biffins need not have worried. The Dukes proved to be good people, welcoming Sarah as one of their own and treating her with 'uniform kindness'. Once more, it wasn't unheard of for a child to be whisked away to start a new life: Bede, Matilda, Geoffrey, Jacques, Jeffrey and Horace had all been taken from their childhood homes to live with strangers.

For Sarah, this was her big break – a thrilling opportunity, a chance to broaden her horizons, to escape the confines of her village and tour towns and cities throughout Britain.

It was the start of a brilliant career. Everywhere she travelled, posters would herald the arrival of the 'celebrated Miss Biffin'. In

1808 alone, she visited Edinburgh, Newcastle, Coventry, Dover, Sandwich and London. Crowds flocked to watch her painting with her mouth and create art that not only rivalled but surpassed her fellow artists, disabled or not. Those who paid to see her didn't come to laugh or mock but marvel at her unexpected dexterity.

'She picked off the table a long-handed pen with her tongue,' one fan recorded, 'and putting the end under a pin on the top of her right shoulder, used it with her lips. She also used the brush in the same manner.' When George Douglas, sixteenth Earl of Morton, commissioned her to paint his portrait, he became suspicious of her talent and took the work away with him between sittings to ensure there could be no trickery.

Sarah wasn't the only woman around embracing her disability. When she was in her teenage years, she might have been aware of Mary Morrell, a woman born without arms who could 'cut the small watch papers and devices, in the most ingenious manner, with a pair of scissors, by means of her toes'.

Then there was 'the surprising Warwickshire young lady', Miss Hawtin. Using her toes again, it was recorded that she 'threads a needle, sews, picks pins, or needles out of a pin-cushion . . . uses the scissors dexterously . . . feeds herself, drinks out of a glass with ease'.

Accounts of Sarah's life are similar. One man, George Long, recorded seeing Sarah in her mid-twenties:

Her appearance was handsome, as seemingly seated on a cushion she deftly plied her needle with her mouth, with which too she threaded it, her work resting on her shoulder stump. She worked both in plain sewing and embroidery, but she also painted miniature portraits, handed round for inspection, and she wrote her name, in an excellent lady's handwriting as we should call it, but executed, as all else, by her mouth alone.

But Sarah was an entrepreneur at heart: she would go on to become a superstar artist, outshining those of non-disabled means. At eighteen years old, it wasn't unreasonable for Sarah – or any young woman – to aspire to become an artist. Although art history books are dominated by male names – the likes of Hans Holbein or Anthony van Dyck or Joshua Reynolds – there were plenty of women artists in British history working at the highest level of society, many of whom eighteen-year-old Sarah could have been aware of.

Start with the Tudor period. We had Susannah Hornebolt, from Ghent. Vasari recorded that she was 'invited to England by Henry VIII and lived there in great honour her whole life long'. Levina Teerlinc was a familiar face at the court of Henry VIII, Edward VI, Mary I and Elizabeth I. She enjoyed a generous income of £40 a year (which was more than what the famous Hans Holbein received).

In the Stuart period there was Artemisia Gentileschi, an Italian woman whose paintings were bought by Charles I, some of which are still hanging in Hampton Court Palace. Then came Anne Killigrew, whom the poet John Dryden described as an 'accomplished young lady . . . excellent in the two sister arts of Poetry and Painting'. She achieved a huge amount in her life, which was cut short at twenty-five by a bout of smallpox. Another shining star was Susan Penelope Rose, daughter of Richard Gibson (one of the court dwarfs who lived alongside Jeffrey Hudson). Horace Walpole recalled she 'painted in watercolours with great freedom'. Fifteen of her miniatures are in the Victoria and Albert Museum in London.

The first Englishwoman to become a distinguished portrait painter was Mary Beale, from Suffolk. Her work rivalled that of Sir Peter Lely, and her paintings hang in the National Portrait Gallery. By the Georgian period, we had Angelica Kauffmann, who painted Queen Charlotte, the wife of George III. There were businesswomen in the art world, too. During the height of the Napoleonic Wars, Hannah Humphrey ran a print-selling empire: commissioning, displaying and selling art from her shop on St James's Street.

So there were plenty of names for young Sarah to take inspiration from. Throughout her life, she created exquisite miniature portraits to an 'almost miraculous degree of perfection' and overcame every barrier to advance her career. In 1821, Sarah was awarded the Large Silver Medal by the Society of Arts and exhibited at the Royal Academy – honours that would have been a career highlight for any artist of the day. His Royal Highness, the Prince of Orange was among her patrons, and 'during a visit to Brussels, he sat for his miniature, with which he was much satisfied, that his Royal Highness presented Miss B with a sum of money far exceeding her demand'.

She was a natural entrepreneur, taking lucrative commissions and travelling to Europe. There was romance, too. At the age of thirty-nine, she had a brief marriage to a man named William Wright, 'a gentleman who had been long attached to her'. At their wedding, when it came to exchanging the rings, Mr Wright pressed the ring to Sarah's shoulder, then put it on a necklace: 'having put it on a gold chain which she wore around her neck, it was placed in the bosom'. The romance was not to last, though: 'the match was unfortunate . . . they never lived together'.

Then – constantly looking forward – Sarah moved to Liverpool, with the hopes of crossing the Atlantic and breaking America.

Her ambitions were scuppered by ill health, and she died in 1850 at the age of sixty-five, at 8 Duke Street (now a smart Georgian townhouse). According to her death certificate, it was a 'disordered stomach and breaking up of the constitution' that finished her off. Her tombstone, which stood at St James Cemetery, Liverpool, declared her to have been:

> *Gifted with singular talents as an Artist,*
> *thousands have been gratified with the able*
> *productions of her pencil, while her versatile*
> *Conversation and agreeable manners*
> *Elicited the admiration of all.*

In her lifetime, Sarah's fame was immense. While her siblings lived their lives in East Quantoxhead, Sarah became a nineteenth-century household name who was even referenced in three Charles Dickens novels. It was recorded that the great portrait painter, Sir Thomas Lawrence, 'would rather have one of his pictures copied by Miss Biffin than by any artist he was acquainted with'.

Today, the Sarah Biffin revival is on. A self-portrait was sold at Sotheby's in 2019 with an auction estimate of £800–£1,200. The final sale price was £137,500. In 2022, Philip Mould & Company dedicated an entire exhibition to her work, 'Without Hands: The Art of Sarah Biffin'.

Her work is magnificent: exquisite miniature portraits, and meticulously rendered studies of feathers. But it is Sarah's spirit that continues to captivate. Newspapers of the day championed 'the earnestness with which she has struggled, and the perseverance with which she has laboured, to attain by her own efforts an honourable independence'. In a world where autonomy for disabled women was virtually non-existent, Sarah overcame every challenge that presented itself. Not only did she excel in a society set up against her, but she used her life-changing physical disability to break through barriers, to go outside the social and cultural norms, such as gaining recognition as a female artist, supporting herself financially, and often going further than non-disabled women of the day.

We can't be certain of the exact circumstances of Sarah in her eighteenth year, but it's clear that already her life was being shaped by her remarkable drive and determination to overcome life's challenges. Nothing is testament to this more than the signature on her paintings. 'Sarah Biffin', she wrote, adding proudly, 'Without hands'.

Another Story

At the other end of the table, conversation was sparkling. Mary, Isambard, Matilda and Vita were enraptured by Jeffrey, leaning in to catch every word. His stories were stranger than fiction.

'Once, there was a great pie that was to be served to the queen. Can you guess what was inside?'

'A little bird,' suggested Fionnghal. 'A Highland corncrake?'

'A small cantilevered bridge, which springs out when the pie is cut,' chimed Isambard.

'A rare ammonite, presented to her as a gift,' piped Mary.

It was the first time that Mary had spoken and, it seemed, that anyone had acknowledged her. Who was this shy girl, with grubby fingernails and a West Country accent? To Vita, she appeared rather an ethereal creature.

'Wrong! Wrong! You are all wrong!' exalted Jeffrey. 'It was something far more glamorous, far more exotic . . . far more dangerous.'

He gave a wry smile. 'It was . . . me!'

But Vita was still looking at Mary. She couldn't put her finger on it. There was something special about Mary. As if the girl could see things differently, as if she could see into another world entirely.

10

Mary Anning

THIRTY-FIVE MILES SOUTH OF East Quantoxhead is another coastline – the south coast of Dorset. If you visited here in the summer of 1817, not far from a village called Lyme Regis, you might have spotted a lone figure, walking in the shadows of the cliffs, turning over rocks and tapping them with a small hammer. This was the eighteen-year-old Mary Anning, and she was doing what she did best. She was hunting for fossils.

Sometimes, among the sea urchins and weed, she would find ammonites: perfectly formed spirals, the preserved shells and once-upon-a-time home of squid-like creatures who lived on these shores millions of years ago. There were plenty of belemnites, too. These were bullet-shaped fossils, long and thin, which were once shells containing tentacles or ink stacks.

To most visitors to Lyme, Mary was as much an enigma as the fossils she collected. Throughout her life, they noted her quirky character, recording her as 'a very clever, funny Creature'. Lady Harriet Silvester found Mary's expertise staggering: 'the extraordinary thing in this young woman is that she has made herself so thoroughly acquainted with the science that the moment she finds any bones she knows to what tribe they belong. She fixes the bones on a frame with cement and then makes drawings and has them engraved'.

Indeed, by her eighteenth birthday, Mary had already established herself as a tour de force in the fossil world, held in high esteem by collectors and self-proclaimed experts (many of them fossils themselves). Lady Silvester noted this, too:

> It is a wonderful instance of divine favour – that this poor, ignorant girl should be so blessed, for by reading and application she has arrived to that degree of knowledge as to be in the habit of writing and talking with professors and other clever men on the subject, and they all acknowledge that she understands more of the science than anyone else in this kingdom.

At eighteen years old, Mary was already a figure of fascination for those who visited her. Perhaps this was unsurprising. This was the heyday of the Gothic, after all. In her youth, the supernatural, the spooky and the spiritual were all the rage. (*Frankenstein* by Mary Shelley was published a year later, in 1818.)

Our Mary's fossil-hunting hobbies matched the goth vibe perfectly. In the shadows of the windswept cliffs walked this lonesome young girl with what seemed to be a sixth sense, enabling her to seek out these strange fossils and reveal the secrets of an ancient world. A world where the creatures took shapes of 'modern bats and vampyres', of unrecognizable living things 'resembling nothing that has ever been seen or heard-of upon earth, excepting the dragons of romance and heraldry'.

The local people of Lyme Regis had always found something a bit strange about young Mary Anning. When she was fifteen years old, she became weirdly attached to a corpse. On 27 March 1815, a ship returning from Bombay found itself in trouble. It sank, with just six of the 160 souls on board surviving. One of these was a beautiful woman, who washed up on the shore. Finding her dishevelled body in the shallows – and enchanted by this Pre-Raphaelite vision – Mary disentangled the weeds from her long hair. Then, when her body was laid at the village church, Mary took care to visit the woman, bringing her flowers and keeping vigil. What was Mary's fascination with this siren of the sea?

Mary was already firmly rooted in the local folklore. Years previously, on a hot summer's day in 1800, the villagers of Lyme Regis headed up the hill beside the village. The landscape was parched from the dry summer. The green, lush grass of the spring had become crisp and arid. The clusters of wildflowers – yellow cow-wheat and pink-veined sea campions – wilted and browned in the cracked ground. In the hedgerows were common rose finches cooling off in the shade, taking a break as they journeyed on their southward migration.

Staggering in the searing heat, and fanning themselves as they went, the villagers – farmhands and dairymaids, fishermen and shepherds – ambled up the lane, out the village. While the adults spoke of politics (perhaps of the recent Acts of Union, which would unite the Kingdom of Ireland and the Kingdom of Great Britain the following year), the children ran ahead, full of excitement. 'Do you think there'll be flips, like this?' some cried. 'Look at me, look at me galloping!' called out others, racing ahead.

The source of such excitement was a visiting troupe of equestrian performers, passing through to demonstrate exceptional feats of horsemanship. There were to be flips, jumps, sideways trotting and every kind of cavalier wizardry.

As the crowd assembled to enjoy the delights of the show, the performances were soon outshone by quite a different spectacle. A huge shadow fell upon the circus and the world turned cold and dark. The sun was nowhere to be seen, hidden behind a mass of black clouds. The horses began pulling away from their reins. Then, suddenly, an enormous flash of lightning filled the sky, and for one moment, everything was drenched with white light. The heavens opened and the thunder cracked, shaking everyone who heard it to their core.

The whole of Devon and Dorset was battered. One visiting admiral, Sir Alan Gardner, declared 'he never experienced it so violent in his life, either by sea or land'. In Exeter, St Edmund's Church was blasted with electrical current, attracted by the iron rod of the weathercock. There was 'scarce any corner or part of the church that did not receive much injury', and the following morning – when the sexton visited to inspect the damage – the 'smell was so sulphurous, that he was almost suffocated'. In another village, Ide, a man was struck, his hat and shoe torn to pieces and landing twenty yards from where he fell.

The crowds in the fields of Lyme Regis felt the might of the storm, too. Some hurried home. Others sought shelter under the boughs of a sturdy elm tree, waiting for the rain to pass. But the lightning seemed to come closer and closer, as if the entirety of God's wrath was unleashed on the people of Lyme Regis. As mothers comforted their crying babies, they huddled together, praying, desperate for the storm to pass.

Their prayers, it seemed, went unanswered. The tree they cowered under was struck directly by a bolt. Electricity surged through its branches, every leaf and bud fizzing with heat. Sparks leapt out of the bark, striking three young women, one of whom was holding a baby in her arms. The impact was immediate: their hearts stopped beating and they fell to the ground, dead.

'Four lives, that great storm took,' cursed the fishermen the following morning, the waters now calm and the sun shining through the mist, 'struck down, those poor innocent souls, and the little baby girl, too.'

But their melancholy was premature. After the lightning strike, the fifteen-month-old baby was rushed home. Here, in a little cottage on the seafront, the lifeless body was placed in warm water. To the astonishment of all in the room, she awoke, spluttering and wailing. It became the stuff of legend in the village: 'The baby's come back to life!' went the gossip, 'Little Mary Anning! She's as alive as you or I!'

So Mary's life began – again – with a miracle. It was reported in the papers on 30 August 1800:

> *A number of people assembled in a field close to the town of Lyme Regis, Dorsetshire, to see some feats of horsemanship, when suddenly arose a most tremendous storm of thunder and lightning. Several persons took shelter under a tree among whom was a woman with a child in her arms. She was struck dead, but the child escaped unhurt. A young girl, about 14 years old, and a young woman about 18, were also struck dead.*

Was there a reason Mary survived the surge of electrical current, pulsing through her little body, when the others perished? Could it be linked to another event, of equal terror? This wasn't, after all, the Anning family's first experience of disaster. Two years previously, their four-year-old daughter (also called Mary) had caught fire in the family house and burnt to death. It was reported in the *Hampshire Chronicle* on Monday, 31 December 1798:

A child four years of age, of Mr R. Anning, a cabinet maker of Lyme-Regis, was left by the mother for about five minutes, with her brother, about three years of age, in a room where there was some shavings . . . the girl's clothes caught fire and she was so dreadfully burnt as to cause her death.

Wasn't it strange? First, the four-year-old Mary, who had been taken by the flames. Then her younger sister (named after the older) had survived an attack of fire, against all odds. And now she'd grown up to be a peculiar, gifted young woman, uncovering secrets of the universe.

Apart from these peculiar events, Mary had as ordinary an upbringing as most Dorsetshire dwellers. As we know, her father, Richard, was a cabinet maker and carpenter by trade. He also searched for fossils in his spare time and encouraged his children to join him. Her mother was Molly, who spent most of Mary's childhood pregnant or tending to young children. Grief was familiar to the Anning household: of Molly's ten babies, only two survived.

This wasn't unusual in a household like the Annings', where cramped conditions encouraged the terrors of smallpox or measles. The house was so close to the seafront that it sometimes seemed the sea was more inside than out. Open the windows, and specks of water would fly in, leaving salt marks on the furniture. During stormy weather, the house was susceptible to flooding, forcing the family to crawl out of an upstairs bedroom window to avoid drowning.

If it wasn't a lightning zap that shaped Mary's character, there may have been a degree of divine intervention. Richard and Molly were Dissenters, a more radical type of Protestant. A two-minute walk from the Anning household was a Congregationalist chapel.

It still stands, a beautiful building, built in the 1750s, with rough-cast walls, plain windows and a grand doorway with Doric pilasters. This was where Mary had been baptized at one month old and, from the age of eight, received a basic education: reading, writing and a smattering of arithmetic.

It was also here – through tuition and regular sermons – that Mary's eyes were opened to a different approach to the world. For example, when public executions were generally accepted, the Congregationalists' texts argued that capital punishment should be abolished. She was told to go against the grain, to question the norm, to think outside the box.

Such teachings found a natural home with Mary, who had a defiant streak: her father, Richard, had led the Lyme Bread Riots of 1800. And now the Congregationalist books seemed to encourage such spirit: 'And shall not the blessed God,' they read, 'who is boundless in Mercy, and full of compassion, pardon the greatest Rebels?' They may not have kicked off revolutionary fervour, but these lessons certainly inspired her independence of thought.

From an early age, Mary was an avid fossil collector. She helped her father, who found a profitable side hustle in selling fossils to holidaying visitors, of which there were plenty. Since the early nineteenth century, Lyme Regis has been a fashionable seaside resort, complete with bathing machines and assembly rooms. It welcomed genteel families, some hoping to recover from bad health, some – perhaps overwhelmed by the glamorous balls, appointments and taking turns around the room – simply needing to 'get away from it all'.

When Horace Nelson's father, Edmund, spent the winters in Bath to treat his bad health, he may well have made a detour down to Lyme Regis. Jane Austen also visited, first in November

1803 and again the following year. So taken was she with the place, she gave it a starring role in her novel *Persuasion*, describing the town in Chapter Eleven:

> *The principal street almost hurrying into the water, the walk to the Cobb [the harbour wall], skirting round the pleasant little bay, which, in the season, is animated with bathing machines and company; the Cobb itself, its old wonders and new improvements, with the very beautiful line of cliffs stretching out to the east of the town, are what the stranger's eye will seek; and a very strange stranger it must be, who does not see charms in the immediate environs of Lyme, to make him wish to know it better.*

As Jane walked the beaches and took in the fresh air on the fossiliferous coastline, did she bump into little Mary splashing in the rock pools? 'Pray, what is it you're doing, child?' Jane may have asked. 'Are you all right here on your own?' To which four-year-old Mary, bucket in hand, may have held out a podgy hand. 'It's an am-am-ammonite, miss. Ancient creatures who lived a long time ago, from before Christ, even.' Was this Jane Austen's first glimpse of prehistoric life, on those blustery Dorset beaches, her bonnet ribbons blowing in the wind?

It was worth Mary's time, all this fossil hunting, because there was good money to be made. The newspapers regularly advertised collections to buy, such as 'a large Collection of Shells, Fossils, and other Natural Curiosities, to any Gentleman of Lady forming a collection for the Cabinet, or in the making of a Grotto'.

Another (more urgent) advert read: 'To be deposed of, A Lot of Fossils, and curious Specimens from different parts of the World, The property of an Aged Widow in great Distress'. Such curiosities had reached the fashionable tastes of high society, too.

After the king's birthday in 1808, it was reported that Princess Mary wore a 'superb dress of silver tissue . . . with a massy border of foil shells, fossils, and stones, studded in festoons . . . shells formed the coup d'œil of this truly elegant and magnificent dress'. Luckily for the Annings, fossils were in.

Mary's father was a big name in the (pretty small) Lyme Regis fossil-collecting scene. In one letter between two fossil-fascinated gentlemen, one reported to the other that 'there is a person at Lyme who collects for sale by the name of Anning, a cabinet maker, and I believe as men are may be depended upon, I would advise you calling upon him at Lyme'.

He also advised his friend that it was worth buttering up the collectors to get the best deals, as was the case with one William Lock. He recommended to 'ask a confounded rogue of the name of Lock to call upon you . . . upon first sight give him a Grog or a Pint, this will buy him to your interest and all crocodiles [fossils] he may meet with will most assuredly be offered you first'.

But later that year, in November 1807, the Anning family found themselves in crisis. While traipsing over the cliffs to the nearby village of Charmouth, Richard Anning lost his footing on the cliffs. He was severely injured by the fall. This, combined with consumption (a condition applied to nearly any disease that 'consumed' the lungs), finished him off. He died in 1810, only forty-four years old. You'll notice that the loss of a parent, at a pretty young age, is becoming a common theme with our eighteen-year-olds.

Now £120 in debt, Molly, Joseph and Mary were facing financial ruin. By 1811, their situation was so bleak that they were enrolled on parish relief. For the next five years, they were supported with money, food and clothing granted by the Overseers of the Parish Poor.

While living in these meagre conditions, with little to support them, Joseph and Mary pursued their fossil searching with greater intensity. From dawn 'til dusk, they traipsed across the stones, clambered around the crumbling cliffs, their fingers feeling the wet rocks disturbed and dislodged in the latest tide. Pulling away the long, leathery fronds of seaweed, and brushing off small creatures – scuttling crabs and rove beetles – the rocks were split to reveal treasures inside: belemnites and ammonites, crinoid and gryphaea.

This brother–sister team developed a fine eye for fossils, and in 1811, they struck paleontological gold. While exploring the boggy slopes of Black Ven, a stretch of coast that was constantly slipping and sliding, Joseph found something that seemed to resemble the head of an enormous crocodile. It was an Ichthyosaurus, a 195-million-year-old marine reptile, with fish bones and scales from its last meal still inside its ribcage. Nearly a year later, Mary located the remainder of the skeleton. It wasn't the first time such specimens had been discovered: there had been one in Somerset and another in Warwickshire. But the Annings' discovery was the first to come to the attention of the gentlemanly scientists in London. As such, it went down in the natural history books as the 'first Ichthyosaurus'. This creature was a strange hybrid. It had flippers like a dolphin, teeth like a crocodile and a pointed snout like a swordfish. Its backbone was like the spine of a fish, but its chest looked like a lizard's.

It was purchased by a local landowner, Henry Hoste Henley, for a whopping £23 (a triumph for the Anning family finances). Hoste Henley loaned it to the London Museum where it was a visitor hit, bemusing everyone who viewed it. Was it a fish, a crocodile, or a 'Lizard Porpoise'?

In her teenage years, Mary continued to patrol the Dorset coast, where she unearthed many such wonders from the past. Sometimes she was accompanied by scholars and scientists, keen to learn from this young font of knowledge.

But all this exploration wasn't without its perils. The coastline was a dangerous place, already taking the life of her father. On one occasion, a cascade of rocks fell around Mary, crushing her dog, Tray: 'The Cliff fell upon him and killed him in a moment before my eyes and close to my feet; it was but a moment between me and the same fate.' On another occasion, a heavy runaway cart hurtled off the road, pinning Mary against a wall. It was yet another one of her miracle escapes.

So, in her eighteenth year, Mary – like her strange finds – was extraordinary. She was fearless, both in disrupting top-level scientific thinking, as well as in her death-defying daily work. She was a fossilist driven by Christian faith, yet for some, her discoveries seemed to disprove God's creation of the world. Forty years before Charles Darwin's *On the Origin of Species*, Mary had an understanding that species were not fixed and that these weird, ancient forms could be the ancestors of modern animals. Mind-blowing stuff for the 1820s.

Mary remained in Lyme Regis her whole life. In her forties, unkind rumours began to spread that she had a drinking problem. In fact, she was taking laudanum to dull the pain of breast cancer, to which she finally succumbed at forty-seven, on 9 March 1847. During her life, she was dubbed the 'Princess of palaeontology', and, in recent years, the Royal Society has recognized her as one of the ten most influential British women in science history.

What I love about Mary is, despite her immense contribution, she was very low key. She didn't need money, connections, equipment, titles or a university education. Her methods were straightforward. Every morning, she stepped out her front door, walked the shores, and looked at the natural world around her – not just a glance, but a proper, long, studied look.

The results were astonishing: she uncovered a time capsule that reshaped how ordinary people and top-level scientists perceived their world. It was an extraordinary achievement for a carpenter's daughter, who – against all odds – shouldn't have survived to her first birthday. Perhaps there really was some magic in that zap of lightning.

About Time

'That's fast!' cried Isambard, as the clock struck eight. He checked his own pocket watch. 'By thirty-four seconds, would you believe!'

He leapt up, took the clock off the mantelpiece and placed it on the table. 'Excuse me, you'll have to finish that later,' he said, sweeping his companions' plates aside to make space.

'Since when are you a clock expert?' asked Matilda.

'Few secrets I learnt from the mighty Breguet.' Dismayed at Matilda's blank expression, he continued, 'Abraham-Louis Breguet? The brilliant horologist? Who makes the best watches and clocks in the world?'

'I don't bother with that sort of technology,' Matilda shrugged. 'A peal of the church bell does enough for me, or I just look at the moon, or the stars. Never failed before.'

Isambard laid out the cogs and screws on a napkin in front of him. 'Maybe – but there aren't any campanologists out at sea! And what do you do on a cloudy night, eh? Has anyone got a screwdriver?' Isambard leant over to take a pin out of Elizabeth's hair. 'Ah! This should do the trick.'

After some tinkering, Isambard replaced the timepiece on the mantel, where it ticked away merrily.

11

Isambard Kingdom Brunel

IF YOU TUNED INTO London radio in the summer of 1821, the traffic report might have gone something like this:

Good morning, London! It's time for your traffic update. It's not looking good I'm afraid. An overturned cart on London Bridge has blocked up the whole city. Fleet Street is chock-a-block as far as the eye can see. Cheapside the same – severe delays, forty-five minutes long. South of the river is a bottleneck – no movement on Tooley Street since sunrise. Drive safe and have a good one.

It wasn't just the roads. From Rotherhithe to London Bridge, the river was jam-packed and full of ships. There were so many boats snuggled up together that it was said you could cross the river by jumping from deck to deck. The cause of all this congestion? In a very short space of time, London had become the biggest port in the world. During 1751, this stretch of the river had 1,682 ships visiting from overseas, with 234,639 tons of goods to be processed. By 1794, this had exploded to 3,663 ships and 620,845 tons.

The problem was that despite the growth, the infrastructure was centuries out of date. Where there was only space for 545 ships, 1,775 were allowed to moor simultaneously, bumping and crashing up against each other. Goods sat unloaded for weeks before they could be processed, leaving them vulnerable to river pirates and night plunderers, scuffle-hunters and mudlarks. 'It's not the pirates or storms or disease which are the difficulty,' shipping merchants might complain, 'it's the nightmare of getting through those damn wharves of Rotherhithe.'

By the 1820s, some adjustments had been made to alleviate the problem. Docks had been built to house the waiting ships, and warehouses to process the goods. But still, deliveries leaving the warehouses were jamming up the roads around the city. The real problem was that it was impossible to easily cross the River Thames. There was the thirteenth-century London Bridge – the same bridge Geoffrey Chaucer would have strolled along, 500 years before. Then came Westminster Bridge (1750) and Battersea Bridge (1771). But the east of the city was a bridge-free zone because ships needed to pass freely along the river without their masts getting snapped off.

What were Londoners to do? Were they doomed to suffer road rage for ever? Luckily, they thought of a solution, which lay deep below the ground: a tunnel. Easier said than done, of course. The first attempt was made in 1799, about twenty-five miles from London, at Tilbury, where in 1588 Elizabeth I famously addressed her armada defence force. But the tunnellers didn't enjoy the same glory, and their plan was swiftly abandoned. Attempt number two came in 1805 when a group of Cornish miners decided to try their hand. But they were used to hard Cornish rock, not the soft London clay. It proved impossible for the tunnel to be built safely without it collapsing or flooding. Works were halted, and the experts declared the endeavour impossible.

One Anglo-French engineer, Marc Brunel, was determined to find a solution. After years of scribbling diagrams on bits of paper, then scrunching them up and throwing them into the bin on the other side of the office, finally – ding! – the lightbulb moment arrived. It was from an unlikely, wriggly source, which appeared to Marc as he inspected some ship's timbers: 'I happened to see before me a piece of condemned timber, a portion of the keel of a ship'. He observed a little worm, which 'had made many erosions . . . I then said to myself these little things have made little tunnels, so might we, by adopting some corresponding means of protection.'

These shipworms would burrow into the hulls, ruining the wood. The soft body of the worm was protected by a hard outer shell at its front, which allowed it to enter, headfirst, with gnawing jaws. They were a menace for a ship's company, but a miracle for an engineer looking for inspiration.

In 1814, Marc Brunel approached Emperor Alexander I of Russia, proposing to tunnel under the River Neva in St Petersburg. The Russians said *nyet*, building a bridge instead. But there was to be more luck in London. In 1818, Marc patented his design and began to recreate the worm's shell on a monumental scale. His invention was the tunnelling shield, a large rectangle of iron scaffolding, eleven metres across, 6.5 metres high, and eighty tons in weight. It created three levels, from which workmen would remove a wooden board in front of them, excavate four inches of the earth, and then replace the board. As every four inches of progress was made, the iron structure would move forward using screw jacks. Meanwhile, behind them, 'a certain number of brick-layers construct the double arch, in brick and roman cement'.

In 1823, Marc produced a plan for a tunnel between Rotherhithe and Wapping, to put his brilliant new invention to the test. Private investments poured in (including from the Duke of Wellington), and the Thames Tunnel Company was formed in 1824.

So how does one go about building a never-before-made tunnel-ling shield? Luckily for Marc Brunel, he was good pals with the Steve Jobs of his day, Henry Maudslay. Just as Jobs promised to change the world through the iPhone, Maudslay understood how innovation in technology could radically, rapidly transform his world.

Such innovation came from absolute precision. Maudslay was a details man. He improved the micrometre (a type of precise measuring device) by a factor of ten, so it could measure down to 0.0001 inches. Then he turned his attention to screw-cutting lathes, making sure the threads (the swirly lines on the shaft of a screw) were accurate. His apprentice, Joseph Whitworth, further developed the concept, and it soon became the de facto British standard.

Marc Brunel had long been impressed with Maudslay's work. In fact, the two men collaborated on an earlier scheme when Marc Brunel had set out to revolutionize the manufacture of pulley blocks on Royal Navy ships.

This had been a big job, as the Royal Navy needed a lot of pulleys. A sailing man-o'-war required up to twenty-five miles of rope, all fed through blocks. HMS *Victory* carried 768 blocks for her rigging and 628 for her guns. Each block varied in size – the largest was twenty-six inches long, the smallest six inches.

Overall, the navy needed 160,000 blocks per year. They were individually hand-made by a workforce of 110 men. Marc Brunel's bright idea was to mechanize the process. He worked with Henry Maudslay to produce forty-two woodworking machines powered by one 32-horsepower steam engine.

By 1807, Maudslay's machines were churning out Brunel's blocks, fulfilling the entire requirement of the Royal Navy. The machine-made blocks were made quicker, cheaper and to a higher standard than ever before, with some still in use for the D-Day landings in 1944. Brunel was able to cut the workforce to ten men and – at the height of the Napoleonic Wars – save the Navy tens of thousands of pounds per year.

And now, in the 1810s, Maudslay and Brunel were working together once more to put the new tunnelling system into action. But this time, as Marc Brunel entered the factory, he was accompanied by another young man. 'Maudslay, let me introduce to you my chief assistant engineer.' An eighteen-year-old boy, the spitting image of Marc, put out his hand: 'Master Isambard Brunel, sir. Pleasure to make your acquaintance.'

Had Maudslay been sceptical of Marc Brunel giving his son such responsibility, he need not have worried. Teenage Isambard was super sharp. The kind of child who would appear on the TV quiz show *Child Genius* and leave Richard Osman proclaiming 'remarkable' to the camera. No one was better suited to act as Maudsley's apprentice than him. Equipped with brains, the best training in the world and stacks of determination, he was raring to get going.

How thrilling it must have been to explore Maudsley's Lambeth factory. This was the equivalent of stepping into a Silicon Valley start-up. 'It is the future, my boy,' Maudslay might have grinned, as he pushed open a door and gestured for Isambard to take a step inside. Here was a city of metal. Huge machines whirring and pounding. Enormous iron structures, as big as double-decker buses, with pistons frantically driving back and forth, hundreds of interconnected cogs spinning, and soot-covered workers scurrying to shovel coal to keep the beast alive.

The sound was deafening, the smell of oil overpowering. But Isambard was transfixed. His eyes widened, his brain sent into overdrive, already calculating the possibilities, processing the potential. 'NEXT ROOM,' Maudslay bellowed through the din, gesturing to a door in the corner.

'This is really where all the ideas happen. See all these young men? These are the brightest minds in London – a bit like you.' This room was the brain of the factory, a hub of innovation where new concepts were thought up. 'Their calculations,' Maudslay continued, 'will create brand-new machines, faster, safer, cheaper and more accurate than before. Then we send the machines to mines, railways, cotton mills and the like, all across the country. If you want to follow in your father's footsteps, my boy, and make some big changes in the world, this is where to begin.'

For eighteen-year-old Isambard, it was music to his ears. He had spent his life waiting for this moment. His destiny as an engineer seemed cast in iron from the moment he was born. His name was of Germanic origin – the first half derived from *isarn*, meaning iron, and the second part derived from either *biart-r* (meaning bright) or *barða* (meaning an axe). He was either iron-bright or iron-axe. Nominative determinism at its best.

Isambard was born on 9 April 1806, in Portsmouth. His bedtime lullabies were a melody of distant, drunken sea shanties, the rustle of sails and the groans and creaks of timber. In 1806, Portsmouth was the beating heart of the Royal Navy, and perhaps the most protected town in Europe, with a network of forts shielding the precious ships inside. It was from Portsmouth that, just a year before, our friend Horatio Nelson had set sail to command the fleet that triumphed at the Battle of Trafalgar.

I know you're itching to hear more about Baby Isambard, but first, let me tell you more about his parents. Their backstories are, to put it frankly, wild. It's a sweeping, cross-continent love story, through revolution and imprisonment, bad timings and miraculous chance. This would be a BAFTA-winning *Atonement*-esque epic . . .

It would start with Sophia Kingdom, his mother. She grows up in Plymouth with her fifteen siblings. As many English girls have been since, young Sophia (played by Keira Knightley) is sent with her sisters to France, to learn French and finesse dinner-party conversation.

On arrival, it emerges this is a terrible mistake. The French Revolution is kicking off. While the others flee to England, Sophia (now gravely ill) is forced to stay. She is a damsel in distress, alone and dying in this dangerous, foreign land. But not all is lost – in comes the heartthrob: a young engineer, Marc Isambard Brunel (played by James McAvoy). Passions flare and the two are engaged to be wed.

But their love is soon thwarted. France is a hotbed of revolutionary tension and – here's the nightmare – Marc is an avowed royalist. He is forced to run for his life. He heads to Le Havre and jumps on a ship bound for New York. But Sophia, being unable to obtain a passport, is trapped in France. As an English girl engaged to an escaped royalist, she gets caught up in the horrors of the 'Reign of Terror' in 1793–94 (a series of massacres and public executions without trial).

Sophia is dragged away in a crowded open cart and imprisoned, to await her turn to be executed (while scratching 'Marc' on the walls of the prison cell, in a heart). As we wait for Sophia to face her grisly fate, everything changes again. The revolutionary leader, Robespierre, falls in July 1794, and the prisoners are free to go. The doors are flung open and, squinting in the sunlight, Sophia emerges, fleeing home to the safety of English shores.

Intermission.

Across the Atlantic, Marc is making a name for himself. After arriving in New York on 6 September 1793, he's become the darling of the architectural scene. He's designed schemes to link the Hudson River with Lake Champlain by canal. He's submitted a proposal for the new Capitol building in Washington, DC. In 1796, he's appointed Chief Engineer of the city of New York. Now an American citizen, Marc designs houses, docks, commercial buildings, an arsenal and a cannon factory.

At a dinner party in 1798, Marc comes face to face with fate again when he first hears of the navy's pulleys. 'Did you know, sir,' a round-faced fellow grumbles, 'every year the Royal Navy needs over 100,000 pulleys for their ships, and all of these are made by hand! Can you believe it!' Between passing potatoes and drinking claret, Marc's mind begins humming once more. He starts furiously designing, staying up all night and throwing scrunched-up paper in the wastepaper basket – until, at dawn, he's cracked it. On 7 February 1799, he sets sail for England, armed with a letter of introduction to the Navy Minister. A month later, he lands at Falmouth.

But in a great, romantic twist, it's not only the Navy Minister on Marc's radar. He sets to work tracking down his beloved, the beautiful Sophia. After six heart-wrenching years apart, not knowing if the other was dead or alive, they reunite, too dumbstruck to say anything intelligent ('Is it raining? I hadn't noticed.'). They marry on 1 November 1799 and walk out of the church as the credits roll in.

EIGHTEEN

Immediate BAFTA.

It was a tale that would go down in history, a love story of extraordinary endurance. It also made Marc and Sophia well prepared for the challenges of parenthood: two daughters, Sophia Macnamara and Emma, and a son, Isambard, followed.

The family moved to London when Isambard was very young, to 98 Cheyne Walk in Chelsea. It's a beautiful white stucco house, now with a blue plaque, which reads 'SIR MARC ISAMBARD BRUNEL 1769–1849 and ISAMBARD KINGDOM BRUNEL 1806–1859 civil engineers lived here'.

In this young boy, Marc created a mini-me. At the age of four, Isambard had been taught drawing. By eight, he had Euclidean geometry under his belt. He had his father's continental looks, too, with distinct olive skin and bright, dark eyes.

From their riverside home, Marc taught his protégé the secrets of his craft. 'Come by the window, Isambard,' Marc might have called over to his son. 'See how the boats stay afloat?' Then, blowing on the windowpane and drawing with his finger to illustrate the point, 'That's because the buoyancy force acting on the vessel is greater than the weight of the ship itself.'

Isambard caught the engineering bug. As a young child, he once passed a newly built store shed at Deptford, in east London. He suddenly quickened his pace, pointed at the building and cried, 'There! Don't you see? It will fall!' The next morning the building was in ruins. Some people thought it was spooky. To Isambard, it was just logic.

When Isambard was sent to boarding school in Hove, he was taught French and became well-versed in Homeric epics. But the standard school curriculum didn't hit the mark, and his mind wandered elsewhere. One letter home in 1820 read: 'I have been making half a dozen boats lately, 'til I have worn my hands to pieces.' While others were planning schoolboy japes or tossing a cricket ball, Isambard made a survey of the local area, assessing how its infrastructure could be improved. 'I have also taken a plan of Hove,' he reported home, 'which is a very amusing job'.

By the age of fourteen, he followed in the footsteps of his mother, all those years before, by crossing the channel to study in France. By now, the terrors of the revolution had passed, and the Bourbon monarchy was restored. Isambard enrolled at the College of Caen and the Lycée Henri-IV in Paris, a hub of mathematical teaching, which he completed in 1822, aged sixteen. Finally, as a sort of finishing school, he served as an apprentice to his dad's old friend, Abraham-Louis Breguet.

Breguet was the king of the watchmaking world (and is still the name of a luxury brand today). Over his career, he delighted the crème de la crème of Europe with his fine designs – Marie Antoinette, Napoleon Bonaparte, Alexander I of Russia and the Duke of Wellington all kept time by Breguet's handiwork. He created the self-winding 'perpetual watch', and the Montre à Tact watch, that could be read by touch, so you could tell the time at night. Breguet also made the 'Marie-Antoinette', the most expensive clock in the world.

Leaning over Breguet's shoulder and watching this master at work, Isambard learnt the secrets of chronometers, watches and scientific instruments. And brilliant Breguet was certainly impressed with his young apprentice, seeing in Isambard the spark of genius. He wrote to Marc on 1 November 1821, pressing the need for Isambard to follow in his father's footsteps: 'I feel that it is important to cultivate in him the happy inventive dispositions that he owes to nature or education, but that it would be a shame to see lost'. Isambard was lucky to be taught by the master. Breguet would die a few years later in 1823. Isambard was – as it were – just in time.

During his teenage years, Isambard must have read his father's letters with great excitement, hearing of his plans for veneers, sawmills and machinery for mass-producing soldiers' boots. How proud he must have been when all of this was recognized with a fellowship from the Royal Society.

But there was a spanner in the works. Due to the Admiralty's failure to pay, Marc Brunel – who had supplied all those pulleys to the navy during the Napoleonic Wars – was sinking dangerously into debt. With £5,000 to pay, and no means of doing it, the family were declared bankrupt, and Marc was sent to debtors' prison.

It was the ultimate humiliation. This was a total and utter disgrace. Going to debtors' prison was an experience known to many members of respectable society in the eighteenth and nineteenth centuries who had spent more than their means. It was almost always men – being responsible for households' financial matters – who were thrown behind bars. However, their wives and children might join them if they didn't have the means to cope on their own.

It was a shame endured by Daniel Defoe, author of *Robinson Crusoe*. Charles Dickens's father, John, also spent several months at the Marshalsea Prison in 1824 (you can still see parts of Marshalsea, a long wall near London Bridge station). With his family behind bars, twelve-year-old Charles Dickens was forced to work at a shoe polish factory. His novel *Little Dorrit* is based on the awful memories of his family living behind bars, and his body of work is littered with children who face hardship as a result of feckless or struggling parents.

For the Brunel family, this period was so dire that it was only ever mentioned as 'the Misfortune'. Marc and Sophia were incarcerated at King's Bench Prison in Southwark. In this moment of desperation, and having been so poorly mistreated by the British government, Marc got in touch with an old pen pal across the seas. Tsar Alexander of Russia was open to helping and suggested the Brunels could relocate to St Petersburg and apply their engineering wizardry there. Correspondence whizzed back and forth between prison and palace.

When word got out that Britain was on the brink of losing one of its best engineers, feathers were ruffled. After pressure from the Duke of Wellington, the government forked out £5,000 to clear Marc's debts, with an agreement that he would abandon the Russian plan. After eighty-eight days behind bars, Marc walked free in August 1821. And, to make good his promise, he was straight back to the drawing board.

Young Isambard finished his studies and returned to London, at which point he turned eighteen. It was during these years that he worked as an apprentice to Henry Maudslay. In 1827, aged twenty, he began his first big project, working as the resident engineer on the Thames Tunnel. Despite Isambard's brilliant capability, the project soon became a nightmare.

The tunnel flooded twice, the workers were left in danger because of poor ventilation, and budgets were exceeded. In 1828, the roof collapsed, and six men perished. Isambard escaped by the skin of his teeth, sustaining serious injuries. The work was stop and go for seven years, finally completed in 1843 as a foot tunnel (and Londoners *still* facing chock-a-block traffic!).

In these early years of adulthood, Isambard struggled to see a successful future for himself. Despondent at his failures, he was resigned to settling for mediocrity, writing in his diary:

EIGHTEEN

It's a gloomy perspective yet bad as it is I cannot with all my efforts work myself up to be downhearted . . . After all let the worst happen – unemployed untalked of – pennyless (that's damned awkward) . . . I suppose a sort of middle path will be the most likely one. A mediocre success – an engineer some-times employed and sometime not – £200/£300 a year, that uncertain.

Yet lurking around the corner was a big break. In March 1833, aged twenty-six, Isambard applied to be chief engineer on the Great Western Railway, a proposed 118-mile line from London to Bristol. In nine weeks, he completed a survey and presented his plans. The endeavour paid off: Isambard got the job.

Once Isambard – with his great brains, determination and ambition – started to build, the momentum gained pace, and soon he was hurtling forward at top speed. Over his lifetime, his output was immense. He was the brains behind Bristol's Clifton Suspension Bridge, the Box Tunnel (the longest tunnel in the world at the time) and London Paddington station – all still working today. His SS *Great Britain* (a great day out in Bristol) was the first iron ship and the first with a steam-powered propeller, rather than a paddle wheel.

He turned his hand to hospitals, too. In 1855, during the Crimean War, Isambard was asked by the British Government to design a portable hospital. It took him six days to complete the designs. It was known as the Renkioi Hospital, able to house many patients with a high standard of hygiene and sanitation. The huts were – according to Florence Nightingale – 'magnificent'.

So how did Brunel achieve so much in his lifetime? How did he get so far, so soon? His childhood offered the best possible preparation for a wannabe engineer: his father was the greatest engineer of the age and Isambard was taught by his father's pals.

But Isambard worked immensely hard, too (incredibly, completing his projects with a team of only thirty-six). One assistant recalled: 'I never met his equal for sustained power of work ... If at all pressed for time he slept in his armchair for two or three hours, and at early dawn he was ready for the work of the day'. Perhaps it explains his one guilty pleasure, tobacco, which 'he indulged in to excess, and probably to his injury'. He died of a stroke in 1859, the same year, by chance, as another great railway engineer, Robert Stephenson (who was also the only son of George Stephenson, the 'Father of Railways').

Isambard was also lucky to be born at the perfect moment, when the fruits of the industrial revolution could be reaped. Had he been born in the Tudor or medieval periods, would his brilliance have had a platform?

Today, Isambard's legacy is everywhere. We live in a Brunellian world, surrounded by the bridges, tunnels, viaducts, buildings and railway lines he left behind. But Isambard was so much more than a prolific engineer. Isambard was a visionary – perhaps the greatest in British history. He harnessed new technology so effectively that it transformed the world in a way most people could have never imagined.

Take the Great Western Railway, which cut the journey time from London to Bristol from a medieval two and a half days to a modern two and a half hours. Then – as if that wasn't enough – at the end of the railway line Brunel built the Bristol docks, where the biggest, fastest ship to ever sail was built.

Now, people could travel from London to New York in two weeks. It was 'the greatest experiment since the creation'. Isambard was shrinking the world, kickstarting global travel and international communications, and laying the groundwork for Britain's standing on the world stage in the late nineteenth century. This was the space race of the day – with Isambard the winner.

In today's risk-averse environment, we tend to play it safe, to fixate on short-term solutions. Isambard – and many of his fellow Victorian innovators – had no time for such caution. The potential was so wonderfully exciting that the risk was worth it. Isambard's technological developments were ground-breaking and unheard of in scope and daring. He put his reputation – and other people's money – on the line. Of course, there were plenty of hiccups, mishaps and miscalculations along the way (such as the 'atmospheric railway' powered by air pumps, which was too expensive to become practical). But with such innovation, full of risk, mistakes are to be expected – and a small price to pay for the eventual success.

Isambard was born in a world of wooden ships with sails, of carriages bumping along the roads. In his lifetime, this world transformed, much of it through his own work. He was born in the Age of Sail, but created the Age of Steam, revolutionizing how we approach engineering, transport and construction.

Of course, at eighteen years old, he always knew the name Brunel would go down in the history books – the question was: would it be Marc or Isambard?

Dessert Arrives

It was that stage of the evening when guests had loosened up: polite conversation became friendly teasing; drinks were spilt and lips became stained with red wine.

Desserts were placed at each setting, but no one paid them much attention.

'I've got a riddle,' announced Bede. 'It's one we used to say at home.'

Jack – who adored hearing about Bede's Anglo-Saxon world – took a fork and tapped his glass to silence the room.

'All right everyone, we're going to hear a good old riddle from our friend Bede. Drumroll please.'

As the others banged the table, Bede, blushing with the attention, stood up: 'When I am alive, I do not speak. Anyone who wants to takes me captive and cuts off my head. They bite my bare body. I do no harm to anyone unless they cut me first. Then I soon make them cry.'

The suggestions came in thick and fast:

'An arrow?'

'A Spanish galleon?'

'A ration book?'

'Hang on, let's go through it step by step,' said Elsie. 'One: it's an

inanimate object. Two: you bite it. Three: it makes people cry. And four: as it's Bede, it's obviously something venerable . . . or should I say, vegetable. It's . . . an onion!'

Bede threw his hands up and clapped, 'You've got it, Elsie! Well done! An onion!'

12

Elsie Inglis

THE ROYAL MILE IS Edinburgh's most famous street. This is the artery of the old city, with Edinburgh Castle perched high at one end and the Palace of Holyroodhouse at the other in the shadow of Arthur's Seat. From above, the Mile looks like the skeleton of a fish with so many little wynds, alleys, lanes, passageways and closes spreading out either side, leading to courtyards, underground streets and never-ending sets of steps.

For most of the year, the Mile is the realm of delivery drivers unloading tartan scarfs, hungover students scurrying to lectures and tourists milling about, perusing shops like Thistle Do Nicely. During the summer months, these smatterings of visitors become an invasion.

In August, the Royal Mile transforms into the heart of the Edinburgh Festival Fringe. If you suffer from claustrophobia, avoid it at all costs! A stroll along those cobbles becomes an attack of leaflets, thesps dressed in ironically bad cardboard costumes, and a racket of sound. There are cries of 'Free student stand-up comedy, starts at two o'clock!' or 'Hard-hitting interpretative dance about drug addiction, four stars!' or 'Family-friendly philosophical meditation on existentialism, starts in half an hour!'.

On Thursday, 29 November 1917, the Royal Mile was also heaving with people. But these were not students, reviewers or tourists. These were mourners, huddled together as the bells of St Giles' Cathedral tolled their sombre lament.

'A large number attending were women,' *The Scotsman* reported, 'the great majority wearing black'. Many who piled into the medieval church were from the Scottish Women's Hospitals, the Women's Army Auxiliary Corps, or the Scottish Federation of Women's Suffrage Societies. There were plenty of Serbians, too: 'tall figures, in light brown military costume', representatives of the Serbian royal family, and the Serbian Red Cross.

At two o'clock, the funeral of Elsie Inglis began. The oak coffin was covered with a Union Jack and a Serbian flag. The Rev. Dr Wallace Williamson took to the pulpit and championed this 'very dear and noble lady, our beloved sister', who represented a 'wondrous union of strength and tenderness, of courage and sweetness, she remains for us a bright and noble member of high devotion and stainless honour'.

At the end of the service, the congregation sang the hymn, 'For all the Saints, who from their labours rest'. The 'Last Post' was played by the Royal Scots buglers. Then – to the accompaniment of Handel's 'Hallelujah Chorus' – the coffin was carried from the church to a gun carriage drawn by six horses. The congregation filed out afterwards, uplifted by 'a thanksgiving instinct', a feeling of 'triumph and hope'.

Next came the cortege from St Giles' Cathedral to Dean Cemetery. As it passed through the city – down the Mound, along

Princes Street, through the West End – vast 'grief-stricken crowds' lined the streets and followed on foot.

Condolences were sent to the family from the high and mighty, celebrating this 'immortal link between Serbia and Scotland'. Queen Mary wrote a letter – published in *The Scotsman* – praising Elsie's 'splendid services' and offering her 'heartfelt sympathy' to relatives. For those who knew Elsie – the 'shawl-draped women holding the bairns of care' – this stately send-off wasn't enough: 'Why did they not give her the V.C.?' they muttered, as the cortege went past.

Who was this woman who was given such prestigious treatment? Who brought Scotland's capital to a standstill? Who was so beloved by so many, in Scotland and in Serbia? Who was championed as Scotland's very own Joan of Arc?

Elsie Inglis was a surgeon and suffragist, whose bravery and tenacity saved thousands of lives. She was a no-nonsense woman, 'a woman of solved problems', and would no doubt have been an avid supporter of Nike's slogan: 'Just Do It'.

To cut to the chase, here's a super-speedy whirlwind tour of the Heroic Deeds of Adult Elsie Inglis. Sit back, relax, and enjoy this PowerPoint presentation – you'll have to imagine the zany graphics and airless atmosphere of a lecture theatre. If you do drop off, please don't snore. First slide. please . . .

SLIDE ONE: CHAMPION OF WOMEN'S HEALTH IN EDINBURGH

Founded the Edinburgh College of Medicine for Women

Opened a maternity hospital, named the Hospice

Often waived her fees and would pay for her patients to recuperate by the seaside

SLIDE TWO: SUPERWOMAN SUFFRAGIST

Elsie was a 'tower of strength' in the suffrage movement

A big name in the Scottish Federation of Women's Suffrage Societies

Her 'unbounded energy and unfailing courage helped the cause forward in more ways than she knew'

SLIDE THREE: THOSE FAMOUS WORDS!

When Britain entered the First World War, Elsie volunteered as a surgeon on the front line

The War Office responded: 'My good lady, go home and sit still.'

Elsie is more determined than ever!

SLIDE FOUR: FIRST WORLD WAR

Raised the equivalent of over £50 million to form the Scottish Women's Hospital

Throughout the war, fourteen medical units were outfitted and over 1,000 women were sent to serve across Europe

Units were mostly run by women nurses, doctors, ambulance drivers, cooks and mechanics

Units were sent to support thousands of allies across France, Serbia, Corsica, Salonika, Romania, Russia and Malta

SLIDE FIVE: SAINT ELSIE

In Serbia, Elsie and her teams worked tirelessly and selflessly to improve the hygiene standards during a deadly typhus epidemic, earning Elsie the nickname 'Mother of the Nation'

Elsie became the first woman to receive the Serbian Order of the White Eagle

'In Scotland,' it was said, 'she became a doctor. In Serbia she became a saint.'

EIGHTEEN

SLIDE SIX: LEGACY AND CONCLUDING THOUGHTS

Elsie was a hero!

She was fearless: 'It was a great day in my life,' she confided to a
friend, 'when I discovered that I did not know what fear was.'

She paved the way for modern women

Her portrait is on the Scottish £50 note

There is soon to be a statue of her on the Royal Mile

SLIDE SEVEN: THANK YOU

Thanks so much for listening, everybody

Are there any questions? None? OK, great

Tea is served in the foyer

That's the career story. That's the woman the public knew and loved. But who was the real Elsie? Where did she come from? Where did it all start?

When her little sister, Eva, wrote a biography (titled *Elsie Inglis: The Woman with the Torch*, published in 1920), she felt it worth starting at the beginning – the very beginning. You had to meet Elsie's ancestors – 'these men and women in their quaint and attractive costumes of long ago' – to get a sense of her. By tracing the Inglis family tree, 'we feel their influence on [Elsie]; we see their spirit mingling with her . . . we see the dim outline of the rock from which she was hewn'.

Elsie was descended from the Inglises of Inverness-shire, in the north of Scotland. They had ancestral links to Robert the Bruce and supported the Young Pretender, Bonnie Prince Charlie. But they were an adventurous bunch, too. One of Elsie's great-grandfathers was the Governor of Java. Another emigrated to South Carolina, dying in a duel fought on 'some point of honour'. Elsie's great-uncle was a friend of William Wilberforce, and later became consul-general in Venice, 'where he died, in 1834, in his gondola!'.

Her grandfathers and father were some of the many Scots who worked for the East India Company (EIC), which was probably the most powerful corporation in history – the ultimate megacorp. From its foundation in 1600, the EIC was granted a monopoly on British trade with the East, which is why, in the eighteenth century, products like cotton, porcelain, tea and silks became à la mode in Britain.

At its height, the EIC dominated global trade between Europe, South Asia and the Far East. It fought numerous wars using its army and navy and conquered and colonized modern-day India, Pakistan, Bangladesh and Burma. After the 1857 Rebellion – a widespread but unsuccessful rebellion against British rule in India – the structure changed. Control of the EIC was transferred to the Crown, aka Queen Victoria. The British Raj (a Hindi word meaning 'realm' or 'empire') began.

This is when Elsie arrived. She was born in India in 1864 and lived there until she was twelve. Her father, John Inglis, was working for the EIC as a civil servant. He was brought up in England, where he attended the East India College at Haileybury, where young men were trained up for life in over-seas civil service. He was a high-spirited pupil, who was once suspended for turning up 'in a state of very questionable sobriety'. Despite this hiccup, John grew up to be a 'dedicated, pious, godly and honest' man, with an unwavering Christian faith, 'simple and profound'. He went to India in 1840, where, apart from one brief return trip to Britain, he spent the next thirty-six years working for the EIC.

Elsie's mother, Harriet, came to India to live with her father (Elsie's grandfather) at the age of seventeen and got married the following year. Harriet was a catch – some eligible bachelors 'drove fifty miles to have the chance of dancing with her!'

The marriage was a fruitful one, as six new Inglises joined the clan. In the late 1850s, John took a break from work, and the family headed back to Britain. The journey took eight months – four months across land from Lahore to Calcutta, then four more sailing the seas around the Cape of Good Hope.

But it was the worst moment to go on furlough. Almost as soon as he'd arrived back in Blighty, John was hastily called back to India, on account of the Indian Rebellion. He parted with his wife, who rejoined him in 1863, leaving her children in Britain. During this second stint in India came a second batch of children. This was the 'second family', and this is where Elsie came into the picture.

So, although Elsie grew up as if she was the eldest child, she was actually child number seven. Elsie – or Eliza Maud Inglis – was born on 16 August 1864, 'a very little thing with a very wee face' and a 'famous pair of large blue eyes'. At four months old, her mother noted how observant she was:

> It is quite remarkable how she looks about her and seems to observe everything. She lies in her bed at night in the dark and talks away out loud in her own little language, and little voice, and she is always ready for a laugh.

More siblings – Eva and Horace – soon followed, and the three of them would spend their childhoods together at Nainital, one of the most beautiful hill stations in the Himalayas. Their veranda had a magnificent view across hills and snow-capped peaks, an outlook of 'silent and majestic stillness'.

Harriet, their 'quiet, strong mother', sat with the children each morning:

There were five minutes when we sat in front of her in a row on little chairs in her room and read the Scripture verses in turn, and then knelt in a straight, quiet row and repeated the prayers after her.

Then, after cocoa on the veranda, they joined their father, John, for a walk:

Three ponies followed behind, each with their attendant grooms . . . father stopping all along the road to talk to every native who wished to speak to him, while we three ran about, laughing and interested in everything.

In the evenings, when John went to bid the children goodnight, 'All order and quietness [was] flung to the winds'.

Elsie and her father, John, were the best of friends, closer than any of the other family members. They were 'special chums', 'comrades, inseparables from the day of her birth'. But there was never any jealousy from the others, and John was sure to treat his children the same: 'Father was always just! The three cups of cocoa were exactly the same in quality and quantity. We got equal shares of his right and left hand in our walks'.

From the very start, Elsie was a natural doctor. Here's an account of the childhood games Elsie and Eva played with their forty dolls:

Elsie decreed once that they should all have measles – so days were spent by us three painting little red dots all over the forty faces and the forty pairs of arms and legs. She was the doctor

and prescribed gruesome drugs which we had to administer.
Then it was decreed that they should slowly recover, so each day
so many spots were washed off until the epidemic was wiped out!

When Elsie was twelve, the family spent two years in Tasmania, where two elder brothers – boys from the first batch of children – had settled.

But even in the wilds of Tasmania, Elsie and Eva were drilled into the British school system. Their school was run by Miss Knott, previously of Cheltenham College for Girls. Here, Elsie revealed her instinct for order and uniform:

In the days when such things were practically unknown, Elsie,
backed by Miss Knott, instituted 'school colours'. They were very
primitive, not beautiful hatbands, but two inches of blue and
white ribbon sewn on to a safety pin and worn on the lapel of
our coats. How proud we were of them.

When Elsie was fourteen years old, the family finally made it to Edinburgh, where Elsie would spend most of her life. They lived at 10 Bruntsfield Place with three servants. It was a large, terraced house (the type now converted into flats), a stone's throw from two glorious stretches of grass: Bruntsfield Links and the Meadows.

The girls caused a stir when they arrived at the Charlotte Square Institution for Schooling. There was a 'certain feeling of surprise' at the arrival of these exotic additions from Tasmania with 'big, earnest brows' and a strange hairstyle, 'parted in the middle and done up in plaits fastened at the back of the head'.

But despite the quirky looks, they settled in fast. Elsie became the joint editor of the school magazine, *Edina* – and the first editor who could make the magazine pay its way. She was a keen croquet player, and 'tolerated no frivolity when a stroke either at croquet or golf were in the balance'.

One particularly characteristic story of Elsie was when she requested permission for the girls to be allowed to play in Charlotte Square Gardens:

In those days, no one thought of providing fresh air exercise for girls except by walk, and tennis was just coming in. Elsie had the courage (to us schoolgirls it seemed the extraordinary courage) to confront the three directors . . .

The directors were 'amiable and estimable men' on their own, but 'the most formidable and awe-inspiring body' as a group. They allowed Elsie use of the gardens – on the strict condition that she could gain permission from the residents of Charlotte Square.

Charlotte Square was the most exclusive of all addresses in the already exclusive New Town area of the city, built in stages between 1767 in 1850 so the well-to-do of Edinburgh could escape the overflowing sewers of the medieval Old Town. The square was designed by the most famous architect of the day, Robert Adam, and over the years there have been more than a few famous residents: No. 6, Bute House, is the official residence of the First Minister of Scotland; No. 9 was the home of medical pioneer Joseph Lister (for whom Listerine mouthwash is named); No. 13 was the home of Sir William Fettes (the businessman who founded Fettes College, to this day Scotland's priciest private school); No. 24 was the birthplace of Field Marshal Douglas Haig; and Alexander Graham Bell (pioneer of the telephone) was born in nearby South Charlotte Street.

This was the kind of crowd Elsie, in her late teens, was dealing with. Very Important People. The types who sat on boards and committees, who were donors or patrons, and who had obituaries in the national newspaper. But Elsie was not to be daunted. She went around the square, ringing each bell and asking the residents whether their very exclusive gardens could be overrun by uproarious schoolgirls.

To her friends, this was nothing short of 'heroic': 'we all felt it was a very brave thing to do'. The permissions were granted. Elsie 'returned from the great exhibition triumphant', and the girls were free to run riot in Charlotte Square.

When she was eighteen years old, Elsie headed to Paris for a year, leaving her family for the first time. In some ways, it was a terrible moment to visit Paris, which had just plunged into the worst stock market crash of the century. But this was also a city of delights. This was the year that Pierre-Auguste Renoir premiered his painting *Luncheon of the Boating Party*. If this was anything like Elsie's eighteenth year – with tables of wine and grapes, and muscly young men wearing vests and boaters – she probably had a good time.

So who was this eighteen-year-old girl? What kind of person had she become? There was no guarantee she would become a national hero. And yet all the ingredients were there: hard work; dedication; a moral compass centred around Christian duty; an interest in medical matters; a father open to the idea of women having a career. For Elsie, those childhood years spent in India normalized the idea of working and living abroad. At the age of eighteen, she was prepared for and familiar with the potential for international travel and work – a skill that would see her leap to volunteer abroad during the First World War. Did her fellow Edinburgh schoolgirls have such a global outlook?

John Inglis was probably the most important figure of

eighteen-year-old Elsie's life: 'no biography of her will be true which does not emphasise the beautiful and deep love and sympathy' between them. This was a 'fellowship', and she was his 'comrade'. They regularly walked together through Edinburgh's streets, when they would have some time to talk together. He treated her as an intellectual equal, answering her questions with the 'utmost cordiality' and an appreciation of her point of view.

This approach – though it might seem totally ordinary today – was quite 'uncommon', and Elsie knew it. She later realized: 'If I have been able to do anything – whatever I am, whatever I have done – I owe it all to my father.' Indeed, John Inglis' open-mindedness freed Elsie of the barriers so many other girls faced.

Here's how Elsie's first 'career chat' went, according to her sister Eva. There was no shouting or scorning. No 'you should have tried harder in your GCSEs', no tears or slammed doors. Just encouragement. It was a model example of parenthood:

> *I remember well the day Elsie came in and, sitting down beside father, divulged her plan of 'going in for medicine'. I still see and hear him, taking it all so perfectly calmly and naturally, and setting to work at once to overcome the difficulties which were in the way, for even then all was not plain sailing for the woman who desired to study medicine.*

This was radical thinking. Not long before Elsie's birth, a guide-book for young ladies was printed: *A manual of etiquette for ladies: or, True principles of politeness*. It considered the entire 'sphere of action' for an eighteen-year-old such as Elsie was nothing more than 'the circle of her own family and dependents'. Pages are devoted to advice, 'to enable you to fill up, in a tolerably agreeable way, some of the many solitary hours you must necessarily pass at home'. The manual trawls through the benefits of chess and backgammon, of singing and learning the pianoforte. 'Every lady should acquire a knowledge of this instrument,' it declares. 'Dancing is likewise essential.' What, I wonder, would the authoress of such an esteemed work consider of Elsie considering – God forbid! – the study of medicine?

Yet as Elsie turned eighteen, the tide was turning – perhaps influenced by the popularity of Queen Victoria, who ascended to the throne at eighteen herself. Doors were finally starting to open for the fairer sex (and not ones that led to another drawing room). Here's how Elsie's biographer, Frances Campbell Balfour, put it in 1918:

> The date of Elsie's birth was in the dawn of the movement which believed it possible that women could have a mind and a brain of their own, and that the freedom of the one and cultivation of the other was not a menace to the possessive rights of the family, or the ruin of society at large.

After qualifying from the Royal College of Physicians, the Royal College of Surgeons in Edinburgh and the Faculty of Physicians and Surgeons of Glasgow (known as the Triple Qualification), Elsie began work at Elizabeth Garrett Anderson's pioneering New Hospital for Women in London, before moving to a leading maternity hospital in Dublin, the Rotunda. In 1894, driven to improve the medical treatment of the Edinburgh poor, she established a practice with fellow student Jessie MacGregor. In 1904, it moved to 219 High Street (part of the Royal Mile) and was renamed the Hospice.

In 1914, when war broke out, Elsie was almost fifty years old. But her most enduring achievements were yet to come. She offered her expertise to the British War Office, who turned her away with the famous line quoted in my slideshow above: 'My good lady, go home and sit still.'

Of course, Elsie did no such thing. She made rallying speeches on 'what women can do to help the war.' She helped establish the Scottish Women's Hospitals for Foreign Service and offered its services to the French and Serbs, both of whom accepted the support.

Soon, Elsie was organizing medical units to be sent to Serbia and Russia, then followed herself, working tirelessly in the heart of a raging typhus epidemic to improve hygiene. As well as a deadly illness, Elsie and her teams faced front-line warfare. In 1915, she was captured and repatriated, only to return to work with the units, refusing to rest until soldiers were guaranteed safe passage out of Serbia. She stayed until the very end, sending a telegram home saying, 'Everything satisfactory and all well except me.'

Indeed, despite her good work, Elsie knew she was dying from bowel cancer. After returning to England, she died the following day on 26 November 1917, aged fifty-three, at the Central Station Hotel, Newcastle. Three days later, the streets of Edinburgh were packed with mourners – many of whom owed their lives to this remarkable woman – to see her funeral cortege pass.

After the war, her legacy lived on, with leftover funds from the Scottish Women's Hospitals for Foreign Service divided between hospitals in Scotland and Belgrade. The Elsie Inglis Memorial Maternity Hospital opened in Edinburgh in July 1925. Today, NHS Lothian runs the Elsie Inglis Staff Development Award – 'The Elsies'– a charitable fund to support and develop individual poten-tial. There is a campaign to install a statue of Elsie on the Royal Mile. In Serbia, Elsie's incredible work has been commemorated, too. In 2015, the British Ambassador to Serbia, Denis Keefe, and the President of the Republic of Serbia, Tomislav Nikolić, unveiled a plaque at the British residence in Belgrade, which was renamed 'Elsie Inglis House'.

It's only fitting that Elsie's remarkable life is remembered so. Perhaps the secret to her success was simple. Sometimes it's doing the basics well that can get us far: being kind, turning up on time, writing a thank-you letter, and not procrastinating. In short, getting the job done. Elsie wasn't a loud, outspoken leader, but – as we saw with her success with the Charlotte Square set – it was her 'quiet, calm and collected' approach that left her 'able to cope with any emergency'.

Not long after her eighteenth birthday, Elsie jotted down the following resolutions (for those looking to follow in her heroic footsteps, this might be a good place to start):

I must give up dreaming – making stories.

I must give up getting cross.

I must devote my mind more to housekeeping.

I must be more thorough in everything.

I must be truthful.

The bottom of the whole evil is the habit of dreaming, which
    must be given up.

So help me, God.

Elsie Inglis.

After Dinner

New groups emerged. Horace, Jacques and Isambard were in heated conversation about ships ('No, Izzy, that's complete rubbish! They left the gunports open – Mary Rose deserved to sink!'). Jack was in deep discussion with Bede ('I can't believe you haven't read Beowulf. It's a classic!'). Jeffrey and Elizabeth were enraptured by Vita's latest relationship drama ('It's not the fact he's only an earl – there's just no spark.').

Vita was proving surprisingly good fun. When she arrived, she was very quiet, almost aloof. She'd kept herself to herself, fiddling with the table flowers. But now she was getting into the swing of things. She whirled around the room, asking everyone – the girls especially – their thoughts, their secrets, their dreams.

13

Vita Sackville-West

NEAR SEVENOAKS IN KENT is a 1,000-acre park. Some of it is rough, rugged land, with boggy valleys. Other parts are open parkland, with long vistas and carefully planted trees that have stood firm for hundreds of years. Mists swirl around horse chestnuts, English oaks, hawthorn and beech, each with a 'knurly tangle of roots . . . coiled above a scarp like serpents'. Among the anthills, where intrepid yellow meadow ants never cease in their work, are fungi of every variety: Saffrondrop Bonnets, Fairy Fingers and purple Amethyst Deceivers.

This is land that, for centuries, has stirred the soul. Henry VIII found it to be 'sounde, parfaite, holesome grounde'. At dawn, the air is filled with the drumming of the great spotted woodpecker, and in the autumn months – during the rutting season – the bellowing of deer, their antlers knocking together as bucks wrestle for the attention of a doe. It is these majestic creatures who rule supreme here, for they are the reason it exists at all. Way back in 1456, Archbishop Bourchier (the man who crowned Richard III) bought the land and fenced it off to make a deer park. The deer were bred to be hunted. Today, they are undisturbed, apart from the occasional interruption of Lycra-clad runners.

In the very heart of the park, perched upon a hilltop, is its crowning jewel. It appears, from a distance, to be a fairy-tale village, with castellated stone towers, gables and turrets, red-brick chimneys and flags fluttering gently in the morning breeze. But on closer inspection, the mullioned windows and shapely gables come into focus, and all becomes clear. This is no village, but one house, a solid mass of Kent ragstone forming a footprint of four acres, and large enough to house a thousand people. Its name is Knole.

In Tudor times, Knole was a royal residence that was visited by all the big names: Henry VIII (for hunting), young Mary I (while her parents were getting divorced), and perhaps Elizabeth I (for some fresh air). After that, it became the grand seat of the Sackville family, one of the oldest names in the land, with records going back to the twelfth century. In the sixteenth century, they were a big name in court circles, and they blinged Knole out to the max. This was the sort of house that might now feature a private cinema, a helipad, and a Damien Hirst in the downstairs loo. All their finery is still in place today, and it's known as a 'Treasure House', pored over by art historians and gawped at by visitors.

But over its long history, where its stones have been worn down by thousands of people – footmen and butlers, posties and farriers – there is one individual to whom Knole meant more than any other. For Vita Sackville-West, the famous writer and garden designer, Knole wasn't just her childhood and ancestral home. It was more than that. Knole was everything.

I first visited Knole in September 2022. We were making a documentary, so the team had to arrive at the crack of dawn to film before visitor opening hours. It was breathtakingly beautiful, the silence only interrupted by our knocks on the enormous wooden gatehouse doors (after ten minutes, we noticed the intercom system on the left). But stepping inside the entrance hall, suddenly everything I knew of Vita made sense. I could imagine her in these rooms, peering out of windows, or gliding up the staircase.

Let me, for a moment, take you back in time. Wherever you're reading this book – perhaps tucked up in bed with a hot-water bottle, or bumbling through Edinburgh on a Lothian bus, or lying on a stripy towel on a beach in Cornwall – we're leaving. Ignore those pink swirls of smoke or the *Doctor Who* theme tune – that's how time travel works these days. Nearly there . . . 1912 . . . 1911 . . . 1910 . . . ding! Open your eyes. We've arrived . . .

The entrance hall of Knole is pretty much unchanged. Still strangely empty and silent, apart from the ticking of a grand-father clock and the sound of a closed door, many rooms away. Out of the corner of your eye, there is movement. From behind a column peers Vita, eighteen years old, with large, unblinking eyes, a scruffy brown fringe, and knotted hair tied up in a bun. She wears a long plain dress with a tear in it, and holds sheets of writing paper under her arm.

'Are you here for a tour?' she inquires, with the impetuous confidence of a grown woman. 'I wasn't expecting one today. My mother and father are away, but I will show you around.'

Despite the rugged appearance, her voice is smooth and polished. She notices you gaze up towards an enormous wooden screen – an explosion of carved swirls and whirls and emblems and heraldry. '1605, they put that in,' she explains. 'It was William Portington, master carpenter to Elizabeth I, I believe.

Never done much for me.' She turns on her heel and walks out of the hall. The tour has begun.

Vita is a strange young woman, wise beyond her years. She knows everything about this house, every nook and cranny of the labyrinth. There are grand state rooms filled with priceless treasures of bygone ages, staircases with one-of-a-kind Renaissance wall paintings, long galleries with walls jam-packed with portraits, jostling for space.

'It's a calendar house,' Vita tells you, as she turns into another gallery (this one adorned with copies of Raphael's work), 'which means there are 365 rooms, one for each day of the year, fifty-two staircases for each week, twelve entrances for each month, and seven courtyards for each day of the week.' It is an anecdote Vita enjoys telling, though it isn't quite true (Knole has around 400 rooms). For Vita, it's more important to convey a spirit of the place, rather than bother over tedious details.

As you pause to marvel at a silver mirror, spectacularly over-laid with garlands of fruits and flowers, Vita calls from afar. You turn and see that she has crawled under a walnut armchair, so only her legs are visible.

'Come here, you must come and look.' As she extracts herself from the space, and you peer underneath – the musty smell of passed centuries filling your nostrils – you see two letters: WP. 'It stands for Whitehall Palace,' Vita explains. 'The Tudor palace that burnt down in 1698. Luckily, the chairs were moved here first!'

It turns out many of the objects here were created for royal residences, some from Whitehall, some from Hampton Court. Leaning from a bedpost of a magnificent four-poster bed, Vita gives the low-down: 'This one is the Spangled Bed, from 1621. Because of the spangles, obviously,' she says, gesturing to the cloth of silver, with embroidery flickering as she moves it. 'It's like looking at moonlight, I always think, as if the stars were captured in cloth.'

Another room. Another magnificent bed. This one was made for King James II, with a Lion and the Unicorn motif, and his monogram, JR. 'And look,' Vita adds, 'a suit of matching armour.'

There is a large chest covered in crimson velvet and overlaid with brass bosses. As Vita opens it up, she reveals a large circular hole, where a pewter bowl would sit. 'The royal seat of easement,' Vita explains, adding, with a wry smile, 'for relieving oneself.'

I'm afraid our time is up. The colour drains from the room, the straight lines of furniture begin to warp, and the pink smoke clouds our view once again. We're back in the present, back to reality.

Aside from showing visitors historic treasures, Vita knew her family history like the back of her hand. She knew every twisting line of her ancestry: the Sackvilles, Dorsets and Sackville-Wests. There was the 6th Earl of Dorset who – as Lord Chamberlain of the Household to William III – was able to buy up furniture from royal palaces. There was the 3rd Duke, who filled the walls with grand paintings and spiced up the interiors with a life-sized nude marble statue of his mistress (which was discreetly moved to the attics when he remarried a wealthy heiress).

The family seemed to become wackier with each generation. Vita's grandfather, Lionel, 2nd Baron Sackville, was a British diplomat. Scandalously, he fell in love with a woman called Pepita, said to be a Romani Spanish dancer (it can be tricky to pin down details, as the family history has been so muddled up with Vita's own romanticization of the past). Lionel and Pepita's relationship lasted nineteen years, and they had seven children, some of whom were placed in a Paris convent.

In 1880, the children returned to England (except for the eldest boy, Max, who was sent to South Africa). Here they were told, for the first time, of their true inheritance. What a shock to be introduced to their aristo family: Uncle Reginald (the Earl De La Warr), Uncle Mortimer (Baron Sackville), Aunt Bessie (Duchess of Bedford) and Aunt Mary (Countess of Derby).

Victoria, the eldest girl, was sent to Washington to live with her father at the British Legation. She arrived in 1881, and was a big hit, charming everyone with her youthful looks and modesty, and strange mix of heritage: the manners of the English aristo, the grace of the French convent girl and, on occasion, a wildness, from her Roma traveller mother.

Marriage proposals came in left, right and centre. The widowed president, Chester A. Arthur, even threw his hat in the ring. But none succeeded. Instead, Victoria kept things in the family. She married her first cousin, also called Lionel, who was six years her junior. It was a tidy solution for family finances: Victoria would marry the man who would inherit Knole, her father's seat.

At the start, Victoria and Lionel were deliciously in love and drunk with passion. On 9 March 1892, a daughter, Victoria, arrived – known as Vita, to distinguish her from her mother. Yet the birth left Victoria so traumatized that she vowed to never again endure it. It was decided: Vita Sackville-West was to be an only child.

On one hand, growing up at Knole was full of excitement. Being an hour's drive from London, her parents regularly hosted glittering society parties with plenty of bright young things and celebrity names. They modernized the place, too, installing all the mod cons: a telephone, electricity, central heating, and bathrooms with running water.

But Lionel and Victoria's passionate love would burn out. While Lionel brought his mistress, an opera singer, to live with him at Knole, Victoria began an affair with John Murray Scott (who played an important role in establishing the Wallace Collection). During Vita's childhood, her mother was away at Murray Scott's various houses: his pied-à-terre on the Rue Laffitte in Paris, or in the Scottish Highlands, at a shooting lodge near Banchory.

Vita sometimes joined her mother on these adventures. But often, she found herself left alone at Knole, her parents wrapped up in their own lives. Left to fend for herself, Vita found comfort in two ways. First, she began writing – plays, poetry, novels – going wherever her pen would take her. Between fourteen and eighteen years old, she wrote eight novels and five plays. They were performed in the dusty attics of Knole, to rapturous applause (with Vita performing her work, as well as playing the part of audience).

She published one play, *Chatterton*, in 1909, and had 100 copies printed. It grapples with some weighty issues, recounting the tragic life of Thomas Chatterton, an eighteenth-century poet who committed suicide at the age of seventeen. Pertinently, this was the same age that Vita was. Did she resonate with his loneliness, his solitude, I wonder? The play is full of passages like this:

> *A poet's work is art, and art is beauty,*
> *And beauty goodness; God would not allow*
> *That goodness thus should perish emptily.*
> *Should art and beauty then be hollowness?*

Pretty impressive for a seventeen-year-old. The play ends with Chatterton's death, and his friend rushing in, full of high drama:

'And he falls on his knees in anguish beside the couch, covering the limp hand with tears and kisses. CURTAIN'.

Aside from writing, the second great comfort in Vita's young life was Knole itself. Knole wasn't just bricks and mortar to Vita, but a real, breathing character, who nourished and nurtured her. 'So I have loved thee, as a lonely child,' she wrote, in an ode to Knole. 'Scarcely a stone of you I had not kissed.' Here – alone – Vita could be herself, free of the fussy, formal clothes her mother insisted she wore. She went full tomboy, wearing a khaki uniform and swinging a cricket bat.

She found friends, too – children from local families, or the household servants. She enjoyed chattering to the maids, helping the cook in the kitchen, or stirring up paint when the decorators came over. Sometimes she'd walk with her grandfather, of whom she was very fond. This was a man who knew little of the grand art on the walls but spent days examining the grounds outside, sometimes accompanied by two domesticated cranes named Romeo and Juliet.

Often, when her parents were in London, Vita gave tours of the house. She may have seemed a lonely figure, floating around these vast rooms alone. But she wasn't truly lonely. There were friends everywhere. 'How do you do, Mr Drake?' she curtsied in the Tudor gallery. 'What's it like in your homeland?' she asked Wang-y-tong, the Chinese pageboy, painted by Reynolds. Nearby were the figures of Summer and Winter, carved as gilt-wood torchères to hold candles ('It must get ever so tiring having to hold those candlesticks all day long!').

Leopards – the heart of the Sackville family crest – roamed the corridors, too. On the staircase, they snarled at passers-by, exposing sharp white fangs fashioned from wood. In the diamonds of windows, little leopards glowed on a background of jewel-like blue. Vita had no trouble imagining them coming to life in the depths of the night, recording in verse:

> *Guard and vigil in the night*
> *While the ancient house is sleeping*
> *They three hundred years are keeping,*
> *Nightly from their stations leaping,*
> *Shadows black in moonlight bright,*
> *Roof to gable creeping.*

Then, the following morning, all back to normal:

> *Rigid when the day returns,*
> *Up aloft in sun or rain*
> *Leopards at their posts again*

She imagined them pacing around behind her: 'Often on the painted stair, As I passed abstractedly, Velvet footsteps, two and three, Padded gravely after me'. When you see Knole through Vita's eyes – with all these companions – perhaps it's no surprise that her diaries are full of impassioned extracts:

> *Knole! Knole! I stretch my hands to you in prayer, You, grey and solid; you, enduring, staid; You do not know what surges beat against your walls; Miss me a little, I who am your soul.*

But, despite being the only child, Vita was a girl, and thus unable to inherit the family title or – to her lifelong anguish – her beloved Knole. Instead, it was bequeathed to her uncle Charles, who became the 4th Baron, and whose descendants still live there today.

How did this strange little girl with her imaginary friends fare outside of Knole? After a run of governesses, she headed to Helen Wolff's school for girls, a day school in Mayfair. There was no talk of career prospects – of becoming a doctor or politician, a writer or actor. There was only one thing these girls worked towards: becoming a prized possession on the marriage market.

In 1910, at eighteen years old, Vita formally 'entered society' and became a debutante. There were 'four balls a week and luncheons every day'. Vita was admired by many an aristo, charmed by her striking, if not conventional, beauty. One of them was Lord Henry Lascelles, whom Vita rejected (which was lucky for Henry, who went on to marry Princess Mary, sister of King George VI).

Even then, at all those sparkling parties, it wasn't the young men – future dukes and earls – who interested Vita. It was the other young women who caught her eye. In her late teenage years, she had grown particularly close to several fellow schoolgirls. There was Violet Keppel, whose mother was the mistress of King Edward VII, and whose descendants include the current Queen Camilla. There was Rosamund Grosvenor, a 'neat little girl who came to play with me'. They weren't always long-lasting, deep-rooted relationships: 'To be frank, she always bored me as a companion,' Vita wrote of Rosamund. 'I was very fond of her, however; she had a sweet nature. But she was quite stupid.'

But there was something more than a friendship there. When she suddenly realized this, at twenty-six, everything seemed to click into place: 'I went into wild spirits; I ran, I shouted, I jumped, I climbed, I vaulted over gates, I felt like a schoolboy let out on a holiday . . . that wild irresponsible day.'

Although Vita eventually married a man, Harold Nicholson, whom she loved and lived with throughout her life, she had countless relationships with women, most famously with Virginia

Woolf. Much of this was kept secret, even from her children, who were forbidden to enter her office. It was only after her death, when her son cut into a locked briefcase to discover her private letters, that the full truth was revealed.

Throughout her life, Vita's early passion for writing was ever-present. She had a gardening column, published collections of poetry and wrote thirteen novels. And although she never expected to return to Knole, it was to reappear in a different form. In 1930, Vita and Harold purchased Sissinghurst Castle, in Kent, which had been owned by the Sackville family in Tudor times. Built as an Elizabethan castle, over the years it had been a prison for captured French sailors from the Seven Years' War, then a parish poor house, then a farm.

It was pretty run-down when Vita and Harold arrived. 'There was nothing but weed, rough grass, a shabby eyesore of a green-house in the wrong place, broken fencing, wired chicken runs, squalor and slovenly disorder everywhere'. But none of this mattered to Vita. In fact, the wildness inspired her. 'It caught instantly at my heart and my imagination,' she wrote, 'I fell in love; love at first sight'. She described Sissinghurst as 'only a cottage, but in its mullioned windows it preserved traces of grandeur'. Those traces of grandeur were, of course, Knole.

It is fascinating to visit Sissinghurst today, because it reveals so much of who Vita was, of where she came from. You can discover every part of her character here: her love of writing, the link to her ancestry, the other women in her life, and her husband, Harold. Together, they created some of the most magnificent gardens in the country – all of which is a testament to Vita and Harold's unconventional love.

It would, in a strange way, all come together for Vita. But at eighteen years old, she was, like many teenagers, blowing in the wind without solid roots. She was in limbo, unsure of who she was, unsure of where she was going, and still trapped by the restraints of her Edwardian childhood. If only Vita had known what thrills – what freedom – lay ahead.

Through the Fire Exit

A shrill bell rang through the room.

'Abandon ship!' yelled Horace.

'Hide! It's the king's men!' cried Elizabeth.

'The toll of the bell! Plague is back!' shrieked Geoffrey.

'Fire!' Jack's voice of authority cut across the group. 'Evacuate!' He pointed to a carved wooden door in the corner, which no one had noticed before. He yanked the handle open, and an icy blast swept into the room.

'Coats!' ordered Jack.

Vivienne snatched coats off hooks and threw one to each guest. Furry, fluffy, woolly and shaggy garments went flying. 'Vintage, be careful!' she warned. Wrapped up, the group scurried out into the cold night air.

Outside, they piled onto a small fire escape. But, just as they were all out of the room, a gust of wind caught on the door, and it swung shut, locking them out.

The horrible truth dawned. They were trapped.

14

Jack Lewis

IN THE SUMMER TERM of 1917, Oxford University gained a new student. He had won a scholarship to University College and was in the books as eighteen years of age, and named Clive Staples Lewis – though everyone called him Jack. 'It's been that way since I was four years old,' young C. S. Lewis might have explained to the porter, as he processed the papers. 'My dog Jacksie was killed by a car, and I took his name, refusing to answer to any other.'

For hundreds of years, Oxford University had been at the forefront of learning – perhaps the most prestigious university in the world. Teaching existed at Oxford in some form from 1096, and the first colleges – University, Balliol and Merton – were established between 1249 and 1264. That's two centuries before Machu Picchu was built, and 500 years before US independence.

What did Jack think, on first impressions, as he got his bearings in this new postcard-perfect city? Did he climb up the grassy mound – the remains of the medieval motte of Oxford Castle? As he strolled along Broad Street, did he notice the memorial to the Protestant martyrs, Ridley and Latimer, who were burnt at the stake at that very spot in 1555? Leaning on the railings, what did Jack think of the Radcliffe Camera, a neat, circular building, perfectly, precisely formed like an enormous navigational instrument, its honey stone glowing in the sunshine?

Jack was a born scholar and a vociferous reader. Had he gone on *Mastermind*, his specialist subject would be 'Anglo-Saxon and Norse Literature'. He could be intimidating – the kind of person whose conversation would be peppered with 'It reminds me of [completely obscure writer who died seventy years ago]', or 'The other day I was reading about [incredibly specific reference to an ancient culture]', leaving you replying, 'Not sure I've read that one actually', and questioning your intellect.

But there was not much chance for intellectual intimidation when Jack arrived at Oxford. This was supposed to be a city of dreaming spires and sleepy tolling bells – but the dream had been rudely interrupted. Oxford was not quite herself. Though the university was still running, many of the libraries were empty, the books unopened and gathering dust. There was another matter to attend to: the city, like the rest of Britain, was three years into a terrible war.

It had all kicked off on 28 June 1914, when the heir to the Austro-Hungarian throne, Archduke Franz Ferdinand, was assassinated in Sarajevo. This provoked an international crisis, culminating in the outbreak of the First World War. By the end of the year, a million British men had enlisted. Oxford University was emptied: by Jack's arrival in 1917, only 15 per cent of the pre-war students were in residence. Oriel College, which had been home to 133 undergraduates, had only ten still in place.

Despite this, the city was busier than ever. For the first time since the 1640s (when King Charles I made Oxford his HQ during the Civil War), the city became a military camp. Battalions billeted in colleges. Soldiers smoked on every street corner. Trucks jammed up the medieval lanes. The stamp of heeled boots echoed down every cobbled street. Somerville College became a hospital for officers. It was here that the poet, Siegfried Sassoon, was sent to recover, 'lying in a little white-walled room, looking through the window onto a College lawn'.

Had Jack wandered into the Examination Schools, past the sweeping Italian marble staircases, he would have stumbled into an enormous space with panelled walls and ornate white plaster-work. Instead of rows of examination desks with students scribbling down answers, there were hundreds of beds, each with a young man fresh from the western front. Their bodies were mangled, and their minds traumatized.

Jack arrived as a student, finally fulfilling his greatest passion for academic study. But, finding the university deserted of both students and dons and operating at the lowest levels, Jack threw himself behind the war effort. On 26 September 1917, he commissioned out of the Officer Training Corps. Instead of poring through texts, he polished boots. Instead of discussing Celtic runes, he barked orders. This was no longer Jack the Undergrad, but Second Lieutenant Lewis, Third Somerset Light Infantry.

It would have surprised younger Jack to know he'd spend his eighteenth year training with the British army in a medieval city in the heart of England. Jack came from somewhere very different – a booming, pounding industrial city that was forging the modern world. It was a 'mighty commercial organization, whose vitality is ever augmenting, and whose influence is already world-wide'. Jack was born on 29 November 1898, in a city at its zenith: Belfast.

If you wanted a ship built at the start of the twentieth century, Belfast was the place to go. There were engineers and boilermakers building the largest ships in the world – including the *Titanic*, which launched in May 1911. It was also a linen centre, earning the nickname Linenopolis. Looms buzzed and whirled all day, powered by women and children. Spinning frames, spindles, fluting rollers, flax cutters, bundling presses and twisting frames were produced in their thousands.

If there was an awards season for industrial output, the Belfast representative would be constantly going up on stage. World's largest tobacco factory? The winner is . . . Belfast! Best Christmas card printing? Belfast. Tea machinery? It was getting embarrassing now. Fan-making works? Handkerchief factory? Largest dry dock? All could be found at Belfast.

It was this industry that brought Jack's family to the city. His grandfather, Richard, was a founding partner in the shipbuilding firm MacIlwaine and Lewis. His maternal grandfather, the Rev. Thomas R. Hamilton, was related to the Ewarts, who were big names in the linen industry.

It was a bustling place to live. As output grew, people flocked to find work. Between 1901 and 1911 – Jack's childhood years – the population increased by 10 per cent, to 385,000. But there was a price to pay for this rapid growth. Though the city appeared to flourish, there were a multitude of horrors behind the stories of success. Henry Whitaker, the city's Medical Officer of Health, regretted that 'it cannot be said to be happy or prosperous when sickness is prevalent; when its deaths-rate is excessive; when, in fact, its very prosperity is founded on the life blood of its people'.

While some enjoyed the fruits of brilliant innovation, many workers lived in overcrowded, Dickensian slums, where poverty and destitution were rife. Alleys piled high with sewage and old cockle shells. The air was thick with smog. A report in 1906 found that the chance of developing tuberculosis was almost double that of England or Scotland. Typhoid was more deadly here than anywhere else in the UK.

Jack's life was a far cry from that of the slums. But in 1907, everyone in Belfast – rich or poor – had good reason to stay at home. The city was riddled with an epidemic of 'spotted fever', a type of cerebrospinal meningitis. The effects were terrifying. A seemingly healthy person might be seized suddenly with fever, enduring vomiting and excruciating head and neck pains.

If the spinal column became infected, the victim was paralysed, their body curving backward in a half-circle, usually remaining so until the end finally came. The few who survived could face a lifetime of blindness, deafness or memory loss. One father, struggling to cope after the death of his wife and child, asked his eleven-year-old son to look after the remaining children while he got dressed. When the boy left, the father hanged himself from his bedpost.

This was the city that Jack grew up in: a city of light and dark, with visions of the future playing out side by side with medieval horrors.

His family lived in a semi-detached house on Dundela Avenue with a large garden, two miles to the east of the city centre. The 1901 census tells us of the family 'and their VISITORS, BOARDERS, SERVANTS, &c., who slept or abode in this House on the night of SUNDAY, the 31st of MARCH 1901'. Here's how the Lewis family were recorded, their details entered in fine, inked handwriting:

SURNAME	FORENAME	AGE	SEX	RELATION TO HEAD
Lewis	Albert James	37	Male	Head of Family
Barber	Martha	28	Female	Servant
Conlon	Sarah Ann	22	Female	Servant
Lewis	Warren Hamilton	5	Male	Son
Lewis	Clive Staples	2	Male	Son
Lewis	Florence Augusta	38	Female	Wife

EIGHTEEN

RELIGION	BIRTHPLACE	OCCUPATION	LITERACY
Church of Ireland	City Cork	Solicitor	Read and write
Presbyterian	County Monaghan	House-Domestic Servant	Read and write
Roman Catholic	County Down	Cook-Domestic Servant	Read and write
Church of Ireland	City of Belfast	Scholar	Read
Church of Ireland	City of Belfast	-	Cannot read
Church of Ireland	County Cork	-	Read and write

So there were Jack's parents, Albert and Florence ('Flora'), his brother, five-year-old Warren ('Warnie'), who, though he could read but not write, was no doubt delighted to be recorded as a 'scholar', and two-year-old Clive Staples, who 'cannot read'. They had two servants: a cook, Sarah Conlon, and a housemaid, Martha Barber.

Jack's father, Albert, was a solicitor, the son of a self-made businessman. His mother, Flora, was a brilliantly clever woman – a mathematics brainiac who graduated from Queen's College, Belfast, and spent much of her time educating her boys.

Jack's grandfather – the Rev. Thomas R. Hamilton – lived ten minutes around the corner in a rectory. One of Jack's earliest memories must have been running to the rectory with his brother Warnie, and arriving, panting and laughing, pulling up their socks. They came face to face with the rectory door knocker – an enormous, grimacing head of a lion. Was it this encounter – this lion that kept watch from the Godly household – that would inspire Jack's writings all those years later?

Opposite the rectory was St Mark's Church, where Jack and Warnie were baptized by their grandfather. This is a magnificent red sandstone building, with a 150-foot-high bell tower soaring to the sky, a beacon for miles around. It was built in the 1870s, so it was less than twenty years old when Jack sat in the pews, gazing at its Gothic arches and colourful wall paintings.

How strange it was that this fantastical medieval time capsule had been created in the most industrialized city in the world. That it wasn't a leftover from a past age, but the creative vision of one man, the architect William Butterfield (who also designed Keble College, in Oxford). In these stones, Butterfield's imagination conjured up a lost world of monks and rituals, of manuscripts and warring knights. It was an impression that stuck firm on young Jack.

Life at Dundela Villas was one of 'humdrum happiness'. Warnie and Jack were inseparable, playing together for hours on end in the garden. One photograph shows Jack sitting on a cart and Warnie holding the string, with long socks, shorts and large straw hats.

Jack had two long-lasting memories from those early years. On one occasion, Warnie was given the lid of a biscuit tin, which he filled with moss, leaves, twigs, petals and flowers – an entire miniature garden. Jack was mightily impressed, writing about it fifty years later in his book *Surprised by Joy*: 'That was the first beauty I ever knew . . . As long as I live my imagination of Paradise will retain something of my brother's toy garden.'

There was something else, too. The house had magnificent views, out to the Castlereagh Hills. These seemed to Jack like distant, faraway lands, impossible to reach. In later years Jack would explain that those childhood years – of gazing at distant hills – gave him a lifelong craving for adventure. He was 'a votary of the blue flower' – or, in simpler terms, he became obsessed with always striving to reach the unreachable.

Sometimes the family went on holidays to the countryside, exploring magnificent landscapes where 'a giant might raise his head over the next ridge'. They visited Dunluce Castle, a dramatic clifftop ruin. Was this the inspiration for Cair Paravel, the fictional castle Jack would write about in later years? The similarities to Dunluce Castle are striking, when reading the Chronicles of Narnia: the fictional Cair Paravel is situated high on a hilltop, surrounded by sandy rockpools strewn with seaweed and miles of 'bluish-green waves breaking for ever on the beach'.

When Jack was seven, the family moved. The next base was 'Little Lea', a red-brick house his father had built. Today it is on Belfast's Circular Road, but for Jack it was 'further out into what was then the country'. Here the adventures were inside: 'long corridors, empty sunlit rooms, upstairs indoor silences, attics explored in solitude, distant noises of gurgling cisterns and pipes, and the noise of wind under the tiles'.

The house was filled to the brim with books. Finding something to read was as easy as walking into a field and 'finding a new blade of grass'. It was Beatrix Potter's books that Jack fell in love with, with their illustrations of anthropomorphic animals. He loved the old *Punch* magazines in his father's study, too: the cartoons of Tenniel, Jack wrote, 'gratified my passion for "dressed animals" with his Russian Bear, British Lion, Egyptian Crocodile and the rest.' Soon, Jack began writing his own stories, with his own anthropomorphic animals, in fantastical worlds of medieval chivalry.

But all was to change in the summer of 1908 when Jack was nine years old. After months of 'strange smells and midnight noises and sinister whispered conversations', Jack learnt a horrifying truth: his beloved mother was dying of cancer. On 23 August – her husband's birthday – she finally succumbed to the disease.

The blissfully happy childhood ended abruptly: 'all settled happiness, all that was tranquil and reliable, disappeared from my life'. There was one more final memento for the boys to cherish her by: a Bible inscribed 'from Mammy with fondest love'.

Two weeks later, Jack was taken down to Donegal Quay:

I am going to school for the first time . . . We reach the quay and go on board the old 'Fleetwood boat'; after some miserable strolling about on deck my father bids us good-bye . . . Soon we are dropping down the Lough and there is the taste of salt on one's lips and the cluster of lights astern, receding from us, is everything I have ever known.

Thus began years of change and uncertainty, as Jack was tossed about from one school to another. First, he joined Warnie at Wynyard House, a prep school in Hertfordshire. It was horrendous and the boys endured physical abuse. Jack considered the school a 'concentration camp', and many suspected the headmaster to be insane. Next came a two-month spell at Campbell College, in Belfast ('I was delighted. I did not believe that anything Irish, even a school, could be bad'). But it was not to last. He was sent back to England. First, Cherbourg School in Malvern, then Malvern College, where he stayed a year.

Jack found it difficult to make friends. His Irish accent was derided by teachers and pupils alike, and he found England a strange place: 'No Englishman will be able to understand my first impressions of England'. It wasn't only his accent the other boys ripped into – his performance on the sports pitch provided more room for ridicule.

The Lewis boys had one working joint in their thumbs, rather than two. This made Jack hopeless at games, not being able to throw or catch. Perhaps it's no surprise he later wrote, 'I conceived a hatred for England which took many years to heal'. His heart also hardened towards God. Having been raised in a Christian household, Jack began to lose faith, turning instead towards atheism.

And there was another black cloud that loomed. On 4 August 1914, Jack, Warnie and their father heard the terrible news: Britain had declared war on Germany. Warnie continued his training at Sandhurst, and Jack, having recently completed his final term at Malvern College, headed for Surrey. There, he continued his education with his brother's tutor, an Irish grammar school teacher called William T. Kirkpatrick.

Kirkpatrick found his new pupil to have a 'maturity of literary judgements which is so unusual and surprising'. Jack developed a fascination for historic worlds of ages past: the ancient literature of Scandinavia preserved in the Icelandic sagas, Greek literature and mythology.

It was at this time that the seeds were planted for new imaginary lands, which would come to fruition many years later:

> 'The Lion' all began with a picture of a faun carrying an umbrella and parcels in a snowy wood. This picture had been in my mind since I was about sixteen. Then one day, when I was about forty, I said to myself, 'Let's try to make a story about it.'

But in his teens there was no time for Jack's fairy stories. The world was at war. Despite getting into Oxford University, it was the Western Front that he prepared for. At eighteen, he was shipped over to France and learnt first-hand the relentless drudgery of conflict. There were 'the boots worn day and night 'til they seemed to grow to your feet'. He struggled through immense weariness: 'I have gone to sleep marching and woken again and found myself marching still'.

On Jack's nineteenth birthday, he arrived at the Battle of the Somme, one of the largest and bloodiest battles of the First World War. In the following months, he experienced the sickening reality of war and witnessed horrors that would stay with him until his dying day. He saw 'the horribly smashed men still moving like half-crushed beetles'. He watched 'men's stomachs fall out on their knees', and the moment a life was taken: the 'shouting faces, while they shouted, freeze into black, bony masks'.

Jack came face to face with his own death, too: 'I felt no fear and certainly no courage. It did not seem to be an occasion for either. The proposition "Here is a man dying" stood before my mind as dry, as factual, as unemotional as something in a textbook. It was not even interesting.'

Did Jack think of these moments, years later, when writing about his characters in the Chronicles of Narnia: 'Peter did not feel very brave; indeed, he felt he was going to be sick. But that made no difference to what he had to do.'

The 'Great War' lasted over four years and led to the deaths of over ten million people, with at least twice as many wounded. Of the five young men Jack became friends with while attending the Officer's Training Corps at Keble College, he was the only one to survive the war: 'I have lost my brothers and my love and all. Nothing is left but me'. It was a harrowing experience for a young man to go through, and it confirmed his atheist suspicions: how could a loving God unleash such barbarity on the world?

Jack's life, at eighteen and nineteen years old, was in total limbo. His world was shaped by external forces over which he had no control. This was a scholar, picked up from a library and tossed onto a battlefield. The usual concerns most of us might face – of career prospects, relationships, or degrees – were irrelevant. Jack's challenge was to get out alive.

When he returned to Oxford after the war, and the university tried to put itself back together with a fraction of its former pupils and staff, Jack resumed a life of high-flying academia. He continued his studies with top marks. In 1925, he was elected a Fellow and Tutor in English Literature at Magdalen College, where he stayed for twenty-nine years until 1954. While at Oxford, he developed a lifelong friendship with 'Tollers' (better known as J. R. R. Tolkien, author of *The Lord of the Rings*). It was in this ancient city – with the intellectual discussions and similar-minded friends – that Jack felt at home, though his childhood memories of the Irish countryside always pulled at his heartstrings. 'Heaven,' he wrote, 'is Oxford lifted and placed in the middle of County Down'.

This academic career path wouldn't have surprised eighteen-year-old Jack. But, as an avowed atheist, he might have been stunned to know he would become one of the most powerful Christian communicators of the age. That he would convert to Christianity in 1931, and write the words: 'I believe in Christianity as I believe that the sun has risen: not only because I see it, but because by it I see everything else.' He would also become famous as a Christian on the airwaves, keeping up morale during the darkest days of the Second World War via a series of BBC radio broadcasts.

But there was more. Jack's fantasies turned to life when they were put to paper as the Chronicles of Narnia, some of the most beloved children's stories ever told. Ironically, it was his experience of conflict that propelled this: 'A real taste for fairy-stories', Tolkien once explained, was 'quickened to full life by war.'

The world of Narnia was, in a thousand ways, a result of Jack's young life: the magic of Northern Ireland's ruined castles, the ever-present Christian faith, the anamorphic animals in Beatrix Potter's books and his father's *Punch* magazines, the beauty of Warnie's miniature garden, the yearning to always explore those distant landscapes. If you ever flick through those pages of fawns and snow and Turkish delight, just remember, you are not only peering into a world created by an author called C. S. Lewis, but stepping through the childhood of that bookish, inquiring young man called Jack.

A Science Lesson

Suddenly, the wind dropped, the fire alarm stopped and dark clouds dispersed to reveal the brilliance of a full moon. A lamppost on the street gave a little light. The group huddled together in their coats. They felt something in the air – something soft and powdery and extremely cold – and all danger was forgotten.

'Snowflakes!' whispered Geoffrey.

'Reminds me of the Arctic,' murmured Horace.

'Or the Himalayan peaks,' added Elsie, blowing some snow off Bede's nose.

'I remember the first time I saw snow,' mused Jacques. 'It was in Venice, so beautiful.'

'I've never understood the science behind snowflakes. Why isn't it just . . . snow?' pondered Mary.

'It's to do with temperature,' Rosalind jumped in to explain. 'The water droplets have to be a certain temperature – under 35°C – to become snowflakes, and the molecules join in a hexagonal structure, each with one oxygen and two hydrogen atoms.'

Impressed with this technical explanation, Mary pushed on: 'And is it true they're all different, each one unique?'

'Well, yes,' Rosalind continued, 'no two are the same, a bit like all of us – totally unique.'

15

Rosalind Franklin

IN THE AUTUMN OF 1938, a sparky eighteen-year-old Jewish girl arrived at Newnham College in Cambridge. She had curly brown hair, an enormous brain, and 'a tantalising naughtiness that could be quite maddening'. She would grow up to change the course of scientific understanding. Her name was Rosalind Franklin.

Rosalind arrived at Cambridge hungry to learn. She took courses in chemistry, extra chemistry, physics, maths, mineralogy and scientific German, and worked towards the tripos exams (named after the historic three-legged stools). For a brilliant young scientist, Cambridge was the place to be. This was where Isaac Newton became Lucasian professor of mathematics at twenty-seven years old, where J. J. Thomson discovered the electron in 1897, and Ernest Rutherford discovered artificial nuclear fission in 1917.

Of course, Rosalind didn't quite follow in their footsteps. When she arrived at university in 1938, she wasn't considered – as a woman – to be a proper student. Women were first admitted to

Cambridge in 1869, but couldn't be granted degrees until 1948 (ten years after Rosalind arrived). Cambridge was the last British university to do so.

Two girls' colleges were established on the outskirts of town: Girton in 1869 and Newnham in 1871, which is where Rosalind was given a room. These colleges were distinctly different from the traditional Cambridge vibe. There were no honey-coloured courts with perfectly square lawns. Instead, they had the spirit of large, comfortable Victorian country houses.

Newnham has red-brick walls with white sash windows, staircases with solid bannisters, Dutch gables and mansard attics. There are seventeen acres of sprawling grounds, too, with white iceberg roses underplanted with black 'Queen of the Night' tulips, formal gardens with ponds, where the air is filled with the sweet scent of lavender, pristinely maintained lawns dotted with limes, oaks and yews, and herbaceous borders of giant alliums, orange poppies and sunshine-yellow peonies.

Newnham was Rosalind's new home, a base from where she could march out to lectures and expand her mind. But this wasn't all calculations scribbled on blackboards, lightbulb moments and lab coats. In many ways, Rosalind ticked off all the usual attributes of a modern Cambridge fresher.

She turned up to lectures, but struggled to hear: it was like 'fragments of conversation one hears when passing someone in the street'. She signed up for the social events and asked her mum to send clothes from home: 'Please send my evening dress (tulip one), evening shoes and evening petticoat. Shoes in the bottom drawer of the wardrobe (gold *or* silver)'.

In the holidays, she went skiing: 'I think I spent one half of the time trying to get up after falling and one quarter slipping down the slope I was climbing up'. But she also spent a good deal of time at après: 'To-day has been spent by most people recovering from last night. There was a fancy dress dance which lasted 'til about four o clock'. Rosalind's fancy dress outfit was her old head-mistress, Miss Strudwick: 'everyone told me I looked like some awful schoolmistress of theirs'.

To her new friends at Cambridge, Rosalind must have been hard to piece together. She could be great fun, teasing others, 'with a burbling, mischievous delight'. But she was also particular, with a forthright attitude and strong opinions. She liked facts, precision and proof, not woolly arguments or inaccuracies.

She'd been like this from an early age. Always questioning, always curious. After reading the Bible as a child, she asked, 'Well, anyhow, how do you know He isn't a She?' This was – according to her younger sister, Jenifer – 'simply logic, not early feminism'. At the age of six, her aunt noted her to be 'alarmingly clever', a little girl who 'spends all her time doing arithmetic for pleasure, and invariably gets her sums right'.

At primary-school age, she was brilliant at maths, though terrible at spelling. She enjoyed learning about geography, the adventures of explorers and history. She was ravenously compet-itive, writing home from her boarding school to update parents on marking injustices:

Somebody must have made some mistake in the adding up and percentaging of last week's marks, for Mrs Blundle got it to 78% instead of 88%. I had 5 tens, 5 eights, a good many nines and 1 seven – I know 1 seven was the only mark I had below eight and Mrs Blundle agreed with that. I was really top, but got put down as fourth, which I cannot possibly have been, as two of the people who beat me did not get one set of marks all through the week higher than me

239

In January 1932, at the age of eleven, Rosalind entered the middle-fourth form of St Paul's Girls School, in London. It was founded in 1904, twenty-seven years before Rosalind arrived. It was a prestigious school and – importantly – a direct bus route from the family home.

At St Paul's, Rosalind found a best friend in Jean Kerslake – a friendship forged through a mutual dislike of another girl. Tensions ran high and Jean and Rosalind's parents were summoned into school on account of behaviours verging on bullying. Jean didn't seem to mind: 'Rosalind and I achieved a certain notoriety which strengthened our alliance'. To calm her down, Rosalind's parents bought her a Persian kitten, Wilhelmina, or Willy, which perched on the arm of her chair when she did her homework.

Perhaps it was unsurprising that Rosalind was a bit of a livewire. Though her parents, Ellis and Muriel, were the epitome of respectability, there were a handful of rule-breaking relatives with 'Bolshevist tendencies'. In 1910, Rosalind's uncle accosted Winston Churchill (then Home Secretary) and tried to strike him with a dog whip. He was reported in *The Times* as 'Mr Churchill's Assailant' and was imprisoned for several months. Then there was Aunt Alice, who had cropped hair, pinstriped clothes and a living arrangement with another woman (never commented on by the family).

At St Paul's, Rosalind's competitive spirit and independence of thought was channelled into high achievement. The vision of the school was forward-looking: 'every girl is being prepared for a career', and 'no woman has a right to exist who does not live a useful life'. School debates included motions such as 'The Entry of Women into Public Affairs and Industry is to be Deplored'. The motion failed to pass, with the High Mistress, Miss Ethel Strudwick, concluding women should not 'be relegated to the home'.

This was punchy stuff for the time. The Sex Disqualification

Removal Bill – which enabled women to join the professions, sit on juries and be awarded degrees – had only passed in 1919. It was just in 1928, when Rosalind was eight, that women were able to vote on the same terms as men. Even Rosalind's father – who was delighted to have such a brainy daughter – took some time to adjust. 'The new generation was different,' Rosalind's younger sister, Jenifer, remembered, 'and it took some time for my father to get used to the idea of women with careers in paid jobs'.

As well as brains and drive, Rosalind was enthusiastic in everything she did. She was a natural St Paul's Girl – or a 'Paulina', as they were known. There were no half-hearted attempts here, none of this glass-half-empty kind of attitude. Rosalind's approach to life was to try your best, with all guns blazing. As a result, she ticked off prizes and scholarships here, there and everywhere. As her best pal Jean remembered: 'Our academic enthusiasm extended to all subjects, and we devoted much time to testing each other's homework and comparing notes . . . We were equally enthusiastic about gym and games'. Rosalind took failure badly: 'I only got B to B+ for that essay, which is very bad,' she wrote home, adding – regarding the teacher who marked it – 'I told you she was an old pig.'

There was only one area where Rosalind was out of tune with the rest. The head of music at St Paul's was the famous composer Gustav Holst, known for his orchestral suite, *The Planets*. Holst found Rosalind a challenge, for she seemed to lack musicality. Suspecting she had a problem with her hearing or her tonsils that was restricting her musical ability, Holst arranged a meeting with Mrs Franklin. It must have been awkward when Mrs Franklin informed the great composer that Rosalind was perfectly healthy – a moment that 'spoilt [Holst's] optimist belief that everyone had music in them'.

Nevertheless, Rosalind found harmony at home. She adored her siblings, parents and grandparents. All were resolutely loyal to one another, caring and respecting, and always writing letters to each other. Rosalind lived with her immediate family at 5 Pembridge Place (known to them as 5PP), in Notting Hill. It's the kind of house you'd see in a Disney film: a white stucco facade, large sash windows (some with balconies) and a grand staircase leading up to the front door. It's perfectly symmetrical: three bays across, three storeys high, with another floor in the basement and more rooms in the eaves.

Had you happened to walk past this house in the summer of 1930, you might well have seen the front door open, and four children pour out – David, Rosalind, Colin, Roland – followed by a portly woman ('Nannie'), with little Jenifer in the pushchair.

Their destination was a good one, and a regular haunt: Kensington Gardens. Here the Franklin children spent many happy days enjoying the delights of the park – the lady selling balloons, the grand memorial to Prince Albert, the Peter Pan statue hidden in the bushes, musical performances at the band-stand. On the return journey, they would pass a building with pointed arches, rounded windows and two soaring towers. This was the New West End Synagogue in St Petersburg Place, where the children came to worship.

The area was home to many Jewish families, as Rosalind's sister, Jenifer, remembered: 'Lazaruses in Pembroke Place, Goldings in Dawson Place, Levines within walking distance'. The district was 'littered with Franklins'. Rosalind's family were a high-powered bunch. Not far away was Great-Aunt Netta (Henrietta Montagu), a suffrage campaigner and educationalist. On another street was Great-Aunt Beatrice, whose husband (Herbert Samuel) would become the first High Commissioner of Mandatory Palestine.

Rosalind's father, Ellis, was a banker in the family business. He made a comfortable living, though he was always meticulous with spending: 'We were brought up never to talk about money – which presumably means we always had enough.' After finishing work, Ellis might potter about the garden, 'growing vegetables and supplying all his family with far more beans than we could eat'. On other nights he visited the Working Men's College, where he volunteered to teach physics to men who couldn't otherwise access it.

As for a maternal figure, the Franklin children had two. First, their actual mother, Muriel, was gentle and intelligent and threw herself into charity work. She taught her children the importance of good manners and writing regularly to grandparents. Her lasting regret was to have only been given 'the conventional Edwardian female middle-class smatter schooling', while her brothers had been sent to university. Muriel wouldn't let the same happen to her daughters, Rosalind and Jenifer.

The other maternal figure was Nannie, a hearty, good-natured woman from Shropshire. She had two club feet and missing toes (the children watched with fascination as she wrapped her feet in bandages to fit inside the surgical boots). Nannie was the one who would tend to cuts and bruises, or brush knotty hair ('Mother was for extras'). Nannie had a no-nonsense approach to discipline: when Rosalind complained of one brother hitting her with a cricket bat, Nannie's response was, 'Well dear, you shouldn't have been teasing him.'

Some of the happiest moments of Rosalind's childhood were at her grandparents' house in Buckinghamshire, which had 'everything [Rosalind] could possibly want'. For days on end, the Franklin children explored tennis courts, woods, ponds, chicken coops and hot houses with exotic fruits. Rosalind wrote about it in her letters (note her unusual spelling!):

We are having great fun here. We went to the farm in the mining and headoverheeled all the way down to the bank . . . We have got a jar of frog's spawn and a newt which we caught in the bulrush pond. We do not no what to feed him on, Monica [a cousin] sais worms and raw meat but he does not eat much.

There were family holidays, too. Each year, the family would rent a large house by the seaside – usually in the Isles of Scilly, Cornwall or South Wales – where they would be joined by various friends and relations. Fathers rolled up their trousers to traipse into rock pools, siblings came together for serious digging operations, and bathing was enjoyed, even in the freezing waters. This was good, wholesome fun, and a chance to get away from London – to go somewhere totally unspoilt. 'I remember the family's horror,' Jenifer recalled, 'when a car park, and all it implied, first appeared on the St David's cliffs.'

The most exciting day of Rosalind's teenage years was 12 May 1937, the coronation of King George VI. Rosalind's father, Ellis, was delighted at the new king, having disapproved of the 'weakness and lack of moral fibre' of his brother and predecessor, Edward VIII. Rosalind adored the day, watching the procession from front-row seats on a club balcony on St James's Street, organized by her grandparents: 'we had a clear view of the whole length of St James's Street, from St James's Palace to Piccadilly'.

After the procession, the Franklins watched the coronation ceremony, then joined the crowds and headed to Buckingham Palace. 'We were not allowed straight through, so we raced along Pall Mall, by Trafalgar Square, and through the mud in St James's Park'. They were in the heart of the throng:

EIGHTEEN

We managed to obtain a very good central position on the steps
of the Victoria Memorial and joined in the cheers and cries of
'We want the King' and 'For he's a jolly good fellow.' At last the
door of the balcony opened – the crowd surged forward, waving
handkerchiefs, gloves and hats, and a terrific cheer went up. It
was a wonderful moment the King, Queen, 2 princesses, Queen
Mary, Dukes and Duchesses of Gloucester and Kent, all came
out. The crowd was solid right back across the Mall and as far
back as you could see.

'I cannot remember a day I have enjoyed more,' Rosalind wrote
to her grandfather, as soon as she got home that evening. 'Thank
you very much for the marvellous opportunity you gave us. Love
from Rosalind.'

In many ways, life seemed good for the young Rosalind
Franklin. But there was a dark cloud that loomed over her teenage
years. Since 1933, when Rosalind was thirteen years old, Germany
had been under the control of Adolf Hitler, and his antisemitic
politics were being implemented with increasing violence. Now,
it was spreading to Britain. In 1936, when Rosalind was sixteen
years old, Oswald Mosley led a march through London's East End.
Mosley declared that Jewish people were 'rats and vermin from
the gutter', and 'fascism can and will win Britain'. The march was
just six miles away from the Franklin home.

As antisemitism worsened in Germany, Jewish refugees began
arriving in Britain, and the Franklins threw themselves into relief
work. Rosalind's father, Ellis, reduced his working hours at the
bank to help the Home Office organize entry permits. Eva
Eisensteadter – a girl whose father was in Buchenwald concentration camp – came to live with the Franklins and shared a room
with Jenifer on the top floor. When Rosalind won a School Leaving

Exhibition for her outstanding performance (£30 a year, for three years, to support her university studies), the Franklin family refused to take the money, redirecting it to a refugee student.

In November 1938, during Rosalind's first term at Cambridge, the situation dramatically worsened in Germany. On Kristallnacht – the Night of the Broken Glass – Jewish-owned stores, buildings and synagogues were attacked. During the pogrom, some 30,000 Jewish men were rounded up and taken to concentration camps. It was the first time Nazi officials made massive arrests of Jews, for the sole reason of being Jewish. *The Times* reported the terror on 11 November 1938:

> *No foreign propagandist bent upon blackening Germany before the world could outdo the tale of burnings and beatings, of blackguardly assaults on defenceless and innocent people, which disgraced that country yesterday.*

Despite the appalling reports from Germany, vicious antisemitism continued to spread in the UK. On 2 September 1938, it was reported in the British press that 'Jewish circles are alarmed at the reported increased activities of antisemitic propagandists in this country'.

In Cambridge, Rosalind was deeply upset at the unfolding events and appalled at her university's apparent indifference. 'Apart from your letters and *The Times*,' she wrote to her parents, 'I would still have no idea that anybody objected to Germany's treatment of the Jews.' Not only did the university ignore the anxieties of Jewish students, but it also seemed to actively support the Nazi cause: in 1938, a joke about 'one man's small moustache' was removed from the Amateur Dramatics Club's Christmas show, for fear of offending Herr Hitler.

Despite this, the university rolled into war preparations, with air-raid precautions and evacuation plans put in place. Rosalind found it ridiculous and unnecessary: 'there is some scheme for digging trenches in the cabbage patch, and rehearsing emptying Newnham into the trenches in five minutes'. These rehearsals could be farcical at times:

> *One of the dons was standing outside my room waiting to blow a whistle at the given signal. The signal came – and the whistle would not blow! However, as everybody expected it, the intermittent squeaks told them what was meant. We then had to assemble at the garden door, dressed, with coats, blankets and gas masks. All ready for grand exit when Mrs P [the tutor] discovered she had the wrong key, so we could not get out! Long delay while the correct key was found . . .*

There was excitement, too. 'There are only two topics of conversation in Newnham at present,' Rosalind wrote in her letters home, '1. Exams and 2. Skeletons'. While the gardens were dug up to create ARP shelters, a pickaxe went straight through the skull of a Saxon skeleton. Newnhamite archaeologists flocked to the scene with dessert spoons and toothbrushes. 'They are really most exciting,' Rosalind wrote of the skeletons. 'They were all facing east, therefore Christian.'

Even in the bleakest of times, Rosalind could find something to keep her spirits up.

At eighteen years old, Rosalind's life was in the lurch. Her family – who never argued – were in turmoil, with Ellis pushing for Rosalind to drop out of Cambridge and help with the war effort, while her mother resisted. In the summer of 1939, the family built their own air-raid shelter at 5PP, and fears abounded of a German invasion. A summer holiday to Norway was cut short when news of the Nazi–Soviet non-aggression pact of 24 August 1939 was announced. Ellis immediately bundled his family onto a ferry from Bergen to Newcastle, the last boat to leave.

In Rosalind's second year, as she returned to Newnham, Britain held its breath and waited for Hitler to attack. In Rosalind's third year, the Blitz struck. Rosalind volunteered as a fire watcher in Cambridge, and when a bomb blasted out the window glass of 5PP, the Franklins took a house in Hertfordshire.

Despite all these difficulties – and the terrifying threat of a German invasion – Rosalind approached life with her usual can-do attitude. It was an attitude that, within two decades, would take her far: she would become one of the most important scientists in history.

Over the course of her career, Rosalind wrote papers on coals, carbons and viruses. But her great legacy was in the field of DNA.

Though DNA had been discovered in the mid-nineteenth century, its function remained a mystery. In her early thirties, Rosalind led a team (which included PhD student Raymond Gosling) that captured 'Photograph 51' at King's College London in May 1952. The camera was set up to take the photograph on Friday, 2 May, which developed on Tuesday, 6 May. It took sixty-two hours to create and produce an X-ray diffraction image of DNA, with greater clarity and more information than ever before.

This has been described as 'arguably the most important photo ever taken'. It demonstrated the double-helix structure of deoxyribonucleic acid – the key molecule that contains the genetic instructions for the development of all living organisms.

The immense importance of Rosalind's work wasn't immediately evident in isolation, being one piece of a complex puzzle. But when another scientist, James Watson, saw Photograph 51 in January 1953, he understood the potential: 'my mouth fell open and my pulse began to race'. It was the final clue that enabled Watson, along with Maurice Wilkins and Francis Crick, to put together research from the previous two decades and understand that DNA was a double helix.

The implications of this breakthrough were monumental. With this knowledge, genetic diseases could be identified, mutations could be reversed, cancer cells could be stopped from multiplying and cells could be made resistant to AIDS. In short, these scientists have saved millions of lives.

Rosalind's role in all this has long been the subject of speculation. For many years, the line has been that the boys took all the credit, that Rosalind's photo was illicitly shown to Watson, allowing him and Crick to deduce the structure and unfairly claim the glory. But recently this has been refuted by some academics, who argue that the image was not the key piece of the puzzle and that Rosalind appears to have expected her data to be shared and was credited at the time.

According to James Naismith (a Professor of Structural Biology at the University of Oxford, and director of the Rosalind Franklin Institute), the Franklin family 'often express the wish that her immense contribution to science is celebrated and that she is not portrayed solely as a woman cheated by men'. The real tragedy of Rosalind's life, Naismith explains, is that while 'she died at thirty-seven from cancer, her career was seen at the time as stellar.'

Rosalind died in 1958. It was four years before the Nobel Prize was awarded to her fellow scientists. The prize is not awarded posthumously, but had Rosalind lived, she should have – and probably would have – been awarded one, too.

Where did this brilliance come from? How did Rosalind push

the boundaries of scientific understanding where so many others had failed? Clearly, being exceptionally bright was in her DNA (though she had yet to realize that!). She was privileged, too, to have access to the best education in the country. Yet there were other forces at play.

According to Jenifer, it was Rosalind's Jewish heritage that was such a key part of her success. Jenifer believed Rosalind was 'always consciously a Jew', in the sense that she valued 'unswerving loyalty to family, a belief in the importance of knowledge (especially in science and medicine) and the virtue of hard work'. These were values embedded by her parents, Ellis and Muriel, who believed so strongly in education, and nourished by her teachers at St Paul's, who pushed the girls to have the guts to go out and change the world.

It is quite incredible thinking of what Rosalind achieved at such a young age, just a few years after arriving in Cambridge as an undergrad. In such a short space of time, she became one of Britain's great scientists, in the league of Lovelace, Fleming and Darwin. Perhaps you can sympathise with how Jenifer put it: 'We, her family, never really understood what she was doing, only felt awe and pride.'

Guilty as Charged

It wasn't funny any more, being locked outside on a fire escape in the cold. Tensions began to rise. 'Your tongue is loose,' snapped Geoffrey, when Vita accused him of standing on her coat.

Elsie became indignant: 'And I don't think there was even a fire in the first place. Was it a practice, then? Or a false alarm?'

'It must have been one of us who set it off!' cried Elizabeth, furious. 'I bet it was one of the boys. Was someone smoking inside? Own up!'

The tension was icy cold. After an uncomfortable few seconds, a voice sounded from an enormous tower of fur: 'It, err, it might have been me.' Richard's face emerged, looking bashful, as he held up the evidence – a packet of cigarettes.

Suddenly, the door burst open. 'There you all are!' cried Jeffrey, holding a full glass of red wine. 'I've been looking for you for ages. Someone threw an enormous fur coat over me. When I emerged, you'd all gone! What on earth have you been doing?'

They all piled back in to continue the party.

16

Richard Burton

'**NOT BAD. BUT TRY** again,' Philip bellowed across the hilltops to his teenage protégé: 'You *must* enunciate the consonants, Rich. Remember what we discussed about the Ts.'

Richard groaned. Once again, he looked down to the book in his hand – *Shakespeare's Greatest Monologues*. The cover was bent round, the corner of page fifty-four turned down. They had been practising, up here on the blustery hills, all afternoon. Richard had lost count of the times he had recited the speech from *Henry V*. They had tried everything – tapping the rhythm, chewing through every word, reciting vowels only, then consonants only. And still, it sounded as mediocre and monotonous as ever.

Richard closed his eyes. He took a long, deep breath, inhaling the cold air into his lungs. For a moment, he was still. He listened to the wind whipping and whistling around him, until his mind was clear. Then – slowly – he opened his eyes and looked at the view ahead. It was a breathtaking sight. Rays of sunlight pierced through the dark grey clouds and speckled the hills with golden light, which moved slowly across the valley, like a stage spotlight.

First it landed on the great, grey viaduct, then the little town below with its chapels and small cottages, and then out to the tempestuous sea beyond. Confronted with this immense natural beauty, Richard's heart swelled. Without thinking, he began to speak.

'What's he that wishes so? My cousin Westmoreland?' Suddenly – for the first time that afternoon – the words began to flow. This wasn't the teenage amateur, hacking and stumbling over prose. This was a young man in total control of his speech. The round vowels travelled joyously in the breeze, the consonants perfectly clear, his sonorous voice booming across the valley, sending birds flying skyward. Gaining momentum, Richard climbed higher up the hills: 'He that shall live this day, and see old age,' he exclaimed to the town below. 'Bedford and Exeter,' he cried to the north, 'Warwick and Talbot,' he cried to the south.

Then, at the peak of the hill, he came to a stop, and lowered his voice, 'And hold their manhoods cheap whiles any speaks,' he paused, and looked up to the skies, 'That fought with us upon Saint Crispin's day.'

Silent at last, Richard found himself panting, with tears in his eyes. It gave him a shock to feel the hand of his tutor, Philip, on his shoulder. 'Bravo, my boy! You've got it!'

Though he was yet to know it, it was this endeavour that – within a couple of decades – would make Richard one of the most celebrated, highly paid actors in the world. An actor who spent $1.1 million on a diamond for his wife. A celebrity whose life was a blur of flashing cameras, dazzling teeth and outrageously beautiful women. A charmer who cast a spell upon everyone he came across: according to Roger Moore, Richard 'had that way with powerful people and they just couldn't say "no".

So – asking for a friend – how did he do it? How can you get to a position of having more money than you know what to do with, having a fabulous job and being absolutely adored worldwide? It had to be an inside job, surely? Were his parents film producers, actors or casting agents who could get their little Richard's foot in the door? Did he spend his childhood hanging around film sets or playing with the offspring of showbiz stars?

What is so mind-blowingly extraordinary is that it was none of those things. There are some very unlikely things that happen in life: being dealt a Royal Flush in poker (odds of 1 in 649,739), a left-handed person dying while using a right-handed appliance (1 in 4,400,000), or dying in a shark attack (1 in 3,748,067). But another addition to that list should be baby Richard becoming the superstar that he was.

Richard was born on 10 November 1925 in the small front bedroom of a terraced house in South Wales, the twelfth of thirteen children in the Welsh-speaking family of Richard and Edith Jenkins. Despite humble origins, he made a big impression: Richard was a 'real whopper' of a baby, weighing twelve pounds.

The Jenkins house was in a mining village called Pontrhydyfen (meaning 'Bridge over the Ford in the River Afan'). It was a hotch-potch of grey stone houses, nestled in a valley. The kind of scene you might see on the front of a biscuit tin. The countryside here was magnificently wild, with rivers rushing through the valleys and ospreys and kestrels soaring through the skies.

But zoom out a bit, and there are some strange features in this countryside: colossal heaps of black dirt, forests cleared to build underground tunnels, and canals and railway bridges to transport goods to docks. Looming over Pontrhydyfen was an enormous four-arched bridge, an aqueduct built in the 1820s to take water to the growing industrial areas in the south.

These were the marks of Wales's Industrial Revolution. Over

the past century, the area had transformed from quiet countryside with small-scale sheep farming to an international industrial centre. Under the heather and gorse of these valleys was everything you needed to produce high-quality iron – iron ore, coal and limestone (to speed up the process).

This quickly became the most important iron-producing region in the world. By 1851, more people were employed by industry than agriculture, making Wales the world's first industrial society. By 1913, there were 620 coal mines in Wales. By 1920, there were 271,000 men working the pits. Pontrhydyfen, Richard's village, was transformed: along with a Co-op and three chapels, there were two local collieries to sustain the families with employment.

Richard's father was known to his family as 'Daddy Ni' (Welsh for 'our Daddy'). He was five foot three but immensely strong, able to 'pick up a thirteen-stone man by the seat of his pants'. He was an expert collier who could 'look at the seam of coal', then tap it, and 'something like twenty tons of coal would fall out of the coal face'. It could be a dangerous life – after one pit explosion, Daddy Ni was so badly burnt he was bandaged with only his eyes and nostrils showing through.

There was 'no nastiness' in Daddy Ni, but he was utterly irresponsible to his family. This was a 'twelve pints a day' man, who never made it to a rugby match because there were too many pubs en route. Money that was needed to support the family, he spent on booze. Sometimes he disappeared for days on end, sleeping rough. After one three-week disappearance, he burst into the kitchen with a toothless twenty-four-year-old greyhound, looked at the astonished family and cried, 'Boys, our troubles are over!'

He, like his father before him, was a regular at the local, the

Miners Arms. In fact, Grandfather Tom – who was wheelchair-ridden after being caught in a mining accident – was something of a legend there. One night, he won a vast amount of money on a horse. Buoyed on by this success, he became wildly drunk and headed home. Whizzing down the hill on his wheels, and crying out the horse's name, Grandfather Tom lost control, crashed into a wall, and was killed instantly. It was a literal case of drinking oneself to death.

The real father figure in Richard's early life was his brother, Ifor. To little Richard, Ifor was the ultimate cool older brother, the epitome of masculinity, and everything Daddy Ni wasn't. He was nineteen years older, rugby-mad and, later on, 'ruled the household with the proverbial firm hand'.

Richard's mother, Edith, was 'little less than an angel', keeping the ship above water: sewing school uniforms, scrubbing the laundry, cooking stews and tarts, and managing accounts. There were plenty of other siblings who doted on Richard, too. Edith gave birth thirteen times, for the first time when she was eighteen, and for the last time at forty-three. The eldest was Tom, born in 1901. Then came Margaret Hannah (who died in infancy), Cecila (known as Cis), Ifor, a second Margaret Hannah (who also died in infancy), William, David, Verdun (named after the First World War battlefield in northern France), Hilda, Catherine (known as Cassie), Edith (always Edie), then finally, the little ones, Richard and Graham.

By the time baby Graham was born in late October 1927, Edith was totally run-down, and no longer as strong as she once was. On the morning of 31 October 1927, Daddy Ni came down the stairs. 'Mae dy fam weed marw', he announced – 'Your mother has died.' The cause was complications in childbirth, which she struggled to overcome. Was it those years of late nights – of going without meals, of waiting up for her husband, of tending to so many children – which finally took their toll? 'Her death was the end of our world,' David remembered, 'and I do not think I have ever fully recovered from that day.'

In this moment of family crisis – as predicted – Daddy Ni walked away from any responsibility. The children had no choice but to step up to the mark. Twenty-one-year-old Ifor postponed his marriage to take command, and ten-year-old Hilda managed the daily chores and shopping. 'They were just marvellous,' a neighbour recalled. 'The boys went their own way. The girls brought themselves up. The little ones were farmed out. Nothing was lacking. They were very strong, you see, the Jenkins in Pontrhydyfen. They keep the chapel going and they cleaned it as well.'

Richard and Graham were sent to live with their adult siblings. Richard with Cis, Graham with Ifor. At two years old, Richard left the wild Welsh countryside of Pontrhydyfen, and headed for his new life with his grown-up sister. They lived in the steel town of Port Talbot, five miles away, where the wind whirled across Swansea Bay and brought tirades of rain.

But Richard's heart was always in the village, and he visited often throughout his childhood. 'When he stayed overnight he would sleep in our bed,' his sister Hilda remembered, 'two of us girls at the top and Richard with the other one at the bottom'. It was a tough gig for Cis, who – on top of her own housework – returned twice a week to Pontrhydyfen to keep the family house ticking over. She would arrive to find piles of unwashed clothes, dirty floors and an empty larder. She cleaned, tidied and cooked, then took the dirty washing home on the village bus. When she missed the bus, she'd walk the five miles, carrying little Richard and dragging the laundry bag behind her.

EIGHTEEN

To Richard's great sorrow, he could never remember his mother, but he would find a worthy replacement in Cis. 'When my mother died,' Rich wrote, 'my sister, had become my mother, and more mother to me than any mother could ever have been.' So, as Richard was sent from his village, he was passed to the safest and most loving of hands.

Along with Cis, Richard was looked after by her husband Elfed, a miner, and lived with their two daughters, Marian and Rhiannon. It was a devout household, and the family would head to chapel three times each Sunday. Richard was a keen, albeit amateur, musician. He had a repertoire of eight hymns: 'The first thing he would do when he got home was go straight to the harmonium and play.' He was a fanatic reader, too. Richard lived in the box room (the only room without gas lighting) and would stay up late, reading by candlelight.

Outside this homely bubble, there was plenty of rough and tumble with a boisterous bunch of local boys. Richard was inseparable from his cousin, Dillwyn Dummer (if either of them caught an illness, they deliberately shared a bed to coordinate time off school). Sometimes they'd follow their gang leader – the fabulously named Leonard Nettle – to the windswept hills, where they'd throw punches and wrestle with a rival gang of boys.

One highlight of Richard's childhood was the moment Ifor gave him a brand-new bicycle. Richard was delighted:

> It was a thing of beauty, and I went everywhere on it. It opened
> up the world for me. I went to Swansea and Newport and
> Aberdare and Mountain Ash – just me and my bicycle. I was so
> proud of that bike, and I was so proud of my brother who gave
> it to me.

By his teenage years, Richard had every reason to be optimistic. He had passed the scholarship exam for Port Talbot Secondary Grammar School. This was his passport to a 'bright future' – not to be a miner, a butcher's boy or go to the steelworks, but have the chance of eventually getting a well-paid and high-powered job.

Here, he thrived. As well as learning English, he threw himself into everything – every club, choir and outing available. He was brilliant at sports (good enough to play rugby professionally). He was clever and witty, chatting back to teachers and – despite bad acne – gaining the attention of the prettiest girls.

When the Second World War started in 1939, Richard was fourteen years old. It became part and parcel of school life. On 15 July 1940, he recorded in his diary: 'We had 3 air raid warnings today. Two of them during school hours. Played cricket tonight with Wherle. I had a scrap with Dai Lodwig. I thought I was going up Cwm [the valley]. I had 73 in arith.'

Yet in his fifth year at school, all these hopes were dashed by 'something of a small family crisis'. When Elfed became ill and unable to work, Richard was forced to leave school and earn his keep. It was a bitter pill to swallow, to say goodbye to the grammar school, and hopes for that 'bright future'. Richard handed in his textbooks and began a job in the haberdashery department at the local Co-op.

This was a total and utter humiliation. 'I broke my heart over him when he went to the shop,' remembered Cis. 'He hated it. Oh – he hated it.' To Richard, the idea of noble, masculine work was heading down the mines, ten hours a day, hacking and heaving coal. Yet here he was, counting coupons and measuring suits, and going by the nickname of 'Jenkins Co-op'.

Was this it? Was this Richard set for life? Perhaps it was all he should expect, being the twelfth child of Daddy Ni, living in a mining town where unemployment was rife. 'What can I do about it?' Richard shrugged, when his old teacher Meredith Jones learnt of his prospects. 'Do, boy?' Jones barked back. 'Get you back to school, boy. But if you want me to help you, you've got to help yourself!'

There were several saviours in Richard's young life. First his mother, then Cis, and now Meredith Jones, who believed that Richard was destined for more than haberdashery. With troubles at home subsiding, Jones persuaded the headmaster to readmit Richard to the secondary school. After an eighteen-month gap, sixteen-year-old Richard returned to education. But he was a misfit. He was troublesome, and confused, with no idea what direction his life should take. This was a boy who knew the world of work, and smoked and drank – yet was forced to wear a school cap.

During these months, Richard was assigned to be a firewatcher. Port Talbot was a prime target for the Luftwaffe, who visited day and night to bomb the steelworks. Richard was the last line of defence. As he sat on the rooftop and looked to the skies, he got to know his fourth saviour. It wasn't an angel, nor a ghostly apparition, but a man. His name was Philip Burton, a failed actor turned English teacher, with a passion for education.

In those long hours watching the steelworks, they put the world to rights and bonded over books and literature. It was through those conversations that Burton saw in Richard a spark: 'I soon became very interested by his undoubted potential,' Burton remembered, 'but for what?' He recalled the moment Richard first opened up about his hopes for a career on the stage: 'When he told me that he wanted to be an actor . . . I was very surprised but instinctively excited and challenged'.

Richard was focused, determined and prepared to do whatever it took. What Philip prescribed was a complete rebrand. First up was changing his voice, his way of speaking. Richard was happy to oblige: 'All right,' he shrugged, 'change 'em.'

Soon, the Welsh twang disappeared. 'His voice,' Philip remembered, 'was rough to begin with but with constant practice it became memorably beautiful'. They headed to the hills to practise. Philip remembered:

I would go further and further away from him, forcing him not to shout but to make certain I could hear him. He soon learned that it was distinctness, not volume, that mattered.

But, as Richard threw himself into thespian training, troubles were unfolding at home. Despite all his popularity, Richard could be a typical irritating teenage boy, chatting back, disrespecting authority and being thoroughly unpleasant. Unsurprisingly, Elfed resented having to support him when most others his age were at work. By Richard's late teens, the tension was unbearable: 'Had a terrible row today,' Richard wrote in his diary. 'Elfed told me to go back to Pont. I walked as far as Cwmavon. I hate the sight of Elfed.'

Seeing his pupil struggling with home life, Philip Burton suggested Rich take the spare room in the house he rented. Elfed was pleased to see him go: 'You take 'im, Mr Burton, you take 'im.' Cis, too, seemed relieved: 'If you take him it would be the answer to my prayers'. On 1 March 1943, seventeen-year-old Richard moved for the third time. His new address was 6 Connaught Street, Port Talbot.

Philip Burton was, in many ways, the father that Richard never had. A man who inspired him, understood him and believed in him. For Philip it was obvious: he should be adopted. It was an offer that Richard jumped at: 'He didn't adopt me; I adopted him'. Philip agreed: 'He needed me, and as I realized later, he set out to get me.' There was a practical benefit, of course. It was thought that being 'Richard Burton, son of a schoolteacher', would increase his chances of entry to Oxford University, which Richard hoped would lead him into the acting world.

But there was a technical hiccup, as Philip recalled:

> When I raised the question with Richard he readily agreed to become my adopted son . . . But when it was found that I was twenty days short of being twenty-one years older than Richard, legal adoption was ruled out.

Instead, Philip Burton became Richard Jenkins's legal ward. The document declared that Richard Walter Jenkins would 'absolutely renounce and abandon the use of the surname of the parent and shall bear the surname of the adopter and shall be held out to the world and in all respects treated as if he were in fact the child of the adopter'. And with that document, Richard Jenkins was no more. Richard Burton was born.

It's interesting to consider more recent theories of boyhood in the context of eighteen-year-old Richard. This adoption seems, at first glance, a pretty radical thing to do. Richard had several father figures: his actual father, Daddy Ni, his older brother, Ifan, and his brother-in-law, Elfed. So why did he need another?

In his acclaimed parenting book *Raising Boys*, the family therapist Steve Biddulph pulls apart this point of life, where there is a particular change for boys. From about fourteen, testosterone levels can increase by up to 800 per cent, and boys become argumentative, restless and moody (this would have been when

Richard was forced to endure the humiliation of the haberdashery counter).

But this is also the exact moment – Biddulph explains – when boys especially benefit from 'other adults who care about them personally or help them move gradually into the larger world'. So it isn't surprising that tensions might have arisen in the household with Cis and Elfred, and it was perfectly natural that Richard might find solace in an external figure like Philip Burton.

Consider Biddulph's analysis of the modern approach to late teenage boys, with teenage years shaped by school and university:

> *I believe this is the age when we fail kids the most. In our society all we offer the mid-teens is 'more of the same': more school, more routines of home. But the adolescent is hungry for something more. He is hormonally and physically ready to break out into an adult role, but we want him to wait another five or six years! It's little wonder that problems arise. What's needed is something that will engage the spirit of a boy – pull him headlong into some creative effort of passion that gives his life wings.*

It is uncanny to read when considering young Richard Burton. That stroppy teenager who resented authority was – through his mentor, Philip – given his creative effort of passion, which did indeed give his life wings.

Already, at the age of eighteen years, this young man had undergone multiple transformations. He had lived in three families, changed his voice and changed his name. This Welsh-born miner's son was on his way to becoming a bright young thing on the theatre scene, with a plummy English accent. It seems evident, at this early stage, that Richard was a man who would forge his own destiny.

Richard and Philip were a great team, and with his guardian's guidance, Richard went from strength to strength. Philip arranged an audition for him in Cardiff, where he bagged a part in a play, *The Druid's Rest*. From then onwards his career took off at lightning speed. Just two years on from being 'Jenkins Co-op', eighteen-year-old Rich appeared professionally on stage, touring at the Royal Court Theatre in Liverpool, and St Martin's Theatre in London.

When *The Druid's Rest* closed, he joined the RAF and spent six months on a special wartime course at Exeter College, Oxford, where he read English while undergoing RAF training. Here he played Angelo in the Oxford University Dramatic Society's production of Shakespeare's *Measure for Measure*. Already at this tender age, Richard seemed to be a master of his craft. A fellow actor, Robert Hardy, recalled:

There were moments when he totally commanded the audience by this stillness. And the voice that would sing like a violin and with a bass that could shake the floor.

Next came roles in theatre, then film, where Richard captivated directors, actors and audiences as he went. The director John Gielgud saw the spark of a genius:

He was marvellous at rehearsals. There was the true theatrical instinct. You only had to indicate—scarcely even that. He would get it and never changed it.

Richard rose to superstar status after being cast as Mark Antony in *Cleopatra*, released in 1963. During filming, he and his American co-star Elizabeth Taylor became lovers. They would marry twice, and like the characters they played – Henry VIII or Mark Antony and Cleopatra – joined the echelons of the most iconic couples in history.

Richard now lived the life of an international superstar, darting between homes in Switzerland and Mexico, between the Dorchester Hotel or his *Kalizma* yacht (named after his daughters, Kate, Liza and Maria). But wherever he was in the world, Wales remained at his core. 'If anything was given to Richard,' his brother recalled of those childhood years, 'it was that feeling of belonging.' Another aspect of his Welsh roots that stayed with him throughout his life was the centrality of alcohol. Though living in vastly different worlds, he retained an addiction, just like his father and grandfather before him.

For all the glamour and accolades, he never felt his work was as 'noble' as the work of men who headed down the mines or tore up the rugby pitch. He may have married the world's most beautiful woman and played Hamlet at the Old Vic, but for Richard, the boyhood dream was embedded strong: for all the glitz and fame, he would still have rather 'played for Wales at Cardiff Arms Park'.

Dance the Night Away

As they clambered back into the warmth of the dining room, safe from danger, Horace turned the music up.

As the speakers blared, Geoffrey made an exaggerated bow and extended his hand to Matilda. She rolled her eyes but, finding herself grinning, took his hand with a nod of approval.

As the two began to twirl around the room, their laughter infectious, chairs were hurriedly shifted to clear the makeshift dance floor. Their revelry reached a fever pitch when Jack broke into an impromptu solo in the centre of the circle, his footwork earning a boisterous round of applause. But with only half an hour left, Vivienne took control. She climbed on a chair and yelled, 'Everyone, take your places!' She pulled the dancers from the floor and pushed them towards their seats.

'Time for the final game!' she announced. 'Spin the Bottle!'

17

Vivienne Westwood

FROM SEPTEMBER 1940 UNTIL May 1941, Britain was under attack. Industrial cities and ports were bombarded by bombs dropped by the German Air Force, the Luftwaffe. London, Coventry, Birmingham, Bristol, Belfast, Southampton, Glasgow, Sheffield, Manchester, Cardiff and Hull were battered, with some areas smashed to smithereens. Over 43,500 civilians were killed. It became known as the 'Blitz' – from the German term Blitzkrieg, meaning 'lightning war'.

It was amid this horror, as Luftwaffe bombers terrorized Britain's skies, and all hell was let loose in the cities below, that another force of nature arrived on the scene. In the Derbyshire countryside, a young woman cradled her precious newborn baby girl. She seemed a sweet, soft, innocent little thing. But inside, there was a fiery spirit. As Britain rebuilt itself in the decades to come, and those battered cities were reborn for the modern age, this little girl would shape that new world, and push the boundaries of what it meant to be modern. She was to become one of the most famous British fashion designers of all time: Vivienne Westwood.

As an older woman (and interviewed many years later by Ian Kelly, in a co-written biography published in 2014), Vivienne reflected that her early years were indications of her grown-up self: 'I think people behave according to their intrinsic character from a very early age.' As a little girl, she always had this inherent feeling she was a 'kind of champion' who was slightly different from the rest. 'I realized that I was unusual . . . I saw myself as somebody who was going to do things.'

So, if we're going to try to piece together Vivienne's character at eighteen, it's important to look at the clues, one by one. Magnifying glasses at the ready! Don your mackintosh and trilby!

First clue: the war shaped everything. 'The first thing you should know about me,' Vivienne explained many years later, 'is that I was born in the Second World War. Rationing. All of that. I didn't have a banana until I was seven. Didn't like it when I did.'

Vivienne's parents, Gordon and Dora, married on 19 August 1939, two weeks after war broke out, and honeymooned in Scarborough, Yorkshire. They lived at 6 Millbrook Cottages, a two-up-two-down labourer's cottage in a terrace of twelve, on the road between the villages of Holingworth and Tintwistle. It was also the main road between Manchester and Sheffield, on the edge of the Peak District. The house was all stone: eighteen-inch-thick stone walls, stone flagged floor, stone pantry, stone boiler. There was an outdoor toilet in the backyard, and a tin bath, which was filled with water warmed on an open fire.

Her birth was announced in the local paper:

SWIRE.

On the 8th April 1941, at the Partington Maternity Home
Glossop. To Gordon and Dora, God's precious gift of a daughter.
Vivienne Isabel. First grandchild for Mr & Mrs E. Ball.

When Vivienne was born, Gordon and Dora were dedicated to the war effort. Dora was a weaver in the local cotton factory, which, from 1939, made uniforms, parachutes, camouflage, webbing and tents. Gordon worked as a storekeeper at A.V. Roe, a famous munitions and aircraft factory just outside Manchester. It was such a vital base that the Luftwaffe made several attempts to destroy it. You can see why: this is where the famous Avro Lancaster bombers were made. Gordon was proud, too, that the family lived near the Derwent Dam, where the Dambusters' famous bouncing bomb was tested.

Here's another clue. Despite the war, Vivienne's childhood – which she spent with her siblings, Olga and Gordon – was idyllic. It reads like an Enid Blyton novel. 'I simply had the greatest childhood,' she recalled. 'We were surrounded by love.' It was a bucolic blur of climbing trees, venturing out to the 'wild and frightening' moors, exploring Snake Pass and Devil's Elbow and Cut-Throat Bridge. There were summer picnics with dandelion and burdock lemonade, craft projects, tea with relatives ('usually at Aunt Ethel's as she was the most well-off'), Harvest Festival, lambs born, and getting snowed in. She would remain nostalgic for this for as long as she lived.

Though her parents ticked all the boxes of loving care, they were 'not remotely scholarly'. That's the third clue to jot in your notebook. The Swires considered reading a waste of time, once paying Vivienne to get rid of her library pass. Instead, physical activities were encouraged: doing, making, running and exploring. Vivienne filled the hours with rudimentary activities: 'I used to live for skipping,' she remembered. 'Skipping is fantastic. Two ropes. The best thing.' There was 'tippling', too – doing handstands against walls and flipping over the other side.

But most of all, Vivienne was a creative child. The type who would always have a Pritt Stick in hand, who'd send off for a Blue Peter badge, who was an expert in papier-mâché. Never-ending sewing, scribbling, reading, drawing. No surface was safe. These obsessions were, as grown-up Vivienne saw it, 'some of the early clues to what I became'.

The war never affected Vivienne in a violent or destructive way. There was perhaps one exception, when a single bomb landed near her home (intended for Manchester, ten miles away), and ceiling plaster fell into the truckle bed where she slept.

It was more in the mundane, day-to-day habits. Vivienne was born into a world of austerity where thrift was a buzzword. Until Vivienne reached thirteen years old, rationing was in place. It started before she was born: petrol in 1939, food in 1940, clothes in 1941 and soap in 1942. Bread, which was usually never rationed during wartime, was put on the ration in July 1946. It would take until 1954 for the last food item – meat – to be de-rationed.

'Make do and mend' was all she'd ever known. It was a great stimulus for a crafty, creative mind, for ordinary objects were constantly reimagined, reinvented and recycled. Her mother led by example, making Christmas decorations from the lids of salt and pepper shakers. This is clue number four – this outlook that would stick with her for life. Many years later, in 2013, she spoke at London Fashion Week and made a plea to the public: 'Buy less. Choose well. Make it last. Quality, not quantity.'

By her teenage years, Vivienne became obsessed with 'immediate Do-it-Yourself' projects. Clothes were becoming her everything. She'd fashion 'quick tops', 'like little bras out of two scarves and sew them together, at a corner, behind the shoulder'.

Perhaps it's no surprise, because (notebook at the ready) Vivienne grew up in a part of the world that had long been associated with textiles. That's the next clue. Textiles to Derbyshire were like pottery to Staffordshire or shipping to Portsmouth. It was the bread and butter of life in these parts. Since the eighteenth century, textile mills and factories had sprung up, powered by fast-running water flowing from the peaks. To the west of the Pennines – the stretch of valleys known as the 'backbone of England' – was Lancashire, where the nation's cotton industry flourished. To the east, in Yorkshire, the woollen industry was established.

By the end of the First World War, 80 per cent of the working population in Glossop (a town three miles from Vivienne's home) was employed in the cotton industry. After the Second World War, the textile trade continued to thrive as the government encouraged exports to finance war debts. Posters were displayed in the villages: 'Britain's bread hangs by Lancashire's thread'. Many people worked in the mills, and all – including Vivienne – would grow up knowing about starched cotton and worsted pinstripes and rugged tweeds. A knowledge that would always feed into Vivienne's later life.

Another trait that emerged in these early years was Vivienne's forthright character, which longed to be the centre of attention. Vivienne had a yearning to be treated like a grown-up. At the arrival of her sister, Olga, on 14 January 1944, Vivienne vowed to 'dead her and put her in the dustbin'. She explained this outburst many years later: 'I was outraged. I didn't know I was going to get her. I was three and from then on, I decided I wanted to be grown up as soon as possible.'

Vivienne certainly considered herself a tomboy, though she never doubted her girlhood:

It had never occurred to me that there was anything better than being a girl. I never wanted to be a boy or to have the perceived

freedoms of a boy. I liked being me, and I happened to be a girl.
I wanted to be a hero and saw no reason a girl couldn't be one.

There were a couple of turning points, too. Faith was an important part of her young life: 'Not to be a Christian would have been a betrayal equal to the acceptance of torture'. But a 'huge, huge' moment in her life – 'a positively Damascene revelation' – was the first time she saw an image of the Crucifixion. Outraged by the suffering depicted, she vowed to challenge oppression: 'I felt I had to become a freedom fighter to stop this sort of thing going on. I really did want to do something to change this horrible world.' That's clue number six, which laid the ground for Vivienne's later work as an activist and humanitarian.

Like Rosalind Franklin's thrill at watching the coronation of King George VI in 1937, Vivienne was treated to the splendour of a royal celebration. Perhaps the most memorable single day of Vivienne's childhood was 2 June 1953: the coronation of Elizabeth II. In true British style, it was miserably wet. After a tea party at Tintwistle Sunday School, the Swires crowded into a nearby house – the 'house that had a television' – clutching soggy Union Jack flags. Twelve-year-old Vivienne watched as twenty-five-year-old Elizabeth Windsor was crowned Queen.

In a world of drab austerity, this was a vivid splash of technicolour, of glamour. A sparkling, shimmering fairy tale. There was ancient ceremony, sumptuous dresses, awe-inspiring music, dazzling crown jewels and the patriotic sense of being British – all viewed through this brand-new bit of technology, the television.

It's an important clue, this one. All these themes would emerge in Vivienne's designs: royalty, tradition, history, aristocracy. She went on to create T-shirts with the slogan 'God Save the Queen'. She played with Scottish tartan and Harris tweed. She chose the royal orb as her company logo. And she saw Elizabeth, this young woman, become a queen – just as Vivienne would do in the fashion world, years later.

Vivienne's secondary school, Glossop Grammar, was three miles from Tintwistle. She'd travel by bus, passing several cloth mills, travelling through a viaduct and into the market town of Glossop. Here, she became a bookworm, devouring Dickens, Keats, Maupassant and Chaucer. For Vivienne, these books 'seemed to talk properly about life and sex and the human condition: the universal in the particular'. She was a clever girl, and proud of doing well. Half a century later she could still remember her marks: 'I got 95 per cent in the English Literature O level and 90 per cent in History!'

She had a sharp, innovative mind, too. One school friend remembered when their class was given the title of 'Bats in the Belfry' to depict. 'We all imagined a church, but she went psychological and did bats in the head. She was smart.'

So let's take a moment to recap our clues, to check the notebook. We've got a brainy, sharp girl with an understanding of materials, an instinct for thriftiness, a nostalgia for the English countryside, a sense of Britishness, an independent mindset, a sensitivity to injustice and a wild creativity.

It is a good list, with plenty of potential – if the circumstances are correct. The problem was, they weren't. Vivienne was a working-class girl in the Derbyshire countryside. Ambitions and aspirations were limited. The careers advice at Glossop Grammar was 'of its time and place'. Vivienne was only aware of four options: school-teacher, hairdresser, nurse or secretary. 'I can't think of anything else that was ever discussed for anybody'.

One fellow schoolgirl, Maureen Purcell, who aspired to be an architect, was told by her mother she 'must be a hairdresser because she was artistic'. Another girl wanted to be a journalist, but 'was told to be a nurse'. The two brightest girls from Vivienne's primary school – 'really clever, highly intelligent girls' – left school at fifteen to go to the cotton mills. Not because they were forced to (the headmaster encouraged them to stay), but for a lack of knowing what else to do.

It is a blessing to the fashion world that, in this void of career encouragement, Vivienne found a ray of hope in her art teacher, Mr Bell. He was 'quite a dramatic presence'. During the war, Mr Bell had been tortured in a Japanese concentration camp – his tongue had been cut, leaving him with a lisp. It was Mr Bell who saw a spark in Vivienne, who encouraged her – at sixteen years old – to visit an art gallery for the first time, to experiment with painting styles, to consider art school: 'He was the one person who said it: "Go on, go."'

There was another coming-of-age moment. In her mid-teens, romance hit Vivienne's life, though it was 'nothing very racy'. Dance halls and cinemas provided good meeting points for the Manchester boys. But it was Butlin's Holiday Resort in Skegness where Vivienne got into the swing of things: she claimed to have 'got off with over a hundred blokes'.

But it wasn't the young men who brought Vivienne a sense of adulthood. It was the new identity she carved out – much to the school's frustration – from her appearance. Red hair one week, a bleached streak the next, and curled so stiff it seemed the rollers hadn't been removed.

At Butlins, she'd seen girls from Essex wear heels and pencil skirts, which she thought 'probably the most exciting garment ever designed'. She saved her money and headed into Manchester: 'This one time I couldn't believe what I saw, something of which I could never have dreamed: stilettos.' She took the new pair to school on a Monday morning and proudly placed them on her desk 'for all to admire'.

Vivienne's idols were hourglass-shaped women – the likes of Marilyn Monroe. As a flat-chested schoolgirl with protruding teeth, there was work to be done. She curved up her body, customizing the school uniform by tightening the skirt and cutting a slit up the back: 'it was like changing from a child to a woman overnight . . . a thrill I'll remember forever.' She started padding her bras, with straightforward logic: 'big tits are what boys are interested in'.

Though Mr Bell had planted the seeds of art school, all this clothing business was still just a hobby. A wage needed to be brought in. She worked at Manchester Woolworths. Then, in July 1957, she took a six-week holiday job at Pickering's cannery as a 'pea pixie' (so named because of the green overall and cap). It was, as Vivienne put it, 'just money'.

But change was coming. Just before turning seventeen, her world was uprooted. She later wrote of this moment: 'everything in my world changed'. Times were tough for Gordon and Dora. From 1951, the British cotton industry was hit by recession, as imports from Hong Kong, India and Pakistan began to flood the home market. Many lost their jobs in Glossopdale's mills, and a few found work in the new chemical and plastic firms. By the end of the decade, the options were scant. 'We had to move,' explained Dora. 'There was no work.'

Dora and Gordon were keen to give their children the best chance in life, and 'when they saw an opportunity, they took it'. Not relocating to Australia, as Gordon had once hoped. Instead, they changed their career path. Here was the logic:

Dad was affected by the Depression and he figured if you worked for the government you would have a salary, and that

running a post office as well as a grocer's meant customers had
to walk all through the shop and buy something on the way.
Mum and Dad worked that out and went from one post office
to the next. And eventually that took us to London.

So the Swire family upped sticks. They travelled to London by
train and were assigned a post office to manage in the leafy suburbs
of Harrow-on-the-Hill, at 31 Station Road. The family lived in
the large three-bedroom flat over the shop, where Vivienne shared
a room with her twelve-year-old sister, Olga.

At first, Vivienne hated it and longed for Derbyshire. Everything
was different and unfamiliar and out of her control. In Derbyshire
there were dance halls with rock 'n' roll bands and 'partners', where
people could talk to one another. A date would involve going to
the pictures where you would 'snog all night on the back row'. In
London, people hung about in cliques and danced to modern jazz
in dark nightclubs. It wasn't to Vivienne's taste. She loathed this
new 'alternative crowd' with their beards and cider.

Perhaps it wasn't surprising that Vivienne found London's youth
scene alienating. For this was the dawn of the teenager. Flicking
through the London newspapers of 1959 – the year Vivienne
turned eighteen – there are endless reports, adverts, comments
and letters discussing the new cultural phenomenon.

In February 1959, it was reported that 'John Elliot, documentary writer for the BBC-TV', was putting together a documentary
on teenagers, by 'visiting coffee bars, council estates, juvenile
courts and skiffle clubs'. In September, the *Sydenham, Forest Hill*
& Penge Gazette reported a shocking new play, where 'teenagers
were left too much to themselves and their emotions', revealing
young people who were 'sophisticated on the surface but became
children when faced by grim realities'. In November, an advert in

the *Daily Mirror* was titled 'TEENAGE PIMPLES can be cleared fast', selling a product that could 'get rid of embarrassing, ugly spots on face, shoulders and back'.

Just a few weeks after Vivienne's eighteenth birthday, in April 1959, it was reported that the hot topic of debate at the congress of the Royal Society of Health was 'teenage rebels'. 'Adolescence is going to get more and more important,' one professor predicted, 'as more training and skill is demanded from adolescents'. Then he warned: 'This is going to increase the tension between how they see themselves and how we see them.'

Debates raged as to how society should deal with the 'waywardness and defiance of modern youth'. A letter in the *South Western Star* (a paper covering Battersea and Wandsworth) declared: 'Let the teenager choose his job and pastimes, within reason, but don't make them old before their time. Work and play will fall in their right places naturally'. In October, in the *Croydon Times*, a column titled 'Teenagers and their Morals' argued that young people should be given more independence: 'Once a child has become an adult he should be treated as an adult. We don't trust children and the hypocrisy of so many adults gets children down'.

In December, a despairing mother, Mrs Kathleen McIntosh, wrote to the *Middlesex Chronicle*, aghast that her teenage sons were reprimanded by the police for loitering:

Teenagers will always congregate, just as their seniors do at pubs or clubs. If they haven't a club then they go to the nearest eating establishment where they munch and gossip or drink their Pepsi-colas. There is nothing wrong in that. Unfortunately, without meaning it, their noisy chatter and boisterous good humour creates a disturbance.

She ended with the suggested alternative approach: 'When a disturbance has occurred has anyone tried phoning the local parson instead of the police?'

It's evident from these debates between parents, teachers and politicians that something was afoot. London was undergoing a youthquake, and Vivienne was in its epicentre. Exactly as Mr Bell had suggested, she joined Harrow Art School for a foundation course in jewellery-making and silversmithing.

She spent time exploring the wonders of London's museums. Vivienne adored the 'pure gold of ancient jewellery' in the British Museum, learning about these people from the past who – as Vivienne saw it – 'held in common with us the human potential for genius and yet whose ideas must have been so different'. She read about the 1947 Kon-Tiki expedition to the Polynesian islands and was 'fired to find out about the Incas'. She was awestruck by the plaster model of a great blue whale, and a display exploring the course of evolution from primitive beginnings.

Alongside expanding her mind, Vivienne pushed her sartorial boundaries. Take a moment to imagine her sitting in the sunshine on the steps outside the British Museum. As curators and academics hurried past in tweed suits and briefcases, they might have been surprised – even shocked – at her appearance. Her clothes were bizarre. Sometimes she built up a huge beehive hair-style on her head. On other occasions, she walked the streets in long pointed shoes that poked out three inches beyond her toes. Had you spotted Vivienne during her 'Trad' phase (aka, dressing like a traditional artist), you might see her in a full skirt, a knitted jumper, a headscarf, carrying a basket for art materials and even – perhaps in the summer months – going barefoot.

But there was one question that Vivienne struggled to answer. The big challenge for eighteen-year-old Vivienne was not a lack of passion or skill. It was a practical one: 'How did you make your living as an artist?' The only way to make money in the arts, she thought, was to sell paintings: 'I was just too working-class to see beyond that one stereotype.'

Disillusioned, she left art school after one term. Time to get serious – she thought. Time to earn a living. At eighteen years old, Vivienne turned away from following her creative instinct. It's a common problem with creative types: the difficulty of finding an outlet for your passion. All the brilliance might be there, but you have to find the correct format, or medium, or social circle, within which to nurture and express it. Until then, it's hard to make anything click. Despite studying at a London art school, with a strong natural ability, Vivienne *still* couldn't see a realistic way forward.

Convinced that the art world wasn't for her, Vivienne rerouted her life. She set out on a perfectly conventional path, preparing to live in a perfectly conventional way. After seeing an advert on the Tube, she started a year-long Pitman's typing course to become a shorthand typist. Unsurprisingly, it didn't sit well: 'I soon realized that I did not want to be a secretary!'

Vivienne wasn't alone in despairing at her career prospects. Despite the post-war boom, there were still plenty of concerns about 'the teenage jobless'. Not long after she had arrived in London, the *Daily Herald* reported, 'Unemployment, particularly among young people, dominated questions in the Commons yesterday. Every year, more and more boys and girls leave school. How many will get jobs?' The letters page of the *North London Press* expressed similar concerns:

> *We have full employment and long may this be so. But many youngsters are in boring occupations (it is the money that*

matters) which demand very little of their intellectual and phys-ical capability and leave them at the end of the day with excess energy to work off, frustration to kill, and self-esteem to establish.

In 1962, Vivienne married her first husband, Derek Westwood, a Hoover factory apprentice (who gave her the famous surname). As a newlywed, Vivienne qualified as a primary school teacher. At that point, her comfortable future seemed set in stone: Mrs Westwood the primary school teacher who was very good at crafting.

It was a chance meeting that changed everything. Her brother, Gordon, brought a nineteen-year-old art student around to Vivienne's flat in Harrow. His name was Malcolm McLaren, and he was striking to look at, with red hair and a face covered in talcum powder. Giving in to her inner creative impulse, Vivienne threw in the towel on a life of convention.

Malcolm was to be Vivienne's second husband, and, though he was awful (he took six days to visit her in hospital after the birth of their son), it was the start of one of Britain's great creative partnerships. While the 1960s was dominated by the hippie move-ment, young Vivienne Westwood and Malcolm McLaren were more intrigued by acts of rebellion. As the 1970s dawned, they opened a small boutique on King's Road in Chelsea, pioneering the punk look: biker clothing, zips, leather and provocative slogans. Malcolm became manager of punk band the Sex Pistols, who wore Vivienne's designs, bringing her into the limelight as a sartorial visionary.

From here, Vivienne's designs went from strength to strength, constantly breaking moulds and pushing boundaries. Starting as the 'Godmother of Punk', over the decades she conquered high fashion and built a global empire.

EIGHTEEN

Her symbol, the orb (introduced in 1986), is a globally recognized representation of rebellion and creativity, of Vivienne herself. Her designs have been flaunted by – and played a part in creating – world icons: Princess Diana, Madonna, Lady Gaga, Rihanna, Elton John, Kate Moss, Gwen Stefani and Angelina Jolie, to name a few.

It is quite incredible that that little girl from Tintwistle who loved to skip became one of the most influential designers of the twentieth century. She was also a pioneer of the sustainable fashion movement and a powerful, passionate advocate for political and environmental causes.

Despite the global dominance, so much can be traced back to youth. On one hand, she was a wartime child. A child born in the Blitz, who frolicked in the Derbyshire countryside, who lived by make-do and mend, who watched the coronation of Elizabeth II as a child, who lived in a world of fabric production. But she was also in the first generation of teenagers, in the sense that we know the term. While drawing upon those themes of childhood, she was unwavering in going against the grain, in waging war against conformity, in pushing the boundaries. When she received an OBE in 1992, for example, she twirled at the photographers to reveal something quite shocking: no knickers.

At eighteen years old, Vivienne probably felt lost, pursuing the wrong career and unsure how to fulfil her true passions. And yet – though her path to success would take several years to reveal itself – she was, in so many ways, already there. Vivienne at eighteen – with that rebellious teenage mindset – is the same woman who would come to rule the fashion world decades later. As Vivienne herself put it, 'I lived all my life as if I'm young'. This was her secret to success. To never grow up, to always rebel, to stay – for ever – a teenager.

Spin the Bottle

Each of the guests took their seats. Vivienne picked up a bottle of red wine, swigged the final dregs and placed it on its side in the middle of the table. 'The rules are simple. We spin the bottle and whoever it lands on must KISS!'

Giggles and shrieks rippled around the room. Richard was delighted. Mary gasped. With great drama, Vivienne spun the bottle. Round and round it travelled, pointing at each face in turn. Sarah . . . Jacques . . . Jeff . . . Vita, until finally, it came to a stop, 'Isambard! Our first champion! And who's the lucky partner?' The bottle cast its spell again, this time landing on Fionnghal. They leant over the table, giggling, and the group erupted with squeals when, for a brief second, blushing Isambard gave her a peck.

The bottle spun again, this time landing on Geoffrey. Whoops and cheers again. Who was it to be? Who would have a kiss from the father of English literature? Only the bottle could decide. Again, it spun, round and round. Everyone held their breath. It finally came to a stop, pointing to the head of the table.

'Rae, it's you!'

18

Rae DeDarre

THERE IS NOTHING LIKE saving the best for last. Our final character is my all-out favourite, Rae DeDarre. This is someone I've always wanted to meet. An intelligent person, with great taste in pretty much everything. Someone who is – I hope – still alive.

But hang on one second. Good heavens! [Note to editor – there seems to be a typo! Stop the press! One second . . . unscramble those letters around . . . chat among yourselves . . . and we're there!] Chapter Eighteen is not *Rae DeDarre*, but you, my *Dear Reader*! There it is! You are the final one of our eighteen! You, who holds this book and reads these lines. This chapter is dedicated to *your* story. To whoever *you* are at eighteen years old, or were, or will be.

Of course, the experience of an eighteen-year-old today will differ massively from that of our eighteen-year-olds of the past. Even since the teenage years of Vivienne Westwood, youth culture has expressed itself in countless ways. In the 1960s, many young people bought into the hippie movement, which stemmed from a resistance to the Vietnam War. They talked about peace, drugs and free love, played folk music on guitars and sported pre-worn clothes or no clothes at all.

The eighteen-year-olds of the 1970s bought into the punk scene. This was Vivienne's revolution, an angry explosion of self-cut and dyed hair, ripped T-shirts, charity-shop trousers and jagged jewellery made from safety pins. There were goths, too, those youths dressed all in black in a neo-Victorian style, who went through an eyeliner pencil each week. In the late 1980s and 1990s, the Acid House movement developed, and ravers descended upon fields or disused warehouses. Young people could prove to be such a menace that the 1994 Criminal Justice Act outlawed music 'characterised by a series of repetitive beats'.

Youth experiences have been shaped by wider changes in society, too, with the development of women's rights and a changing population. Our prime ministers reflect this. Since Vivienne Westwood was a teenager, there have been two female prime ministers, Margaret Thatcher and Theresa May. In 2023, Rishi Sunak became prime minister, a man with East African-born Hindu parents of Indian Punjabi descent.

According to the 2021 census, in England and Wales, the population was 59.5 million (up 3.5 million since 2011). Women were 51 per cent of the population, and 82 per cent of the population was white. North Norfolk had the highest median age (fifty-four years), with Nottingham, Cambridge, Oxford and Manchester the lowest (all thirty-one years).

For young people, the greatest difference in their lives is probably higher education. Today, over 40 per cent of eighteen-year-olds apply to university. In 2016, young women were 35 per cent more likely to go to university than men (a fact that Rosalind Franklin would have found heartening). Though the limitations of class and gender are far less apparent than they have been historically, white working-class boys are now the least likely to enter higher education.

There has been a revolution in travel, too. For the first time, cheap flights across the world are part and parcel of daily life and the norm for the young. A quick glance at the Ryanair website at the time of writing showed flights under £20 to over thirty destinations in Europe. A weekend in Rome – once unthinkable to our ancestors – is perfectly possible. Travelling, studying, working or living abroad are all options.

Young people today live in the digital, always-connected world. Everything from the food shop to your next relationship is forged through a screen. While letters or the fax machine once reigned supreme, we can now stay in touch with friends, family, doctors or colleagues at every minute of the day.

The lives of young people today are remarkably different from what they have been in the past. This chapter – your chapter – proves to be an interesting one!

So tell me! I'm all ears. Is eighteen-year-old you a cricket-obsessed hip-hop artist from Argyll, hoping to become a solicitor? Perhaps a soon-to-be medical student, whose real dream is to clean gravestones and make ASMR videos about it on TikTok? Maybe you are a child star performing on stage at the Liverpool Empire, too afraid to tell your Tiger Mum you want to join the RAF?

Perhaps you're already working in the job you'll do for the rest of your life. Perhaps you've been in prison, won a Nobel Prize or have been expelled from school. Perhaps you are totally ordinary, totally as expected.

Are you someone who has hundreds of friends, or do you prefer a close-knit circle? Are you kind or caring, selfish or daring? Can you see your career mapped out already? Has it already started?

Have you met your soulmate? Do they know who you are? Are you cared for by a loved one? Or are you a carer for someone else?

Whatever the story, and whatever the insecurities, anxieties, hopes, challenges, views, dreams and worries, they are all totally valid. All remarkable. The human condition doesn't much change. Your insecurities, anxieties, hopes, challenges, views, dreams and worries were felt in some way by all the other teenagers at the dinner table. They are as important a part of history as Jacques Francis finding his feet in a foreign country, or Jack Lewis missing his mother, or Sarah Biffin's determination to sew.

The joy of history is it's everything that has ever happened and everyone who has ever lived. Whatever your story is or was, it is worthy of being told. Perhaps there is a voice in your head thinking, *Why on earth would anyone be interested in little old me?* Because we are so familiar with our own stories, they seem real and believable, but pretty mundane. Just stuff happening. One thing, after another. In contrast, the lives of people in the past seem exciting and glamorous and shocking and so hard to imagine. Yet those people lived and breathed and gossiped and laughed and sneezed in just the same way as we do today. And what's more, they probably found their lives mundane or ordinary, too.

And this is reassuring! Just like Isambard, your big break might be just around the corner. Or a totally unpredictable event – like the arrival of Bonnie Prince Charlie in Fionnghal's story – might be soon to change your world for ever.

Just as we are fascinated by the stories of Elsie, or Vita, or Isambard, or Sarah, your story is part of history, and will be fascinating, valuable evidence for future historians – big name or not. What will those historians write about you? Will it be 'The

Extraordinary Life of . . .' or 'The True Story of . . .'? Would they pick up on your parents' story, or your friends', or that of a teacher?

This is your chance to fill in the gaps. Take your time. I'll grab a cup of tea. The floor is all yours . . .

Lights Up

At eleven o'clock, the party comes to an end.

Empty party poppers litter the floor. The remnants of a smashed glass sit on the side table. A small leather purse with gold coins lies forgotten on the side. The mantelpiece clock ticks on.

As the guests file out of the room and stumble down the stairs, there are plans to hop into taxis and horse-drawn carriages, steam trains and parents' cars. Promises are thrown about of seeing each other again soon.

There is a call up the stairs. 'You coming, Rae?'

You do a final sweep, and, just as you reach for the door, you catch yourself in the mirror. In the reflection, you see an eighteen-year-old who is complicated and unusual, who has so much to offer and – in a totally unique way – is utterly wonderful.

'Just coming!' you cry. And as you pull open the door, and head down the stairs to join the others, you step forward into the rest of your life. Ready for whatever the future may hold. Ready for whatever is written in the stars.

CONCLUSION

Some Final Thoughts

I set out to write this book hoping to get to know the eighteen-year-olds of Britain. To discover who they are, who they have been for the past thousand years. I hope you'll all come to your own, different conclusions (especially with the inclusion of Chapter Eighteen!). But here is what has stuck out to me.

Most striking is the high proportion of young people whose families were disjointed or torn apart. Many were familiar with losing loved ones through plague, disease, execution or accident. Many, too, were separated from their biological families at a very young age, and replaced them with a surrogate family, be they monks or sailors or something else entirely. They left to start a career, join a monastery, marry a foreign king, or go to boarding school. Some were forcibly taken, with no choice in the matter.

Today, all this upheaval would be considered highly traumatic. What would a modern therapist make of eighteen-year-old Elizabeth I? Where to start! Executed mother, dead father, four stepmothers, sexual abuse from a stepfather (who was summarily executed), beloved half-siblings who are also rivals? Better get comfortable on that couch.

It's also notable – and heartening – to see how many of our young friends' lives were transformed by another person. Someone who understood their passion and helped them nurture it. For Elsie Inglis, it was her father, who never questioned her ambition. For Rosalind Franklin, it was those St Paul's mistresses who believed so passionately in girls' education and careers. For Richard Burton, it was his mentor, Philip Burton, who launched him into the acting world. For Vivienne Westwood, it was her art teacher, Mr Bell, who encouraged her creative instincts when no one else did.

It is a testament to the power of inspiring teachers and mentors out there, who can make an incalculable difference to a young life. A lesson to all of us about how a few words of encouragement can go a long way – and adversely, how damaging an unkind snigger or an offhand dismissal can be. It's kind – and cool – to be supportive of other people 'having a go'.

I hope you can also see, now, how early years and childhood are vitally important in understanding a person. It's been interesting, too, to force myself to imagine these lot as living, breathing people. By bringing these figures from the past into the room with me – with *you*.

In imagining coming face to face with someone, we are forced to think what they were really like. How they'd interact or laugh or joke. I must be the only person to have ever linked this group via a table plan (available to peruse on the following pages). How would an eighteenth-century sailor interact with a sixteenth-century princess? What part of their personality would make them act in that way? What about their cultural and historical contexts? I'd encourage you to try it out with other historical figures. It is a good exercise, for it forces us to refocus, to consider these people on their terms. We use the names *they* were familiar with: Horace, not Horatio, Fionnghal, not Flora, Jack, not C. S. Lewis. You see, there is *some* method in the madness.

But the overwhelming conclusion I'm drawn to? I'm impressed. I'm impressed at what young people have achieved, have put up with and have endured. That, despite trial and tribulation, in the face of cruelty or disadvantages acting against them, they can pull through with flying colours.

What does it mean for British teens of today? Most teenagers live with their family and go to school. They aren't expected to have achieved much outside of that. And yet there is a perceived crisis at hand. That they are disconnected and dissatisfied, addicted to technology and incapable of socializing. It is – perhaps – a valid concern. But not their fault. It is largely a result of environment: nurture, not nature. When put in difficult or dangerous situations, we've seen that young people will rise to the challenge.

I'm sure parents, teachers and social workers will have strong and differing opinions on this, based on years of experience. Of course, it is a fine line, and every case – every teen – is different. However, my instinct is that learning to overcome difficulty produces the best results in people. Who knows which mopey teenager would – if push came to shove – have the brilliance of Isambard Kingdom Brunel, or the spirit of Empress Matilda, lurking beneath their mop of hair?

This is encouraging, for there are real challenges lying ahead for today's young, waiting to be tackled: the onset of AI, the social disconnect created by technology, the difficulties of a changing environment, ongoing political discord, international crises. But every age has its own challenges, and there is no reason this generation can't find the answers, as many generations have before. We are, after all, materially and medically better off than ever before, with incredible access to knowledge and learning. If moments of world-changing genius are soon to come upon one of us, it's comforting to know that – unlike our ancestors – they are less likely to be interrupted by agonizing toothache or crippling gout.

If we look at the long course of history, and eighteen-year-olds within that, it's hard to pin down what unites their experiences. Each of them – by virtue of birth, chance or societal convention – are at different stages of life. Some have already enjoyed a career peak. Others have no idea of the challenges to come. Lady Elizabeth might have struggled to believe what her future had in store, that she was to sit on the throne for forty-five years. Likewise, Vivienne Swire, that eccentric eighteen-year-old who started a typist course, might have screamed in amazement to know she would become one of the greatest fashion designers of all time. Eighteen, then, is not the be-all and end-all. It's not even the beginning, but another stepping stone on a complicated and unpredictable path.

Perhaps eighteen is not really an age at all. Perhaps we should think of it as a mindset, an outlook, which all of us can inhabit. A time at the start of adulthood, of self-doubt and uncertainty. Being eighteen is to not know what the future holds. The contours of your character are indistinct, even to yourself. But this uncertainty can also be a blessing. For this is the moment to consider all options, to recast the die, to throw the net wide.

Imagine adulthood as a garden. We enter through a gate, leaving childhood behind – a place we can glance at over the fence, but never actually return to. Being eighteen is to lean on the gatepost and look at the garden ahead, map in hand. There are hundreds of paths to choose from. Some lead to pristine lawns, rose gardens, bluebell woods, lily ponds or vegetable allotments. There are abandoned water butts with lurking toads, streams with banks of wild garlic, dense woodland with ancient, gnarly trees, and boiling greenhouses with tropical, poisonous plants. There are treehouses and garden sheds, green pools and rusty trampolines, upturned gnomes and dried-up fountains, crumbling walls and rickety fences. There are beauties to stop and admire: arches of rambling roses, and dragonflies dancing on water. But there are dangers, too: wasps that sting and rabbit holes that, if you're not looking, can twist an ankle.

Some of us take the main path, content to settle down in a deckchair, basking in the dappled sunlight. Some of us divert from the path to swim in streams, tumble down hills or clamber up trees, risking life and limb. Some are given the wrong directions, ending up in the sculpture park when they hoped to be in the wildflower meadow.

But that's not a problem. All of us, at any point, have the option to return to the starting gatepost, to take a new path and begin a new journey. It is at this moment we champion this daring eighteen-year-old outlook. We revisit that place of uncertainty, of risk, of potential, of excitement. And from here we venture forth down a new path.

Life can be full of difficulties and challenges – those stings of a nettle, those lurking rabbit holes. But by taking that unknown path – by embracing the spirit of being eighteen – the rewards can be manifold. Who knows what sun-dappled orchards or gently flowing streams await?

TABLE PLAN

Matilda

Isambard	Vita
Mary	Jeffrey
Richard	Fionnghal
Elizabeth	Jacques
Horace	Sarah
Rosalind	Jack
Geoffrey	Vivienne
Elsie	Bede

Rae

PLACES TO VISIT

ST PAUL'S CHURCH, JARROW
The monastery at Jarrow is where Bede spent most of his life. You can still see parts of the original Anglo-Saxon monastery in the chancel of St Paul's Church. Look out for the dedication stone on an inner wall of the tower, which dates to 23 April 685.

DURHAM CATHEDRAL, DURHAM
Though he was originally buried at Jarrow, Bede's remains were moved to Durham in the eleventh century. Today he is interred in the Galilee Chapel at Durham Cathedral, beside St Cuthbert. His tomb is marked with the Latin words 'HIC SUNT IN FOSSA BEDAE VENERABILIS OSSA' (Here are buried the bones of the Venerable Bede). Make sure to visit the Undercroft Café.

TOWER OF LONDON, LONDON
In the heart of the Tower of London is the White Tower, the old keep built by William the Conqueror during the early 1080s. It's here that King William's granddaughter – Empress Matilda – may have stayed in her youth before she travelled to Germany.

MAINZ CATHEDRAL, GERMANY

On 25 July 1110, Matilda was crowned 'Queen of the Romans' at the magnificent Mainz Cathedral. Romanesque in style, this is a 'cathedral mountain' of red sandstone with three naves. What did Matilda think of this vast space when she came here as a child?

SOUTHWARK CATHEDRAL, LONDON

This beautiful church is one of the oldest in London, and not far from where Geoffrey Chaucer grew up in Vintry Ward. Here is where John Gower (a close friend of Chaucer) was buried, in a grand tomb beautifully coloured in vivid red, gold and green. Look out for Hodge, the cathedral cat.

WESTMINSTER ABBEY, LONDON

When Geoffrey Chaucer died in 1400, he was buried in the south transept of Westminster Abbey. In 1556, the present grey Purbeck marble monument was erected to Chaucer's memory. It reads, 'Of old the bard who struck the noblest strains/Great Geoffrey Chaucer, now this tomb retains./If for the period of his life you call,/the signs are under that will note you all./In the year of our Lord 1400, on the 25th day of October./Death is the repose of cares.'

THE *MARY ROSE*, PORTSMOUTH

On 11 October 1982, over 400 years after Jacques Francis dived down to recover its treasures, the *Mary Rose* was finally raised from the seabed. Today, the recovered ship is on display. There are also thousands of recovered Tudor objects and relics, including the skeleton of Hatch, the carpenter's dog.

THE DOLPHIN HOTEL, SOUTHAMPTON

Though this hotel has a grand Georgian facade, there are original medieval timbers and stone vaulting inside, and records date back to at least 1454. It was here that Jacques Francis and his fellow divers stayed while working on salvaging the *Mary Rose*. In later years, it became a popular coaching inn. Jane Austen celebrated her eighteenth birthday there in 1793.

HATFIELD HOUSE, HERTFORDSHIRE

The Old Palace at Hatfield House was built around 1485 and acquired by Henry VIII from the Bishop of Ely in 1538. From then on, it was used as a nursery for his three children. It is here – inside these red-brick walls and formal gardens – that Mary, Elizabeth and Edward spent much of their childhoods. In 1558, Elizabeth was sitting under an oak tree in the park when she learnt of her succession to the throne.

OAKHAM, RUTLAND

The charming market town of Oakham is where Jeffrey Hudson was born. There are many wonderful buildings to explore. The great hall of the Norman castle still stands, which – because of a centuries-old tradition that implores important visitors to donate a horseshoe – has over 200 horseshoes hanging inside. Make sure to visit Oakham Market Cross, a structure dating from the sixteenth or seventeenth century. It has a central stone shaft surrounded by eight timber posts, supported by a tiled roof. Next to it is a set of stocks. Did Jeffrey play here with his siblings, I wonder?

THE BANQUETING HOUSE, LONDON

This was the crowning glory of the sprawling Whitehall Palace, the rest of which burnt down in 1698. It was designed by Inigo

Jones, and its ceiling was decorated with Rubens paintings. It was here that grand feasts and masques were held for the Stuart court, and the likes of Jeffrey Hudson performed for royals and dignitaries.

FLORA MACDONALD MONUMENT, SOUTH UIST

At the end of a remote farm drive in South Uist are the foundation walls of a house. This is believed to be where Fionnghal nic Dhòmhnaill lived as a child. Within the cottage is a large monument with a plaque, which reads: 'Clan Donald raised this cairn of remembrance to their kinswoman Flora MacDonald daughter of Ranald, son of Angus of Milton South Uist. She was born in 1722 near this place and spent her early life in the house that stood on this foundation. When pursuit was drawing near to the Prince in the Long Island she greatly aided him by her heroism and endurance to gain shelter in the Isle of Skye.'

FLORA MACDONALD'S GRAVE, ISLE OF SKYE

In a windswept cemetery, not far from Kilmuir, is the final resting place of Fionnghal. The original monument was destroyed in a gale in 1871, and replaced by the current design in 1880. It is an imposing 28-foot-high Celtic Cross made of granite. The epitaph – taken from the account of Dr Samuel Johnson – reads: 'Her name will be mentioned in history and if courage and fidelity be virtues, mentioned with honour.'

HMS *VICTORY*, PORTSMOUTH

Since 1823, HMS *Victory* has been permanently at anchor in Portsmouth harbour. This is the famous ship that Nelson commanded at the Battle of Trafalgar in 1805. It is quite incredible to pace up and down the decks, as Nelson might have done, or to explore the Great Cabin, where battle plans were drawn up.

BURNHAM THORPE, NORFOLK

Burnham Thorpe is the village where Nelson was born and spent his childhood. His father, Edmund, was the rector at the church from 1755 to 1803 and lived with his family at the old parsonage (which no longer stands, having been pulled down in 1803). The graves of Nelson's mother and father are on the north side of the church chancel, and the graves of a brother and sister are in the churchyard. Across the green is the village pub – the first of many to be named the Lord Nelson.

CHURCH OF ST MARY, EAST QUANTOXHEAD, SOMERSET

This is the fourteenth-century church where Sarah Biffin was baptized. The baptism record reads: 'Daughter of Henry and Sarah Biffin was baptised on the 31st October born without arms or legs'.

LYME REGIS MUSEUM, DORSET

This wonderful seafront museum was built on the site of Mary Anning's childhood home. A blue plaque outside reads: 'The famous fossilist was born here in a house on the site of Lyme Regis Museum. The house was her home & her fossil shop until 1826.' It is a joy to step out from the museum and – while walking the Jurassic coastline – trace young Mary Anning's footsteps.

THE NATURAL HISTORY MUSEUM, LONDON

The Fossil Marine Reptiles gallery in London's Natural History Museum displays specimens collected by Mary Anning and her brother Joseph in the early 1800s. There are also some of the most complete fossils of prehistoric sea animals to see, including a female ichthyosaur fossil with evidence of six unborn young in her womb.

BRUNEL MUSEUM, LONDON

This delightful little museum is located at the entrance to the Thames Tunnel, the world's oldest underwater tunnel, which Brunel worked on as a young man. Visitors can head down into the tunnel shaft, a space that once served as the Grand Entrance Hall. You can still see where the early steam trains coated the shaft walls in soot.

SS *GREAT BRITAIN*, BRISTOL

One of the most fascinating historic locations I've ever visited, SS *Great Britain* is a testament to Brunel's brilliance. When she was launched in 1843, this was the largest ship ever built, fitted with a 1,000-horsepower steam engine – the most powerful yet used at sea. Instead of using conventional paddle wheels to drive his ship, Brunel opted for a screw propeller. Perhaps it's no surprise SS *Great Britain* was called 'the greatest experiment since the creation'.

NAINITAL, INDIA

This Himalayan lake town is where Elsie Inglis was born in 1864, and spent much of her childhood. In the centre of the town is an emerald lake, often filled with colourful sailboats. According to mythology, the lake was formed when the eyes of the goddess Sati fell at this spot, as her body was being carried by Lord Shiva after her death.

CHARLOTTE SQUARE, EDINBURGH

This beautiful square was designed by Robert Adam in 1791 and is today the official residence of the First Minister of Scotland. Number 23 Charlotte Square was once the location of Edinburgh's Institution for Educating Young Ladies, where Elsie Inglis attended with sister Eva.

DEAN CEMETERY, EDINBURGH

After lying in state in St Giles Cathedral in Edinburgh, Elsie Inglis was buried in Dean Cemetery. There are plenty of famous names here, including Robert McVitie, the man who invented the digestive biscuit, and Sir Thomas Bouch, whose engineering errors gave us the phrase 'botched job'.

KNOLE HOUSE, KENT

Sitting within Kent's last medieval deer park, Knole is one of the largest and grandest houses in the country, its walls adorned with Reynolds, Gainsboroughs and van Dycks. This was the childhood home of Vita Sackville-West, whose family members still live there today.

SISSINGHURST CASTLE, KENT

This is where Vita Sackville-West lived in the 1930s with her diplomat and author husband, Harold Nicolson. Here are some of the finest gardens in the country, shaped by Harold's architectural planning of the garden 'rooms', and Vita's colourful planting.

ST MARK'S CHURCH, BELFAST

St Mark's church is a landmark of east Belfast, its 150-foot-high bell tower visible from many miles around, and designed in red sandstone by William Butterfield in the Gothic revival style. It was here where Jack Lewis's grandfather, Thomas Hamilton, was rector and where Lewis was baptized on 29 January 1899. The lion on the front door of the rectory is popularly believed to be the inspiration for Aslan from the Chronicles of Narnia.

HOLY TRINITY HEADINGTON QUARRY, OXFORD

This delightful little church, built in 1849, is where Jack Lewis worshipped for over thirty years. He is buried in the churchyard. Inside is the 'Narnia Window' and the pew where the Lewis brothers used to sit.

NEWNHAM COLLEGE, CAMBRIDGE

Newnham College is where Rosalind Franklin lived while an undergraduate, during the Second World War. It was established in 1871 as a house where young women could stay while attending lectures in Cambridge (though they weren't granted degrees until 1948). The gardens are beautiful and open for public visits.

PONTRHYDYFEN, WALES

Nestled deep in the beautiful Afan Valley, five miles from Port Talbot, is the picturesque former coal-mining village of Pontrhydyfen. The front bedroom of the small, terraced house of 2 Dan-y-Bont is where Richard Burton was born, on 10 November 1925. A short walk away is the Miner's Arms, where Richard's father and grandfather were regulars.

TINTWISTLE, CHESHIRE

This picturesque Peak District village is where Vivienne Westwood was born in 1941. She spent her childhood here until the family moved to Harrow, London. The name 'Tintwistle' is thought to derive from the word 'twisla', meaning a fork of a river or valley (the village is situated above the meeting of Arnfield Brook and the River Etherow).

MY LIFE AT 18

I asked a few people what advice they would give to their eighteen-year-old self or to eighteen-year-olds today. Here's what they said . . .

'When I was eighteen, I knew that I wanted to gain a better under-standing of human biology and then use that knowledge to improve human health in some way. It took me forty years, but I got there in the end! So, once you know what you want to achieve, don't give up.'

Sarah Gilbert,
vaccinologist who led the team that developed
the Oxford coronavirus vaccine

'It's smart to develop the habit of planning and preparing before you take action. This will be vital to your future success – at every stage of your business development. Once you have started on your journey, you will be relying on that thoroughness and accuracy of your early research and development. Always give yourself time to pause and focus, to bring this vision into the present. At this point, I suggest a little nap, just to revisit that dream. You know, the one where your business planning works out perfectly. Ah, sweet dreams!'

Levi Roots,
businessman

'When I was eighteen, I knew everything! So that was convenient. However, it also wasn't true. Advice to my younger self would probably have fallen on deaf ears, but I would've just given myself a little hug, told myself not to listen to the critics in my head and let myself know how many amazing, supportive and wise people I'll meet along the way, who will provide grounding and fun and love and friendship. It's not the easiest path, being a singer, but there are adventures to be had and you get used to the twisty ups and downs of it all. Plus I'd thank eighteen-year-old me for the kernel of optimism I've always carried. It's served me well.'

Sophie Ellis-Bextor,
singer and songwriter

'I never learnt to stay still or to think, really, as the pressing need to paint, draw, talk and play was too great. Now I *wish* I had lived abroad and learnt to speak a language. And stayed in bed more. I look at what I did then and think: *Did it really seem up to scratch?* I don't feel any different at sixty-one.'

Matthew Rice,
artist

'Like most illustrators, I'm freelance and always have been. Looking back to when I was starting out, it's striking how my very first jobs, just after art school, served as stepping stones, one commission leading to the next. They were crucial in beginning the path that brought me to where I am now, with amazing, unexpected opportunities along the way. My advice to someone about to embark on their working life is to give your best to every job you do, because you never know where it could take you!'

Nick Sharratt,
illustrator

EIGHTEEN

'Have courage and be yourself. Don't try to be the person you think everyone else wants you to be.'

Lara Maiklem,
mudlarker

'Don't get too bothered if you don't know what you want to do with your life. I messed about with my mates and got in trouble . . . a lot. But I also carried on doing the things I was into as a child: exploring abandoned buildings – what I thought were spooky churches and ruins. Later, I somehow managed to make a career out of repairing these places. Be true to who you were as a child. Some of the most interesting people I've met didn't have a clue at eighteen what they wanted to do with their lives – and still don't in their fifties and sixties.'

Andrew Ziminski,
stonemason

'As a kid, I knew I wanted to work in radio because of all the warmth and fun and stories that came out of what was, back then, a small box in the corner of my room. It has never disappointed me! Your young self is your true self. Stick with your dreams as long as you can!'

Fi Glover,
journalist and broadcaster

'I was a knife thrower's stooge at a holiday camp when I was eighteen – not an occupation upon which to build a career! I didn't have a clue what I really wanted to do. Which was just as well, as it turns out, because most of the jobs I've been lucky enough to do (BBC arts editor, director of Tate Media, artistic director at the Barbican) didn't exist back then. Sometimes no plan is the best plan. Let serendipity be your guide.'

Will Gompertz,
journalist, author and art critic

'My words of wisdom to my eighteen-year-old self? Don't worry, no matter how confident your peers may seem, they are all as bewildered by life as you are. Just remain open, curious and generous and you'll be OK.'

Roderick Williams,
baritone and composer

'People don't care what you do. And, when they do start caring, positively or (most importantly) negatively, it means you're doing it well.'

Daisy Tempest,
luthier

'Ever since the age of eleven, I have known what I wanted to be and do. I have always visualized my future in my head. I have also never taken myself too seriously – as opposed to my passion, pottery, which I treat with the utmost respect. Never take yourself too seriously; it might take you down a path that can truly open doors. Who knew that me dressed as Adele singing a bad version of "Rolling in the Deep" would give me the opportunity to be a judge on the telly?!'

Keith Brymer Jones,
potter and ceramic designer

'It's really easy to live someone else's life by mistake. It's not that you shouldn't listen to other people – the advice of others is really important and often wise. But, in the end, what you do every day is ultimately what you're doing with your life – and you're the only one who sees the whole of it. So live the life you know in your heart is yours – and don't waste energy or time worrying about what everyone else thinks you should do. Don't waste time waiting for "real life" to start. It's happening now; get involved, get stuff wrong – it's fine – and laugh easily, always.'

Lucy Winkett,
priest

'When I was eighteen, I wanted to change the world and I shouted loudly about it. I still want to change the world in many of the same ways and I still shout a bit. But I've added more persuasion and humour to the mix. I think that's been more effective.'

Mary Beard,
classicist

'Try hard. Be kind. Remember you will fail at things – that's OK. Don't let the fear of failure stop you. Be brave. Trust yourself; you're wiser than society gives you credit for. Oh, and spend more time outside. Your mind and body will thank you.'

Mary-Ann Ochota,
anthropologist, broadcaster and author

'When I was eighteen, I had no concept of the amount of time that I had. Think of something you want to do – and then, even if it takes years, do it. Those years will seem to collapse into minutes when seen in retrospect.'

Dan Snow,
historian

'There are a couple of mantras that I've lived by since I was eighteen and, now I'm in my fifties, I know them to be true. Firstly, I worked with my father. When I left school, he was a time-served bricklayer from the 1950s – incredible knowledge. I just wish I'd listened more when I was eighteen! When he died, way before his time, this became even more evident! Take more time and learn from your elders as you don't know when they'll be gone. Also, I realized that if you take a half-hearted attitude to your work then you'll always receive a half-hearted outcome. Put simply: the more you put in, the more you get out.'

Lynn Mathias,
flintknapper

'When I first visited a prison, I was amazed by how many talented, ambitious and charismatic people were locked up inside, so I started recruiting them to work in our business. Twenty-two years later, we have over 600 ex-offenders as colleagues. Give people a second chance – they change lives and help organizations thrive.'

James Timpson,
businessman and philanthropist

'At eighteen, I was absorbed in the life of a busy working kitchen in the West End of London, doing shifts of 12–15 hours a day. It didn't matter that I was only being paid £15 a week – I was full of passion and enthusiasm, keen to learn everything and proud to wear my tall white chef's hat. Today, almost fifty years later, I'm still sharing my love of cooking – now without the hat, but all those vital ingredients I learnt remain. Which proves that, if you work hard and never give up on your dreams, anything is possible.'

Ainsley Harriott,
chef

'Let me *paws* to think . . . I would tell eighteen-year-old Hodge to remember how lucky he was to have been given a second chance and to take advantage of living in such an a-*meow*-zing place! Not every cat gets a whole *cat*-hedral to themselves.'

Hodge,
Southwark Cathedral cat

A NOTE OF THANKS

Thanks must go to all the historians who have shared their vast expertise and so kindly helped in a variety of ways – advised on details, checked chapters, recommended contacts or offered words of friendly encouragement: Nicola Tallis, Andrzej Stasiak, Sarah Foot, Kevin Dawson, Miranda Kauffmann, Sarah Gristwood, Matthew Lewis, Gordan Pentland, Marion Turner, Andrew Lambert, Ellie Smith, Ian Kelly, Tristan Hughes, Catherine Hanley, Alister McGrath, Tom Rubython, John Jacob Woolf, Lara Anderson and Jacqueline Riding. At every stage of this journey, everyone I've spoken to has been wholly supportive and generous – a wonderful reflection of the history world.

Many thanks to the brilliant Joshua Hales and the dynamo-researcher Eleanor Kochman for their assistance; and to Mike Harpley, Ríbh Brownlee, Melissa Bond, Caroline Hardman, Helen Purvis and everyone in the teams at Pan Macmillan, Hardman & Swainson and Knight Ayton Management for all their brilliance, expertise and support.

Thank you to the teams who run the London Library, the Chalke History Festival speakers' tent, the Blackwell's Oxford cafe, various Landmark Trust properties, National Trust cafes, the French

House and the Soho Bar of the Groucho Club, for providing such stirring settings in which to write.

And to the millions of you on TikTok, Instagram and the rest, who have accompanied me in exploring so many wonderful historic places and whose enthusiasm for learning knows no bounds, thank you. I look forward to many more adventures together.

Thanks to all my wonderful friends and family. But, most importantly, I must thank the eighteen-year-olds of the past, present and future.

Alice Loxton
Groucho Club, London
Exactly ten years after her eighteenth birthday
(martini in hand)

NOTES

page

18 'You might see the world': Little, Lester K. (ed.), *Plague and the End of Antiquity: The Pandemic of 541–750* (Cambridge: Cambridge University Press, 2007), p. 12.

25 'The dedication of the basilica of St Paul': Wood, Ian, *The Origins of Jarrow: The Monastery, the Slake and Ecefrith's Minister* (Jarrow: Bede's World Studies), p. 3.

29 'I have spent the whole of my life': Wright, Robert J., *A Companion to Bede: A Reader's Commentary on the Ecclesiastical History of the English People* (Michigan: William B. Eerdmans, 2008), p. 2.

42 'Matilda, the daughter of Henry': Chibnall, Marjorie, *The Empress Matilda: Queen Consort, Queen Mother and Lady of the English* (Oxford: Blackwell's, 1993), p. 26.

45 'England, formerly the seat of justice': Dalton, Paul & White, Graeme J. (eds), *King Stephen's Reign (1135–1154)* (Woodbridge: Boydell and Brewer, 2008), p. 80.

50 'William de Breusa also testifies': Giraldus De Barri, *The Itinerary of Archbishop Baldwin Through Wales*, trans. Richard Colt Hoare, 1806.

55 'And at first it carried off': Horrox, Rosemary (trans. and ed.), *The Black Death* (Manchester: Manchester University Press, 1994), p. 250.

55   'But see (with what intense bitterness of heart)': Bothwell, James, 'An Emotional Pragmatism: Edward III and Death', in Dodd, Gwilym & Taylor, Craig (eds), *Monarchy, State and Political Culture in Late Medieval England: Essays in Honour of W. Mark Ormrod* (York: York Medieval Press, 2020), p. 58.

65   'the disaster was caused': 'Spain: July 1545, 21–25', in *Calendar of State Papers, Spain, Volume 8, 1545-1546* (London, 1904). pp. 184–95, via British History Online.

68   'One of them, who had a pewter tankard of beer in his hand': Kauffman, Miranda, *Black Tudors* (London: Oneworld, 2018), p. 43.

71   'As for slaves and bondmen': Kauffman, *Black Tudors*, p. 16.

101 'A Master-Cook!': Johnson, Ben, *The Staple of News*, Act IV, Scene II (1625).

112 'only three rooms': MacLeod, Ruairidh H., *Flora MacDonald: The Jacobite Heroine in Scotland and North America* (London: Shepheard-Walwyn, 1995), p. 3.

114 'There is a pleasure on the heath': Keats, John, 'Lines Written in the Highlands', from *Poetry Manuscripts at Harvard*, ed. Jack Stillinger (Boston: Harvard University Press, 1990), p. 88.

133 'A stock of warm clothing': Constantine John Phipps Baron Mulgrave, *The Journal of a Voyage undertaken by order of his present Majesty, for making discoveries towards the North Pole*, 1774, p. xxviii.

134 'The very ice in which they were beset': Mulgrave, *The Journal of a Voyage*, p. 64.

135 'His hair already stood on end': Mulgrave, *The Journal of a Voyage*, p. 60.

137 'a feeling that I should never rise': Southey, Robert, *The Life of Nelson* (London, 1898), p. 18.

138 'After a long and gloomy reverie': Southey, *The Life of Nelson*, p. 18.

147 'At the age of eight years': Sarah Biffin, 'An Interesting Narrative and proposals for a print of Miss Beffin to be dedicated, by

permission to HRH the Princess Augusta', 942 BIF/10, Liverpool Record Office, p. 1.

149 'her appearance was handsome': Long, B. S., 'MINIATURES', *Journal of the Royal Society of Arts*, 83 (4312) (1935), pp. 815–31.

152 'Gifted with singular talents': 'Sarah Biffin's Epitaph', *Daily Post & Mercury*, 20 February 1925.

158 'It is a wonderful instance of divine favour': Thomson, Keith, *Fossils: A Very Short Introduction* (Oxford: Oxford University Press, 2005), p. 29.

161 'a number of people assembled': *Hull Advertiser*, Saturday, 30 August 1800.

162 'A child four years of age': *Hampshire Chronicle*, Monday, 31 December 1798.

164 'The principal street': Austen, Jane, *Persuasion* (Oxford: Oxford University Press, 2008), p. 80.

183 'It's a gloomy perspective': University of Bristol Archives. Ref No: DM1306/2/1/folio 25.

195 'it is quite remarkable': Campbell Balfour, Frances, *Dr Elsie Inglis* (Legare Street, 2022), p. 19.

196 'Elsie decreed once': Campbell Balfour, *Dr Elsie Inglis*, p. 23.

197 'in the days when such things': Campbell Balfour, *Dr Elsie Inglis*, p. 28.

198 'In those days, no one thought': Campbell Balfour, *Dr Elsie Inglis*, p. 31.

200 'I remember well the day': Campbell Balfour, *Dr Elsie Inglis*, p. 40.

201 'The date of Elsie's birth': Campbell Balfour, *Dr Elsie Inglis*, p. 25.

213 'A poet's work is art': Sackville-West, Vita, *Chatterton: A Drama in Three Acts* (Sevenoaks: J. Salmon, 1909), p. 12.

215 'Guard and vigil in the night': Sackville-West, Vita, *Orchard and Vineyard* (London: John Lane, The Bodley Head, 1921), p. 50.
'Knole! Knole!': Stevens, Michael, *V. Sackville-West: A Critical Biography* (London: Michael Joseph, 1973), p. 41.

230 'I am going to school': Lewis, C. S., *Surprised by Joy* (London: HarperCollins, 2010), p. 23.

232 "The Lion' all began': DeGregorio, Scott (ed.), *The Cambridge Companion to C. S. Lewis* (Cambridge: Cambridge University Press, 2010), p. 266.

239 'somebody must have made some mistake': Maddox, Brenda, *Rosalind Franklin: The Dark Lady of DNA* (London: HarperCollins, 2003), p. 35.

244 'We are having great fun': Glynn, Jenifer, *My Sister Rosalind Franklin* (Oxford: Oxford University Press, 2012), p. 15.

245 'We managed to obtain': Maddox, *Rosalind Franklin*, p. 36.

247 'One of the dons': Glynn, *My Sister Rosalind Franklin*, p. 48.

259 'It was a thing of beauty': Rubython, Tom, *And God Created Burton* (London: Myrtle Press, 2011), p. 60.

262 'I would go further and further away': Rubython, *And God Created Burton*, p. 43.

263 'When I raised the question with Richard': Bragg, Melvyn, *Rich: The Life of Richard Burton* (London: Hodder and Stoughton, 2012), p. 38.

264 'I believe this is the age': Biddulph, Steve, *Raising Boys: Why Boys Are Different – and How to Help Them Become Happy and Well-Balanced Men* (Thorsons, 1997), p. 20.

265 'There were moments': Bragg, *Rich*, p. 50.
'He was marvellous at rehearsals': Bragg, *Rich*, p. 69.

270 'SWIRE': Westwood, Vivienne & Kelly, Ian, *Vivienne Westwood* (London: Picador, 2015), p. 45.

273 'It had never occurred to me': Westwood & Kelly, *Vivienne Westwood*, p. 50.

277 'Dad was affected by the Depression': Westwood & Kelly, *Vivienne Westwood*, p. 73.

281 'We have full employment': *North London Press*, 30 January 1959.

SELECT BIBLIOGRAPHY

Aberth, John, *The Black Death: A New History of the Great Mortality in Europe, 1347–1500* (Oxford: Oxford University Press, 2022)

Bagust, Harold, *The Greater Genius?: A Biography of Marc Isambard Brunel* (Shepperton: Ian Allan, 2006)

Bede, *The Ecclesiastical History of the English People* (Oxford: Oxford University Press, 2008)

Bleakly, David, *C. S. Lewis: At Home in Ireland* (Bangor: Strandtown, 1998)

Borman, Tracy, *Anne Boleyn & Elizabeth I: The Mother and Daughter Who Changed History* (London: Hodder and Stoughton, 2023)

Bragg, Melvyn, *Rich: The Life of Richard Burton* (London: Hodder and Stoughton, 2010)

Brindle, Stephen, *Brunel: The Man Who Built the World* (Phoenix Press, 2006)

Buchanan, R. Angus, *Brunel: The Life and Times of Isambard Kingdom Brunel* (London: Bloomsbury, 2006)

Campbell Balfour, Frances, *Dr Elsie Inglis* (Legare Street, 2022)

Castor, Helen, *She-Wolves: The Women Who Ruled England Before Elizabeth* (London: Faber & Faber, 2011)

Chibnall, Marjorie, *The Empress Matilda: Queen Consort, Queen Mother and Lady of the English* (Oxford: Blackwells, 1993)

Curry, Anne & Hughes, Michael (eds), *Arms, Armies and Fortifications in the Hundred Years' War* (Woodbridge: Boydell and Brewer, 1999)

Dalton, Paul & White, Graeme J. (eds), *King Stephen's Reign (1135–1154)* (Woodbridge: Boydell and Brewer, 2008)

DeGregorio, Scott (ed.), *The Cambridge Companion to Bede* (Cambridge: Cambridge University Press, 2010)

Dennison, Matthew, *Behind the Mask: The Life of Vita Sackville-West* (London: HarperCollins, 2015)

Douglas, Hugh, *Flora MacDonald: The Most Loyal Rebel* (Cheltenham: The History Press, 2003)

Emling, Shelley, *The Fossil Hunter: Dinosaurs, Evolution, and the Woman Whose Discoveries Changed the World* (London: Palgrave Macmillan, 2011)

Fraser, Flora, *Pretty Young Rebel: The Life of Flora MacDonald* (London: Bloomsbury, 2022)

Fuhrmann, Horst, *Germany in the High Middle Ages: c.1050–1200* (Cambridge: Cambridge University Press, 1986)

Fuller, Thomas & Nichols, John (eds), *The History of the Worthies of England* (London: Printed for F.C. & J. Rivington etc., 1811)

Garth, John, *Tolkien and the Great War: The Threshold of Middle-Earth* (London: HarperCollins, 2004)

Glynn, Jenifer, *My Sister Rosalind Franklin* (Oxford: Oxford University Press, 2012)

Hanley, Catherine, *Matilda: Empress, Queen, Warrior* (New Haven: Yale University Press, 2020)

Hollister, Warren C., *Henry I* (New Haven: Yale University Press, 2003)

Horrox, Rosemary (trans. and ed.), *The Black Death* (Manchester: Manchester University Press, 1994)

Hunneycutt, Lois L., *Matilda of Scotland: A Study in Medieval Queenship* (Woodbridge: Boydell Press, 2003)

Jenkins, David, *Richard Burton: A Brother Remembered* (London: Century, 1993)

Kaufmann, Miranda, *Black Tudors: The Untold Story* (London: Oneworld, 2018)

Knox, William W. J., *The Lives of Scottish Women: Women and Scottish Society 1800–1980* (Edinburgh: Edinburgh University Press, 2006)

Lavery, Brian, *Nelson's Navy: The Ships, Men and Organisation, 1793–1815* (London: Bloomsbury, 2020)

Lewis, C. S., *Surprised by Joy* (London: HarperCollins, 2012)

Leyser, Henrietta, *Beda: A Journey Through the Seven Kingdoms in the Age of Bede* (London: Bloomsbury, 2015)

Little, Lester K. (ed.), *Plague and the End of Antiquity: The Pandemic of 541–750* (Cambridge: Cambridge University Press, 2007)

McLaren, Eva Shaw, *Elsie Inglis* (Legare Street Press, 2022)

MacLeod, Ruairidh H., *Flora MacDonald: The Jacobite Heroine in Scotland and North America* (London: Shepheard-Walwyn, 1995)

Maddox, Brenda, *Rosalind Franklin: The Dark Lady of DNA* (London: HarperCollins, 2003)

Morris, Marc, *The Anglo-Saxons: A History of the Beginnings of England* (London: Hutchinson, 2021)

Mortimer, Ian, *The Time Traveller's Guide to Elizabethan England* (London: Vintage, 2013).

Mortimer, Ian, *The Time Traveller's Guide to Medieval England* (London: Vintage, 2009)

Mortimer, Ian, *The Time Traveller's Guide to Regency Britain* (London: Vintage, 2020)

Mortimer, Ian, *The Time Traveller's Guide to Restoration Britain* (London: Vintage, 2018)

Mulvagh, Jane, *Vivienne Westwood: An Unfashionable Life* (London: HarperCollins, 2003)

Page, Nick, *Lord Minimus: The Extraordinary Life of Britain's Smallest Man* (London: HarperCollins, 2001)

Perry, Maria, *The Word of a Prince: A Life of Elizabeth I* (Woodbridge: Boydell and Brewer, 1996)

Phipps, Constantine John, *The Journal of a Voyage Undertaken by Order of His Present Majesty, for Making Discoveries Towards the North Pole, by the Hon. Commodore Phipps, and Captain Lutwidge* (Newbery, 1774)

Pierce, Patricia, *Jurassic Mary: Mary Anning and the Primeval Monsters* (Cheltenham: The History Press, 2014)

Rice, Matthew, *Rice's Architectural Primer* (London: Bloomsbury, 2010)

Riding, Jacqueline, *Jacobites: A New History of the '45 Rebellion* (London: Bloomsbury, 2016)

Rubython, Tom, *And God Created Burton* (Northampton: Myrtle Press, 2016)

Sackville-West, V., *Knole and the Sackvilles* (Legare Street Press, 2022)

Sackville-West, V., *Pepita* (London: Vintage, 2016)

Sugden, John, *Nelson: A Dream of Glory* (London: Vintage, 2012)

Tallis, Nicola, *Young Elizabeth: Princess. Prisoner. Queen.* (London: Michael O'Mara, 2024)

Turner, Marion, *Chaucer Here and Now* (Oxford: Bodleian Library, 2023)

Turner, Marion, *Chaucer: A European Life* (Princeton: Princeton University Press, 2020)

Webb, Simon, *In Search of Bede* (Durham: The Langley Press, 2010)

Westwood, Vivienne & Kelly, Ian, *Vivienne Westwood* (London: Picador, 2015)

Whaley, Joachim, *Germany and the Holy Roman Empire: Volume I: Maximilian I to the Peace of Westphalia, 1493–1648* (Oxford: Oxford University Press, 2013)

Without Hands: The Art of Sarah Biffin (London: Paul Holberton Publishing, 2022)

Wood, Ian, *The Origins of Jarrow: The Monastery, the Slake and Ecefrith's Minister* (Jarrow: Bede's World, 2008)

Wright, Robert J., *A Companion to Bede: A Reader's Commentary on the Ecclesiastical History of the English People* (Michigan: William B. Eerdmans, 2008)

Here are some other *very* useful resources:

History Today
BBC History Extra
Oxford Dictionary of National Biography
British Newspaper Archive
British Library website
National Trust Collections
Historic England Research Records
The London Library
Bibliography of British and Irish History
JSTOR
Oxford Art Online
The Sunday Times Digital Archive
The Telegraph Historical Archive
British History Online
English Heritage website